Lecture Notes in Computer Sci

Commenced Publication in 1973
Founding and Former Series Editors:
Gerhard Goos, Juris Hartmanis, and Jan van Leeuwen

Anna Sperotto   Guillaume Doyen
Steven Latré   Marinos Charalambides
Burkhard Stiller (Eds.)

Monitoring and Securing Virtualized Networks and Services

8th IFIP WG 6.6 International Conference
on Autonomous Infrastructure,
Management, and Security, AIMS 2014
Brno, Czech Republic, June 30 – July 3, 2014
Proceedings

 Springer

Volume Editors

Anna Sperotto
University of Twente, Enschede, The Netherlands
E-mail: a.sperotto@utwente.nl

Guillaume Doyen
Troyes University of Technology, Troyes Cedex, France
E-mail: guillaume.doyen@utt.fr

Steven Latré
University of Antwerp, Belgium
E-mail: steven.latre@uantwerpen.be

Marinos Charalambides
University College London, UK
E-mail: marinos.charalambides@ucl.ac.uk

Burkhard Stiller
University of Zurich, Switzerland
E-mail: stiller@ifi.uzh.ch

ISSN 0302-9743   e-ISSN 1611-3349
ISBN 978-3-662-43861-9   e-ISBN 978-3-662-43862-6
DOI 10.1007/978-3-662-43862-6
Springer Heidelberg New York Dordrecht London

Library of Congress Control Number: 2014941086

LNCS Sublibrary: SL 5 – Computer Communication Networks
and Telecommunications

Typesetting: Camera-ready by author, data conversion by Scientific Publishing Services, Chennai, India

Printed on acid-free paper

Springer is part of Springer Science+Business Media (www.springer.com)

Preface

The International Conference on Autonomous Infrastructure, Management, and Security (AIMS 2014) is a single-track event integrating regular conference paper sessions, a keynote, lab sessions, and the PhD Student Workshop into a highly interactive event. This year AIMS has re-defined its "DNA" and was even more focused on PhD students and young researchers. One of the key goals of AIMS is to provide early-stage researchers with constructive feedback by senior scientists and give them the possibility of growing in the research community by means of targeted lab sessions on technical and educational aspects of the research activity.

AIMS 2014, which took place from June 30 to July 3, 2014, in Brno, Czech Republic, was hosted by the Masaryk University as the eighth edition of a conference series on management and security aspects of distributed and autonomous systems. It followed the already established tradition of an unusually vivid and interactive conference series, after successful events in Barcelona, Spain, in 2013, Luxembourg, Luxembourg, in 2012, Nancy, France, in 2011, Zürich, Switzerland, in 2010, Enschede, The Netherlands, in 2009, Bremen, Germany, in 2008, and Oslo, Norway, in 2007.

This year, AIMS 2014 focused on monitoring and securing virtualized networks and services. This theme is addressed in the technical program with papers related to monitoring, security, and management methodologies in the application areas of wired and wireless networks, Internet-of-Things, and Cloud infrastructures. AIMS 2014 was organized as a 4-day program structured to encourage the interaction with and the active participation of the conference's audience. The program consisted of technical sessions for the main track and PhD sessions, interleaved with a keynote, an "Education Session Talk," and three lab sessions. The AIMS 2014 keynote presentation was given by Martin Rehak, Cisco Systems, on "Security Analytics: Finding a Needle in the Hay Blower". These lab sessions offered hands-on experience in network and service management topics and they were organized in practical exercises preceded by short tutorial-style teaching session. The first lab session presented the "Fast Network Simulation Set-up" tool chain, aiming at facilitating the set-up of complex scenarios for network simulations. The second lab session covered the topic of network management using software-defined networking. Finally, the third lab session focused on security and the session introduced the "Cybernetic Proving Ground", a testbed for Cloud-based security research. Finally, and in line with its educational mission, this year the conference also included an "Education Session Talk", which was given by Aiko Pras on the topic of scientific publications and with the goal of providing guidelines for PhD students and young researchers on publication venues and the advantages and drawbacks of related metrics to which each researcher is nowadays subject to.

The technical program consisted of three sessions — covering the topics of emerging infrastructures for networks and services, experimental studies for security management, and monitoring methods for Quality-of-Service and security — and included nine full papers, which were selected after a thorough reviewing process out of 29 submissions. Each paper received three or four independent reviews, followed by a shepherding process aimed at tutoring those nine accepted papers through the preparation of the camera-ready paper version and to the paper presentation.

The AIMS PhD Student Workshop provides a venue for doctoral students to present and discuss their research ideas, and more importantly to obtain valuable feedback from the AIMS audience about their planned PhD research work. This year, the workshop was structured into four technical sessions covering security, management of virtualized network resources and functions, software-defined networking, and monitoring. All PhD papers included in this volume describe the current state of these investigations, including their clear research problem statements, proposed approaches, and an outline of results achieved so far. A total of 13 PhD papers were presented and discussed. These papers were selected after a separate review process out of 27 submissions, while all PhD papers received at least three independent reviews.

The present volume of the *Lecture Notes in Computer Science* series includes all papers presented at AIMS 2014 as defined within the overall final program. It demonstrates again the European scope of this conference series, since most of those papers accepted originate from European research groups. AIMS 2014 proved to be a conference with a strong educational goal, as indicated by the good number of submissions and the attractiveness of the PhD Student Workshop.

The editors would like to thank the many people who helped make AIMS 2014 such a high-quality and successful event. Firstly, many thanks are addressed to all authors, who submitted their contributions to AIMS 2014, and to the lab session speakers, namely, Lorenzo Saino, Niels Bouten, Maxim Claeys, Jeroen Famaey, Jakub Čegan, Martin Vizváry, and Michal Procházka, and the keynote and educational session speakers Martin Rehak and Aiko Pras. The great review work performed by the members of both the AIMS TPC and the PhD Student Workshop Committee as well as additional reviewers is highly acknowledged. Thanks go also to Petr Velan and Jeroen Famaey for setting up and organizing these lab sessions and the test-bed hardware. Additionally, many thanks are addressed to the local organizers at Masaryk University for providing all logistics and hosting the AIMS 2014 event.

Finally, the editors would like express their thanks to Springer and in particular to Anna Kramer for the smooth cooperation in finalizing these proceedings. Additionally, special thanks go to the AIMS 2014 supporter, the European FP7 NoE FLAMINGO under Grant No. 318488.

April 2014

Anna Sperotto
Guillaume Doyen
Steven Latré
Marinos Charalambides

 Masaryk University

 NoE FLAMINGO

Organization

General Chair AIMS 2014

Pavel Čeleda   Masaryk University, Czech Republic

Technical Program Committee Co-chairs

Guillaume Doyen   Troyes University of Technology, France
Anna Sperotto   University of Twente, The Netherlands

PhD Student Workshop Co-chairs

Steven Latré   Universiteit Antwerp, iMinds, Belgium
Marinos Charalambides   University College London, UK

Labs Co-chairs

Petr Velan   Masaryk University, Czech Republic
Jeroen Famaey   Ghent University, iMinds, Belgium

Publications Chair

Burkhard Stiller   University of Zürich, Switzerland

Local Co-chairs

Iva Krejčí   Masaryk University, Czech Republic
Jan Vykopal   Masaryk University, Czech Republic

AIMS Steering Committee

Burkhard Stiller   University of Zürich, Switzerland
Olivier Festor   Telecom Nancy, University of Lorraine, France
Ramin Sadre   Aalborg University, Denmark
Guillaume Doyen   Troyes University of Technology, France
David Hausheer   Technical University Darmstadt, Germany
Aiko Pras   University of Twente, The Netherlands

Technical Program Committee

Alessandro Finamore	Politecnico di Torino, Italy
Alex Galis	University College London, UK
Alexander Clemm	Cisco Systems, USA
Alexander Keller	IBM Global Technology Services, USA
Alva L. Couch	Tufts University, USA
Anandha Gopalan	Imperial College London, UK
Bertrand Mathieu	Orange Labs, France
Bruno Quoitin	Université de Mons, Belgium
Burkhard Stiller	University of Zürich, Switzerland
Danny Raz	Technion, Israel
David Hausheer	Technical University Darmstadt, Germany
Filip De Turck	Ghent University, iMinds, Belgium
Gabi Dreo Rodosek	University of Federal Armed Forces, Munich, Germany
Georgios Karagiannis	University of Twente, The Netherlands
Grégory Bonnet	University of Caen Lower Normandy, France
Isabelle Chrisment	TELECOM Nancy, Université de Lorraine, France
Jan Kořenek	Brno University of Technology, Czech Republic
Jérôme François	INRIA Grand Est Nancy, France
Jürgen Schönwälder	Jacobs University Bremen, Germany
Kurt Tutschku	Blekinge Institute of Technology, Sweden
Lisandro Zambenedetti Granville	UFRGS, Brazil
Martin Waldburger	WIK-Consult, Germany
Martin Žádník	Brno University of Technology, Czech Republic
Mauro Tortonesi	University of Ferrara, Italy
Michelle Sibilla	Paul Sabatier University, France
Olivier Festor	Telecom Nancy, University of Lorraine, France
Philippe Owezarski	LAAS-CNRS, France
Piotr Cholda	AGH University of Science and Technology, Poland
Radu State	University of Luxembourg, Luxembourg
Ramin Sadre	Aalborg University, Denmark
Raouf Boutaba	University of Waterloo, Canada
Remi Badonnel	INRIA, TELECOM Nancy, Université de Lorraine, France
Róbert Szabó	Budapest University of Technology and Economics, Hungary
Thomas Bocek	University of Zürich, Switzerland
Vojtěch Krmíček	Masaryk University, Czech Republic

PhD Student Workshop Committee

Aiko Pras	University of Twente, The Netherlands
Alberto Schaeffer-Filho	UFRGS, Brazil
Arosha Bandara	The Open University, UK
Bradley Simmons	York University, Canada
Carol Fung	Virginia Commonwealth University, USA
Clarissa Marquezan	Duisburg-Essen University, Germany
Daphne Tuncer	University College London, UK
Desislava Dimitrova	University of Bern, Switzerland
Dimitrios Pezaros	University of Glasgow, UK
George Pavlou	University College London, UK
Giovane Moura	Delft University of Technology, The Netherlands
Javier Rubio-Loyola	CINVESTAV, Mexico
Jeroen Famaey	Ghent University, iMinds, Belgium
Joan Serrat	Universitat Politecnica de Catalunya, Spain
Kostas Tsagkaris	University of Piraeus, Greece
Lefteris Mamatas	University College London, UK
Luciano Paschoal Gaspary	UFRGS, Brazil
Maxwell Young	Drexel University, USA
Ning Wang	University of Surrey, UK
Paulo Simoes	University of Coimbra, Portugal
Steven Davy	Waterford Institute of Technology, Ireland
Stylianos Georgoulas	University of Surrey, UK
Sven van der Meer	Ericsson, Ireland

Reviewers

Detailed reviews for papers submitted to AIMS 2014 were carried out by the Technical Program Committee as well as the PhD Student Workshop Committee as stated above and additionally by the following reviewers:

Abdelkader Lahmadi	Matthias Wichtlhuber
Christian Koch	Natalie Matta
Corinna Schmitt	Nikolay Melnikov
Gaëtan Hurel	Patrick Truong
Hammi Badis	Piotr Wydrych
Juan Pablo Timpanaro	Reaz Ahmed
Leonhard Nobach	Rida Khatoun
Lisa Kristiana	Vaibhav Bajpai

Keynote — Modern Security Analytics: Finding a Needle in the Hay Blower

Martin Rehak

Cisco Systems
Prague, Czech Republic
marrehak@cisco.com

Abstract. Detection of advanced security threats is one of the exciting problems of current computer science. The field, which has been traditionally considered an art, rather than science, has been undergoing major transformation due to the rapid evolution of attacks staged by government actors and organized crime, rather than by hobbyists and enthusiasts from the past. In order to keep the pace with these attackers, a mix of approaches from machine learning, "big data analytics", game theory and distributed computing is necessary to deliver a robust, scalable, and affordable solution to this problem.

This keynote will concentrate on the stream analytics, *i.e.,* the application of highly efficient machine learning methods to data in flight, prior to their serialization and more in-depth analytics steps. We will follow one case of malware detection on its path through the system, and we will also show that a bit of an art is still necessary to make science work in a highly adversarial environment.

Educational Session — Where to Publish?

Aiko Pras

University of Twente, The Netherlands
a.pras@utwente.nl

Abstract. In this educational session talk we stress the importance of publishing your research results at the right venues. First, we identify the workshops, conferences, magazines, and journals in the area of network and systems management, but also in the broader networking area. We will discuss the quality of some of our conferences and journals, as perceived by experts in our field, as well as people outside our area. In addition, we present acceptance rates, acceptance procedures, conference and journal rankings, as well as impact factors. Although some Ph.D. students may believe that a main goal is to publish as many papers as possible, this talk will stress that there are other important metrics, such as some key venues and the number of citations. We will discuss the pros and cons of the H-index, a metric that is currently quite popular for judging quality of people as well as conferences, but has several limitations. The talk concludes with explaining the importance of publishing in journals indexed in Thomson's Science Citation Index (SCI), or alternatives like Scopus. It also explains CPP, JCS, and FCS factors.

Lab Session 1 — Fast Network Simulation Setup

Lorenzo Saino

University College London, United Kingdom
l.saino@ee.ucl.ac.uk

Abstract. Arguably, one of the most cumbersome tasks required to run a network experiment is the setup of a complete scenario and its implementation in the target simulator or emulator. This process includes selecting an appropriate topology, provision nodes and links with all required parameters and, finally, configure traffic sources or generate traffic matrices.

Executing all these task manually is both time-consuming and error-prone. The Fast Network Simulation Setup (FNSS) tool chain addresses this problem by allowing users to generate even complex experiment scenarios with few lines of Python code and deploy them in the preferred target simulator. FNSS currently supports ns-2, ns-3, mininet as well as custom-built C++, Java, and Python simulators. The lab is divided in three parts.

In the first part, participants will be familiarized with various models and data sets of networks topologies. They will also learn the most commonly used models to assign link capacities, delays and buffer sizes and how to synthetically generate realistic traffic matrices. The second part will provide an overview of the FNSS tool chain. Participants will learn how to install and configure it and they will be walked through its main features. Finally, in the third part, participants will learn through live coding examples how to easily generate complex simulation scenarios and how to deploy them on a number of different simulators or emulators.

Lab Session 2 — Deploying OpenFlow Experiments on the Virtual Wall Test-bed

Niels Bouten, Maxim Claeys, and Jeroen Famaey

Ghent University, iMinds, Belgium
{niels.bouten|maxim.claeys|jeroen.famaey}@intec.ugent.be

Abstract. Software-defined networking (SDN) greatly increases network management flexibility by decoupling decision making (i.e., control plane) from traffic forwarding (*i.e.*, data plane) in network equipment. This enables network control to become directly programmable, and allows intelligent software components to dynamically reconfigure the network based on service requirements and network conditions. OpenFlow is without a doubt the most widely known implementation of the SDN concept. It is a protocol which structures the communication between the network's data and control plane and provides granular traffic control.

The goal of this hands-on lab session is to familiarize the participant with the concept of SDN in general and with OpenFlow in particular. We will explore OpenFlow's capabilities to dynamically reroute traffic, guarantee bandwidth, and differentiate flows. Participants will be given the opportunity to apply their acquired knowledge by setting up an OpenFlow-based experiment that guarantees the Quality-of-Service requirements of a networked video application. The experiment will be run in a live network setting, facilitated by the Virtual Wall test-bed.

The Virtual Wall is a test-bed facility for setting up large-scale network topologies. The Virtual Wall nodes can be assigned different functionalities and organized in arbitrary network topologies on the fly. As such, it is a generic experimental environment for advanced network, distributed software and service evaluation, and supports scalability research. The facility has been made available to the research community through different FP7 FIRE projects. The lab session will provide a brief theoretical introduction about the Virtual Wall's capabilities in preparation of the hands-on part.

Lab Session 3 — Cybernetic Proving Ground: A Cloud-Based Security Research Test-bed

Jakub Čegan, Martin Vizváry, and Michal Procházka

Masaryk University, Czech Republic
{cegan|vizvary|prochazkam}@ics.muni.cz

Abstract. Cyber attacks have become ubiquitous and in order to face current threats it is important to understand them. However, studying these attacks in a real environment is not often viable. Therefore, it is necessary to find other methods of examining the nature of the attacks. This lab session will present Cybernetic Proving Ground (CPG) that is being developed at Masaryk University. The CPG is a cloud-based framework that allows users to instantiate and run miscellaneous security and forensic scenarios.

The CPG provides a generic way to simulate and study a wide range of cyber attacks. It facilitates an establishment of isolated virtual environments that researchers can use to pursue controlled analysis of the attacks. Using virtualization and clouds, we managed to provide an environment, where it is possible to configure any common network configuration. Therefore, we are able to fulfill needs of many types of security scenarios. The user can use the CPG to set up isolated environments very quickly without the necessity of knowing details about network configuration or deploying auxiliary services such as a monitoring infrastructure.

The lab session is divided in three parts. In the first part of the lab session, participants will learn how to access the CPG infrastructure and how to configure a scenario. The second part of the lab session will focus on running a security scenario. The participants will take part in the scenario as each of them will have a machine to control. An overall status of the CPG scenario will be monitored in the course of the simulation. We will show how to use CPG to easily generate network scenarios, deploy them to simulate and evaluate experiments in a large cloud-based environment.

Table of Contents

Experimental Studies for Security Management

Ph.D. Student Workshop — SDN and Content Delivery

Monitoring Methods for Quality-of-Service and Security

Ph.D. Student Workshop — Monitoring and Information Sharing

Trade-off-based Adoption Methodology for Cloud-Based Infrastructures and Services

Radhika Garg and Burkhard Stiller

Department of Informatics IFI, University of Zurich, Switzerland
{garg,stiller}@ifi.uzh.ch

Abstract. Adoption and consequent management of cloud-based infrastructures and services is driven by business requirements and objectives within an organization. The decision of either to move from a legacy system to a cloud-based system or to move from one cloud solution to another is based on various factors. A potential customer, therefore, should evaluate (a) relevant factors affecting the adoption of a cloud and (b) impacts cloud services will have on multi-faceted objectives of an organization. Existing methods for such an adoption process do not evaluate these two aspects for the decision of cloud adoption. Thus, this paper fills this gap by introducing a new Trade-off-based Adoption methodology for Cloud-based Infrastructures and Services (TrAdeCIS), which is based on the impact cloud-based services will have on the organization. This methodology developed will support organizations in decisions concerning (a) the selection of cloud service provider, (b) the type of cloud service to be adopted, and (c) the suitable type of cloud to be adopted. TrAdeCIS is illustrated based on a survey conducted with 10 organizations, who have adopted or plan to adopt cloud-based solution to fulfil their advanced IT requirements.

1   Introduction

Organizations are increasingly concentrating on adopting new and emerging IT solutions to fulfill their business requirements and objectives. A cloud computing environment foresees advantages for organizations such as lower IT administration and managed service costs and a better business continuity and disaster recovery process [1], [13]. However, there are   also disadvantages in terms of loss of control of services and/or data [19] as well as lower security, privacy, and reliability [9], [10]. Therefore, in a decision of either moving from a legacy infrastructure to a cloud-based solution or switching the cloud provider, contradicting and interdependent factors must be evaluated in full. These factors can be based on technical, economical, legal, and business oriented requirements and objectives. The difficulty in the decision of cloud adoption exists because of multiple criteria of selection, and due to the presence of more than one alternative solution. The current decision methodology for the selection of the best available cloud-based solution for IT requirements in organizations is an ad-hoc process, which does not only fail to achieve a trade-off between multiple contradicting factors, but also lacks a quantitative validation of this decision made.

A. Sperotto et al. (Eds.): AIMS 2014, LNCS 8508, pp. 1–14, 2014.

Researchers have suggested a generic framework for such a decision using multi-attribute decision algorithms [14], [16]. However, this work did not incorporate that (a) attributes can be mutually dependent, and (b) a trade-off-based decision is required based on multi-faceted business objectives. Hence, the need of a highly integrated yet flexible methodology for the decision of cloud adoption was distinctly identified [22]. The methodology developed and followed in this paper is called Trade-off-based Adoption methodology for Cloud-based Infrastructures and Services (TrAdeCIS) and is motivated by those gaps still existent in terms of identifying trade-off strategies for a cloud adoption and the management of cloud-based infrastructures and services. Trade-off strategy means altering the importance allotted to business objectives so that the best possible technical solution, based on traditional IT metrics, such as availability, response time, scalability, or efficiency, can be selected. Therefore, the methodology discussed in this paper focuses on the impact of business processes and business-level objectives on cloud adoption and vice versa. The aim of this approach is to find the best possible technical solution on an acceptable business value. This methodology can be used for a cloud-based decision concerning cloud-service providers, the cloud type, and services that should be migrated to the cloud. The application case of cloud-based solutions, has been selected due to its current importance, the demand from companies to see guided help, and to formalize the methodolgy in a concrete setting.

The methodology developed in this paper consists of following three steps: First, the identification of relevant factors, based on which the available alternative solutions will be evaluated. The list of such factors for this paper is retrieved based on the survey conducted with organizations who plan or have adopted cloud-based solutions for their IT needs. The following two steps of the decision support system are based on two multi-criteria decision analysis methods: (a) The Technique for Order of Preference by Similarity to Ideal Solution (TOPSIS), and (b) the Analytic Network Process (ANP) [12], [17]. These two methods are chosen due to their inherent nature of being able to compare components of an adoption scenario and to rank alternatives under consideration. While TOPSIS is used to rank alternative solutions based on technical requirements, ANP is used to establish a trade-off-based decision for multiple contradicting Business Performance Metrics. These algorithms will be used within the envelope of business-level objectives, so that a holistic method is achieved for the decision regarding adoption of cloud.

This paper is structured as follows. Sec. 2 discusses relevant research work and gaps existent in a cloud adoption process. Sec. 3 provides an in-depth view of TrAdeCIS for establishing the trade-off-based decision methodology for adoption of clouds in an organization. Sec. 4 illustrates the new methodology based on results obtained from the survey conducted. Finally, Sec. 5 summarizes and concludes the paper.

2   Terminology and Related Work

Business-driven IT management deals with fulfilling IT requirements by evaluating impact of IT on business processes and vice versa. However, business objectives are contradicting in nature and, therefore, a trade-off strategy is necessary. Such a strategy can fulfil IT requirements in a best possible way by balancing various requirements and goals. The term business value or return value refers to the impact IT (in the context of this paper, a cloud-based solution) has on organizational performance using process-level, economic, and operational metrics, called Business Performance Metrics (BPM).

In order to compare related work to TrAdeCIS, it is divided into two groups. Category one consists of current efforts in cloud adoption and management of cloud resources and services concentrating on technical aspects, such as resource provisioning [7] or migration and implementation processes [4], [11]. Category two comprises of methodologies for the decision of cloud adoption for an organization. Research on a cloud adoption decision process suggests various approaches such as Goal-oriented Requirement Engineering (GRE) [22], [2] and a quantified method of Multi-Attribute Decision Analysis (MADA) [14], [16]. These approaches present a method of decision making based on evaluating various factors that impact such a decision. However, they are not integrated and do not incorporate business-level objectives and requirements. For example, the effect on the net profit after adopting cloud-based services cannot be addressed by such methods.

However, from the cloud providers perspective, the last few years have seen research on business-driven IT management [5], [8], [18]. These approaches concentrate on managing the ever increasing scale of cloud-based resources and services, by providing business level objectives-driven cloud management for the cloud provider. These are holistic approaches as cloud providers have to consider the context where services are used in order to make any service management related decision.

As shown in Tab. 1 the comparison of related work to TrAdeCIS is based on four key features, "Yes" describing the presence and "No" denoting the lack of that feature.

Table 1. Feature Comparison of Cloud Implementation and Adoption Methods

Features	Implementation Methods	MADA	GRE	TrAdeCIS
Relevant Factor Identification Method	No	No	Yes	Yes
Quantified Decision Method	No	Yes	No	Yes
Business Objectives Consideration	No	No	No	Yes
Trade-off-based decision	No	No	No	Yes

A cloud adoption decision methodology based not only on monitoring technical requirements and factors but also targeting to reach a overall governance process, itself based on business-level policies and objectives, does not exist for a potential cloud customer. The overall adoption decision for a cloud becomes more complex when services and resources are distributed in diverse legacy infrastructure.

Therefore, TrAdeCIS establishes a novel methodology, with which an organization can take a decision based on a trade-off strategy of business objectives. TOPSIS and ANP serve as underlying mathematical models to support this decision of establishing a trade-off strategy. The capability of ANP and TOPSIS to work with interdependent and conflicting factors, effecting the decision, qualifies them to be applicable. Both methods have also been used for solving decision problems with certainty and making forecasts in various fields of science, manufacturing, and finance [6], [15], [21].

3   The Development of TrAdeCIS

The overview of the methodology developed in this paper to establish trade-off-based decision for the selection of (a) cloud service provider, (b) cloud service to be adopted, and (c) the suited type of cloud to be adopted, is shown in Fig. 1. As the decision to move from legacy infrastructure to cloud-based solution or to switch the cloud provider is effected by several factors, TrAdeCIS begins with the selection and prioritization of these factors. The selection and prioritization of these factors is based on the technical requirements, and business objectives and policies of organization. Once TrAdeCIS is implemented as a decision support tool, it will include a generalized list of factors, which organizations planning to adopt cloud-based solutions should consider. This list of factors will be based on data collected from (a) survey conducted with organizations who have adopted or plan to adopt cloud-based solution, and (b) academic and industry literature on relevant factors in such a scenario. However, TrAdeCIS would provide flexibility to the organizations to adapt this list of factors based on use-case specific details. This process of identification and prioritizing factors is discussed and presented in Sec. 4. Once an organization identifies its requirements and business objectives TrAdeCIS is an easy, efficient, and a structured approach for making a decision for adoption of cloud-based solutions, which involv multiple attributes and objectives. This is possible because TrAdeCIS is a fully quantitative approach based on mathematical models with clearly identified steps.

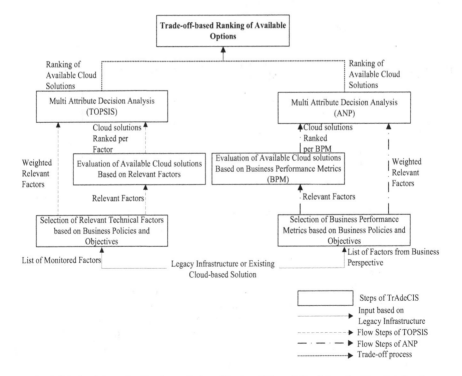

Fig. 1. Methodology for Business Driven Trade-off-based Decision for Cloud Adoption

3.1   Business Layer

The first step for making a decision for the adoption of a cloud-based solution is driven by business level considerations of an organization who plans to a adopt cloud-based solution. Based on the status of current infrastructure (*e.g.*, resources, processes interdependencies), and business goals and policies (*e.g.*, availability level, risk) relevant factors for the evaluation of alternative new cloud-based solutions are selected. To illustrate the process of selection of relevant factors consider an organization dealing with private information of its clients. Such an organization will target to have a control over such data to make sure data is not lost and tampered by anybody. Therefore, privacy of data and data control are two most important factors to be considered. Criteria which serve as benefits are considered positive (*e.g.*, bandwidth, availability) while those which are risk or cost prone are considered to be negative (*e.g.*, latency, cost) [14]. Also, depending on the criticality of the business goal,selected on the basis of business policies, relevant factors can be given a relative rank. Criticality of business goals is a metric to define the relevance as it is defined in an organization for each process and service for evaluating IT operations, for example, in terms of, risk in terms of vendor lock-in, technical requirements of availability, latency, security, and business goals and vision of reducing operational cost, increasing available resources.

3.2   TOPSIS

Once relevant factors are identified and prioritized a multi-attribute decision making algorithm is required to rank alternative solutions. TOPSIS is such a technique for solving decision problems   by determining the relative advantage of available alternatives [12]. An optimum alternative is mathematically at the shortest geometrical distance from the best solution and at largest geometrical distance from the worst solution. The alternative solution that is at the maximum distance from the worst solution has the least risk attached to it. With this method it is possible to compare a set of alternatives by identifying priorities for each factor and normalizing score for each factor. This gives the advantage of identifying how an alternative scores per attribute in form of the following steps:

1. TOPSIS assumes that there are m alternatives and n attributes/criteria and the score of each option with respect to each criterion is known [20]. Let $X = (x_{ij})$ and $m \times n$ a matrix represent x_{ij} the score of alternative i with respect to criterion j. Let J be the set of benefit attributes (to be maximized) and J' be the set of negative attributes or criteria (to be minimized).

2.The matrix X is normalized to form a normalized decision matrix. This step transforms the attributes having different dimensions into non-dimensional attributes, hence allowing comparisons across criteria. Normalized weights are obtained as

$$r_{ij} = \frac{x_{ij}}{\displaystyle\sum_{\substack{1 \le i \le m \\ 1 \le j \le n}} x_{ij}^2}$$

3. Construct the weighted normalized decision matrix, where each weight is represented by wj for $1 \le j \le n$. Multiply each column of the normalized decision matrix by its associated weight. An element of the new decision matrix is $v_{ij} = w_{ij} \times r_{ij}$.

4. Determine the ideal positive solution $A^* = [v_1{}^*, v_n{}^*]$, where $v_j{}^* = \max(v_{ij})$, if $j \in J$ or $\min(v_{ij})$ if $j \in J'$. Determine the ideal negative solution $A' = [v_1', v_n']$, where $v_j' = \min(v_{ij})$, if $j \in J$ or $\max(v_{ij})$ if $j \in J'$.

5. Determine the separation from the ideal solution for every alternative *j*. Distance from the positive solution is $S_i{}^* = \sqrt{\sum(v_j{}^* - v_{ij})^2}$ and that from the negative solution is $S_i' = \sqrt{\sum(v_j' - v_{ij})^2}$ for $1 \le j \le m$.

6. Calculate the relative closeness to the ideal solution $C_i{}^* = \dfrac{S'_i}{S_i{}^* + S_i'}$. Give highest rank to the option with $C_i{}^*$ closest to 1.

Using this method TrAdeCIS obtains a ranked list of available alternative cloud-based solutions, which are evaluated on technical parameters based on business objectives and policies as shown in Sec. 4.2.

3.3   Evaluation of Alternatives Based on Business Performance Metrics

While the alternative solutions, in the previous step, were ranked based on the relevant factors from the technical and operations perspective, this step evaluates the alternative solutions from the business value perspective. This is important so that returns in terms of business value can be quantified and measured for each of the alternatives. These factors fall in the category of cost, time, profitability, or quality, for example, earned value, planned dollar expenditure per month, workload vs. utilization, and speed of cost reduction. Therefore, based on the business objectives and policies, appropriate BPM are identified and ranked. Each alternative is then evaluated for each of these metrics.

3.4   Trade-off-based Decision Using ANP

The final step is the most crucial step as it lets decision makers evaluate alternative solutions from the perspective of a return value. ANP evaluates the decision by considering the interdependence of attributes as well as the influence of alternatives in a decision making process [17]. The ranking obtained here can be different than the one obtained from TOPSIS. This happens because factors used to evaluate alternatives in ANP are BPMs as identified by organizations. ANP provides the flexibility of altering weights allotted to factors to establish a trade-off in TrAdeCIS. Establishing a trade-off is necessary so that the best technical solution is selected at an acceptable return value. The possibility of calculating the interdependence of attribute and ability to forecast benefits, costs, and risks qualify ANP for establishing a trade-off strategy for cloud adoption. In this method criteria and alternatives are considered as nodes in a network as shown in Fig. 2. Each node can be compared to all other nodes it has a relation with, thus, a logical overview of those steps is given here only [17]:

1. ANP makes a pare wise comparison of all nodes with respect to the objective. An equally spaced scale is also chosen to assign priorities.
2. These priorities are represented in a matrix and the normalized principle Eigen vector is computed. As a result local priorities for all connections are obtained.
3. Steps 1 and 2 are repeated for all connections to obtain the unweighted super matrix.
4. The unweighted super matrix is normalized to calculate the weighted super matrix.
5. The limit matrix is now calculated, which is the weighted super matrix raise to the power of k+1, where k is an arbitrary positive integer. This gives the ranking for alternative solutions with respect to the objective.

After applying ANP, a ranking of alternatives is obtained, which is based on the evaluation of available alternative solutions on the basis of BPMs identified by organizations. In this step, if the ranking obtained is different from the one obtained using TOPSIS (as different factors are considered), priorities given to factors can be adjusted in order to achieve the same ranking as with TOPSIS. These priorities represent the trade-off between the return value and technical features of a selected solution.

4   Illustration of the Method Based on Survey Results

This section illustrates the new methodology using parameters and their respective weights, based on interviews conducted with 10 organizations, who adopted or plan to adopt a cloud-based solution to fulfil their IT requirements. A qualitative research approach is followed in order to investigate diverse and complex data in depth [3].

Table 2. Organizations Overview

Company	Domain of Expertise	Size of Company[a]	Geographic Scope Served
C1	ICT Provider	60000	Europe, USA, Singapore
C2	Health Insurance	450	Switzerland
C3	Telecommunications	20000	Switzerland
C4	IT Infrastructure provider	5000	Europe, USA, Australia, China
C5	Financial Services	2600	Worldwide
C6	Property and Life Insurance	4000	Switzerland
C7	Professional Services	180000	Worldwide
C8	Networking Solutions	67000	Worldwide
C9	ICT Association	-	Switzerland
C10	Financial Services	140000	Worldwide

[a] Number of employees as per June, 2013

As shown in Tab. 2, organizations that participated in the survey vary in size, the scope of their expertise, and their geographical scope. Therefore, their IT requirements also vary. In turn, the aim of these interviews was to understand parameters these organizations evaluate before making a decision to make any changes in their existing IT infrastructure. These interviews were semi-structured so that those interviews could be adapted according to individual circumstances, such as focusing on specific areas or discarding questions, which did not apply. This survey helped in collecting a list of factors (e.g., availability, functionality, scalability), which depending on the use-case specific details were considered by organizations before adopting any cloud-based solution. In order to illustrate TrAdeCIS only the data collected from company C2 is used. This helps in evaluating a specific use-case in depth using TrAdeCIS. However, this methodology can be applied to any of the other use-case specific data obtained from other organizations. All the other use-cases are that of similar nature, and discussing them in depth would not provide any new insights to the illustration of TrAdeCIS. The plan of C2 is to scale the existing infrastructure in order to accommodate requirements of the peak season. Therefore, C2 required to evaluate the best available cloud-service provider.

4.1   Business Layer

Business requirements for C2 were to increase scalability and availability of the existing infrastructure as the business profitability depends mainly on the web-based platforms and applications that are used by customers and partners of C2. Also, as these applications dealt mainly with private and sensitive data of clients, privacy and security were also important aspects. In addition, as per the legal and regulative requirements, compliance and location of data storage were also critical factors for evaluating the alternative cloud-based solutions. After, finding the list of factors, C2 was asked to give both the weights of attributes and ranking of alternatives by numbers in the range of 1 to 10. As TOPSIS normalizes weights and rankings, the range and the number chosen to rank the alternatives does not matter, as shown in Sec. 4.2., These factors along with their relevant priorities (as identified by C2) are shown in Tab. 3. This table also consists of ranking of each of the available alternative service providers (A1, A2, A3) per factor, which were being considered by C2.

Table 3. Ranking of Alternatives per Attribute

Factors	Weights	A1	A2	A3
Functionality	3	7	6	5
Privacy	7	9	4	10
Availability	6	4	3	2
Scalability	5	5	8	5
Compliance	4	1	2	3
Storage Location	2	3	1	6
Simplicity	1	4	2	7

4.2 Ranking the Alternative Solutions Using TOPSIS

Alternatives are ranked in TOPSIS on the basis of distance from positive ideal and negative ideal solution as explained in Sec. 3.2. Applying formal steps of TOPSIS on the data shown in Tab. 3 positive ideal and negative solutions are calculated as shown in Tab. 4.

While the positive ideal solution is the set of the maximum values {2.001, 4.988, 4.460, 2.340, 1.068, 2.356, 0.843} for all these factors amongst all alternatives, the negative ideal solution is the set of minimum values {1.410, 1.995, 2.230, 3.745, 3.208, 0.388, 0.240}.

Table 4. Positive Ideal Solution and Negative Ideal

Factors	A1	A2	A3
Functionality	2.001	1.710	1.410
Privacy	4.489	1.995	4.988
Availability	4.460	3.342	2.230
Scalability	2.340	3.745	2.340
Compliance	1.068	2.136	3.208
Storage Location	1.178	0.388	2.356
Simplicity	0.481	0.240	0.843

In these sets element 4 and 5, namely scalabilty and compliance, are considered to be negative factors, *i.e.*, they contribute to risk and cost of the decision. Therefore, in the positive ideal set maximum value is taken and in the negative ideal solution minimum value is considered. The next step of TOPSIS is to find the distance of the alternative solutions from the positive and negative ideal solutions as shown in Tab. 5 and Tab. 6.

Table 5. Distance from the Positive Ideal Solution

Factors	A1	A2	A3
Functionality	0.000	0.073	0.3111
Privacy	0.201	8.883	0.000
Availability	0.000	0.553	2.166
Scalability	0.000	1.625	0.000
Compliance	0.000	0.531	2.133
Storage Location	0.723	1.999	0.000
Simplicity	0.117	0.324	0.000
S_i^*	1.009	3.740	2.147

Table 6. Distance from the Negative Ideal Solution

Factors	A1	A2	A3
Functionality	0.311	0.083	0.000
Privacy	6.143	0.000	8.830
Availability	2.214	0.553	0.000
Scalability	1.625	0.000	1.625
Compliance	2.133	0.536	0.000
Storage Location	0.320	0.000	1.999
Simplicity	0.051	0.000	0.260
S'_i	3.574	1.082	3.572

Depending on the value of relative closeness of the alternative solutions (A1, A2, A3) to the ideal solution(c_i*) the ranking of these alternatives is identified. c_i* for three alternatives are {0.2363, 0.071, 0.2361}. As seen from this example, A1 and A3 perform almost similar at these attributes due to similar c_i*. In this case establishing a trade-off strategy is most relevant as the final decision can be now based purely on business performance metrics. In other cases, especially when there is a substantial difference in c_i*, a trade-off strategy is mandatory, since a customer can judge the level of compromise that is to be made on returns to be expected. Trade-off are necessary as the best possible solution based on technical attributes might not be the most profitable as per business value and vice versa.

4.3   Evaluation of Alternatives Based on Business Performance Metrics

This step expects organizations using TrAdeCIS to identify and prioritize BPMs for measuring expected return in terms of business value for each alternative. The process of ranking each of the available alternative solutions (here, A1, A2, A3), per factor or BPM, is based on the experience of organization, and the market history of the service or cloud-solution. For example, if the market history of alternative A1 is better than A3, A1 will be ranked higher for the considered factor.

As obtained during the discussion with *C2* the BPMs are migration time, cost reduction, and workload versus utilization. These are the only factors by which *C2* decided to evaluate the business value of the available alternatives as *C2* planned to serve the peak load requirements with minimum cost. Also, as this service is very critical, the business migration time should be the least possible, and critical workloads should be handled by the service provider by prioritizing resources. C2 identified that its cost reduction is twice as relevant as migration time. Remaining relevant priorities as identified by *C2* for these factors are shown in Tab. 7.

Table 7. Relative Priorities of BPMs

Business Performance Metrics	Migration Time	Cost Reduction	Workload vs. Utilization
Migration Time	1	1/2	1/3
Cost Reduction	2	1	1/3
Workload vs. Utilization	3	3	1

4.4   Illustrating Trade-off-based Decision Using ANP

The ranked alternatives obtained in previous step of TrAdeCIS using TOPSIS, are now evaluated with respect to BPMs identified and ranked by the C2. As shown in Fig. 2 in ANP factors and alternative solutions are represented as nodes and inter-connections between them are marked with their relative importance, which is obtained by pair-wise comparison of each node. In this example, the decision is to be made for alternatives A1 and A3 as they scored same when evaluated using TOPSIS.

Following these steps as explained in Sec. 3.4, the normalized Eigen vector is calculated and priorities are found by TrAdeCIS. Hence the obtained unweighted super matrix is shown in Tab. 8. After normalizing the unweighted super matrix, the limit matrix is obtained as shown in Tab. 9. In ANP each alternative is evaluated independently of other alternatives. Now A3 gains higher priority owing to its high ranking in cost reductions, which overrule the high performance of A1 in the other two attributes (performance of alternatives in each of the attribute in Tab. 5). Therefore, A3 gives higher returns than A1 — it is a better solution in terms BPMs (migration time). cost reductions, and workload vs. utilization). However, as proven by TOPSIS A1 is a better alternative with respect to attributes important for the service. Now, if *C2* desires to change the priorities of BPMs it can happen that A1 is again chosen. If this happens then the best technical solution will be chosen at a trade-off of return value. On the other hand, if A3 is chosen then the solution with best return value will be chosen at a trade-off of technical specifications.

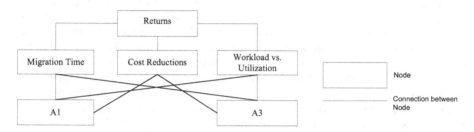

Fig. 2. Connection of Nodes in ANP

Table 8. Values Obtained in Unweighted Super Matrix

	Returns	Migration Time	Cost Reduction	Workload vs. Utilization	A1	A3
Returns	1	0	0	0	0	0
Migration Time	16	1	0	0	75	13
Cost Reduction	25	0	1	0	13	75
Workload vs. Utilization	59	0	0	1	13	13
A1	0	50	20	67	1	0
A3	0	50	80	33	0	1

Table 9. Values Obtained in Limit Matrix for Returns

	Returns	Migration Time	Cost Reduction	Workload vs. Utilization	A1	A3
Returns	0	0	0	0	0	0
Migration Time	0	18	18	18	0	0
Cost Reduction	0	26	26	26	0	0
Workload vs. Utilization	0	6	6	6	0	0
A1	36	0	0	0	18	18
A3	64	0	0	0	32	32

5   Summary, Conclusions, and Future Work

This paper has determined and discussed the existing gap between adopting cloud services and evaluating the impact cloud-services will have on business processes and organization. To fill this gap the concept of establishing a trade-off strategy is introduced — the new TrAdeCIS methodology — by which an organization can evaluate available alternative cloud-based solution based on the impact selected alternative will have on business. To establish this trade-off strategy two multi-attribute decision analysis methods are applied: TOPSIS and ANP. While TOPSIS is used to rank alternative solutions based on attributes from the technical perspective, ANP identifies a trade-off strategy based on returns expected. Thus, TrAdeCIS quantifies this process of decision making for a cloud adoption by (a) identifying relevant attributes and their relative importance, (b) ranking attributes on the basis of requirements, and (c) establishing the trade-off strategy on the basis of returns expected. This paper also illustrates TrAdeCIS based on survey results collected from organizations who have adopted or plan to adopt cloud-based solutions for their IT requirements.

It can be concluded that the current ad-hoc process of cloud adoption in organizations can be replaced with the quantitative methodology of TrAdeCIS. This approach developed fills the gap of evaluating cloud-based solutions not only from the technical perspective, but also from the view of impact it will have on the organization.

The next step of this work is to implement TrAdeCIS as a working prototype, which will be tested and evaluated with further organizations, who plan to adopt cloud-based solution for their advanced IT needs. This will help to evaluate the impact of TrAdeCIS in full and in such a decision making process of these organizations, all in comparison to existing, though, functionally restricted related work.

Acknowledgments. This work was partly funded by FLAMINGO, the Network of Excellence Project ICT-318488, supported by the European Commission under its Seventh Framework Programme.

References

1. Armbrust, M., Fox, A., Grith, R., Joseph, A.: A View of Cloud Computing of Cloud. Communications of the ACM 53(4), 50–58 (2010)
2. Beserra, P., Camara, A., Ximenes, R., Albuquerque, A.B., Mendonca, N.C.: Cloudstep: A Step-by-Step Decision Process to Support Legacy Application Migration to Cloud. In: 6th International Workshop on the Maintenance and Evolution of Service-Oriented and Cloud-Based Systems (MESOCA), pp. 7–16. IEEE, Trento (2012)
3. Blaxter, L., Hughes, C., Tight, M.: How to Research. McGraw-Hill International (2010)
4. Chang, V., Wills, G., Walters, R.J., Curie, W.: Towards a Structured Cloud ROI: The University of Southampton Cost-Saving and User Satisfaction Case Studies. In: Sustainable Green Computing: Practise, Methodologies and Technologies, pp. 179–200. IGI Global (2012)
5. Chhetri, M.B., Vo, Q.B., Kowalczyk, R.: Policy-based Automation of SLA Establishment for Cloud Computing Services. In: IEEE/ACM 12th International Symposium on Cluster, Cloud, and Grid Computing (CCGrid), pp. 164–171. IEEE, Ottawa (2012)
6. Deng, H., Yeh, C., Wills, R.: Inter-company Comparison Using Modified TOPSIS with Objective Weights. Computers and Operational Research 27(10), 963–973 (2000)
7. Ferrer, A., Hernandez, F., Tordsson, J., Elmroth, E., Zsigri, C., Sirvent, R., Guitart, J., Badia, R., Djemame, K., Ziegler, W., Dimitrakos, T., Nair, S., Kousiouris, G., Konstanteli, K., Varvarigou, T., Hudzia, B., Kipp, A., Wesner, S., Corrales, M., Forgo, N., Sharif, T., Sheridan, C.: OPTIMIS: A Holistic Approach to Cloud Service Provisioning. Future Generation Computer Systems 28(1), 66–77 (2012)
8. Fito, J.O., Macias, M., Julia, F., Guitart, J.: Business-Driven IT Management for Cloud Computing Providers. In: 4th International Conference on Cloud Computing Technology and Science (CloudCom), pp. 193–200. IEEE, Taipei (2012)
9. Geczy, P., Izumi, N., Hasid, K.: Cloudsourcing: Managing Cloud Adoption. GlobalJournal of Business Research 6(2), 57–70 (2012)
10. Greenwood, D., Khajeh-Hosseni, A., Smith, J., Sommerville, I.: The Cloud Adoption Toolkit: Addressing the Challenges of Cloud Adoption in Enterprise. Arxiv preprint, arXiv:1003.3866 (2010)
11. Khajeh-Hosseini, A., Greenwood, D., Sommerville, I.: Cloud Migration: A Case Study of Migrating an Enterprise IT System to IaaS. In: 3rd International Conference on Cloud Computing (CLOUD), pp. 450–457. IEEE, Miami (2010)

12. Hwang, C., Yoon, K.: Multi Attribute Decision Making: Methods and Applications. Springer, Berlin (1981)
13. Li, A., Yang, X., Kandula, S., Zhang, M.: Cloudcmp: Comparing Public Cloud Providers. In: ACM SIGCOMM Conference on Internet Measurement, pp. 1–14. ACM, Melbourne (2010)
14. Menzel, M., Schoenherr, M., Tai, S.: The (MC2)2 Criteria, Requirements and a Software Prototype for Cloud Infrastructure Decisions. In: Software: Practice and Experience. Wiley Online Library (2011)
15. Niemira, M., Saaty, T.: An Analytic Network Process Model for Financial-crisis Forecasting. International Journal of Forecasting 20(4), 573–587 (2004)
16. Saripalli, P., Pingali, G.: MADMAC: Multiple Attribute Decision Methodology for Adoption of Clouds. In: 4th International Conference on Cloud Computing (CLOUD), pp. 316–323. IEEE, Washington DC (2011)
17. Saaty, T.: Fundamentals of the Analytic Network Process-dependence and Feedback in Decision-making with a Single Network. Journal of Systems Science and Systems Engineering 13(2), 129–157 (2004)
18. Sedaghat, M., Hernandez, F., Elmroth, E.: Unifying Cloud Management: Towards Overall Governance of Business Level Objectives. In: IEEE/ACM 11th International Symposium on Cluster, Cloud, and Grid Computing (CCGrid), Newport Beach, CA, USA, pp. 591–597 (May 2011)
19. Sultan, N.A.: Reaching for the "Cloud": How SMEs can Manage. International Journal of Information Management 31(3), 272–278 (2011)
20. Wang, J., Liu, S., Zhan, J.: An extension TOPSIS for Fuzzy MCDM Based on Vague Set Theory. Journal of Systems Science and Systems Engineering 14(1), 73–84 (2005)
21. Wang, T., Chang, T.: Application of TOPSIS in Evaluating Initial Training Aircraft under a Fuzzy Environment. Expert Systems with Applications 33(4), 870–880 (2007)
22. Zardari, S., Bahnsoon, R.: Cloud Adoption: A Goal-Oriented Requirements Engineering Approach. In: 2nd International Workshop on Software Engineering for Cloud Computing, pp. 29–35. ACM, Honolulu (2011)

ESPRESSO: An Encryption as a Service for Cloud Storage Systems

Seungmin Kang[1], Bharadwaj Veeravalli[1], and Khin Mi Mi Aung[2]

[1] National University of Singpore, Singapore
{kang_seungmin,elebv}@nus.edu.sg
[2] Data Storage Institute, A*STAR, Singapore
mi_mi_aung@dsi.a-star.edu.sg

Abstract. Cloud storage systems have become the primary storage space for cloud users' data. Despite the huge advantages and flexibility of the cloud storage services, many challenges are hindering the migration of users' data into the cloud. Among them, the data privacy needs to be considered. In this paper, we design and implement an encryption service namely ESPRESSO (Encryption as a Service for Cloud Storage Systems) to protect the users' data by using advanced encryption algorithms. The flexible design and the standalone property of ESPRESSO allow cloud storage service providers to easily integrate it without heavy modification and implementation of their infrastructures. ESPRESSO was integrated into two open-source cloud storage platforms: OpenStack/Swift and Nimbus/Cumulus. The real experiments were conducted, and the results assess the performance and effectiveness of ESPRESSO.

Keywords: Cloud storage system, encryption, data privacy protection.

1 Introduction

With significant investment, many cloud storage systems are providing cloud users high data availability and the flexibility in data management, and they become the primary storage space for users' data. Thus, instead of storing and managing data in local servers, most of users nowadays are moving their data into the cloud and paying for storage and management service by a pay-per-use model. In this sense, cloud users are sharing a common storage space offered by Cloud Service Providers (CSPs). This characteristic raises several challenges which are hindering the migration of users' softwares and data into the cloud [1]. Among them, the security and data privacy are the most important challenges needed to be solved to attract users [2]. While consumers have been willing to trade privacy for the convenience of cloud storage services, this is not the case for enterprises and government organizations. This reluctance can be attributed to several factors that range from a desire to protect mission-critical data to regulatory obligations to preserve the confidentiality and integrity of data. The latter can occur when the customer is responsible for keeping personally identifiable information (PII), or financial and medical records [3]. Driven by the

A. Sperotto et al. (Eds.): AIMS 2014, LNCS 8508, pp. 15–28, 2014.

need to secure growing cloud data storage systems as well as high profile security breaches, data protection in cloud storage systems has become a hot topic in both academia and industry [4,5,6,7]. While the current approaches, which rely on a user-centric authentication service, can be broken by authentication attacks, encryption emerged as one of the most effective means to protect sensitive data no matter where it lives [8].

With an encryption tool, users can encrypt data on their local machine before uploading the encrypted data to a cloud. However, this approach introduces an additional burden for users to manage the encryption key and operate the encryption tool. Furthermore, users are required to equip local machines which are able to handle such a compute-intensive task that incurs the time overhead. These issues make the user-side encryption approach difficult to realize, especially when users are using scarce resource devices such as smartphones. A server-side encryption approach is therefore needed. On one hand, CSPs can provide the encryption to users as an added value service with minimal additional cost. On the other hand, this encryption can be offered as a free charge service. It then becomes a competitive advantage of a CSP against other CSPs to attract users and increase the CSP's reputation.

Among existing CSPs, only two commercial CSPs: Google Cloud Storage [9] and Amazon S3 [10] offer a server-side encryption service. However, the encryption services developed by Google and Amazon cannot be adopted by many other CSPs which want to offer the server-side encryption to users such as Microsoft Azure [11], GoGrid [12], RackSpace [13]. This observation inspires us to design and implement a standalone encryption service, ESPRESSO, for such CSPs to integrate without heavy modification and implementation of their infrastructures. Furthermore, we aim at providing a configurable and flexible encryption service for both CSPs who can choose the encryption algorithm based on their preference, and users who can specify the critical level of their data. The data with higher critical level needs to be more securely protected. Last but not least, we aim at providing ESPRESSO as a transparent encryption service which makes users perceive no difference between with and without the encryption service in terms of latency and complexity of data management operations.

The paper is organized as follows. Section 2 presents the problem statement including threat model and design goals of ESPRESSO whose the architecture is described in Section 3. Section 4 presents the detailed implementation of ESPRESSO. The integration of ESPRESSO into the Swift and Cumulus storage systems is presented in Section 5. Section 6 presents the experimental results which assess the performance and effectiveness of ESPRESSO. The related work is discussed in Section 7 followed by the conclusion of the paper in Section 8.

2   Problem Statement

2.1   The System and Threat Model

In this paper, we consider the CSPs which provide a data storage service. To protect the data privacy, an encryption service is used to encrypt the data before being stored in the cloud, and decrypt the data whenever users need to access the data. Depending on the deployment location of the encryption service, different threat models can be introduced. Below, three threat models will be analyzed.

1. The first model applies the user-side encryption approach. Users deploy the encryption software on their local machine and flexibly operate the service without needing to trust any third party. However, users are generally not expert in the security domain. The user's machine therefore suffers the security risks such as key exposure attacks or attacks from malicious programs. Moreover, it is not an easy task for non-expert users to take full responsibility of encryption key management such as key generation, key storage and keeping those keys always safe. Yet, if users are using scarce resource devices such as mobile devices, performing the encryption on such devices may not be possible since the encryption is considered as a compute-intensive task.
2. Users can rely on a third party who offers the encryption service. The third party takes full responsibility for managing the data encryption, protecting the encryption server and preventing the exposure of the users' encryption keys. Assuming that the encryption service is resistant to the security risks, users still have the sole concern on the adversarial behavior of the third party. With the curiosity and economic purpose, the third party might collude with malicious users to harvest data contents when it is highly beneficial [14]. Moreover, this model requires further effort from users to retrieve the encrypted data to their local machine before uploading to the cloud.
3. CSPs play the role of the third party presented in the second model. CSPs deploy the encryption software on a server in its trusted domain as one of its components. Users therefore benefit all advantages but also suffer the security risks as mentioned above. The operation overhead might be lesser since users do not need to manage the encrypted data. Instead, users upload the plaintext data to the CSP who will forward the data to the encryption server to encrypt before storing the encrypted data in storage servers.

As described, each model has advantages and disadvantages. Assuming that users trust the third party in the second model and the CSP in the third model at the same level, we believe that the third model brings users the most advantages. Depending on the model, the encryption service may be designed and implemented differently to assure that it efficiently operates at high performance. We present in the next section the design goals of ESPRESSO, the encryption service for CSPs as we advocate the third model presented above.

2.2   Design Goals

Several design requirements should be carefully considered since the design directly affects the overall performance of the system.

Architectural requirements. The encryption service should include two main components. The first component is the encryption key management. To increase isolation among users, a CSP may use different keys to encrypt different users' data and a user may have multiple keys for different data. To prevent leaking one's key to another, the encryption key must also be encrypted. Additionally, since the data availability is an important requirement of a cloud storage system, keys need to be replicated to be available when requested.

The second component is the data encryption management. ESPRESSO needs to provide the flexibility for both CSPs and users. Since ESPRESSO can be used by different CSPs, it should support multiple encryption algorithms. A CSP may choose its preferred algorithms to process users' data, e.g., Swift may use AES while Eucalyptus may use Blowfish. For users, the service should allow them to specify a desired critical level for their data. Currently, the CSPs, which offer server-side encryption, support only a single key length option, e.g., Google Cloud uses 128-bit keys. However, users may have different levels of security. Financial or medical records need to be more securely protected (using 256-bit keys) than entertainment data like musics or movies (using 128-bit keys).

Choosing supported encryption algorithms and critical levels of data. Given that CSPs offer different encryption algorithms and key lengths, choosing the supported encryption algorithms and critical levels of data is also important to achieve the flexibility. There exists many encryption algorithms in the literature including symmetric and asymmetric algorithms with their own advantages and disadvantages. A symmetric algorithm eases the implementation, however, it may not provide high level of security while an asymmetric algorithm is more complex to manage its key pair. Additionally, an asymmetric algorithm may take longer time for data encryption and decryption.

On the critical level of data, the longer key length is, the higher security level is guaranteed, however, it also takes longer time for encryption and decryption of data. Therefore, choosing the key length for each security level should take into account the tradeoff between the security level and the processing time.

APIs for integration to cloud storage platforms. As a last requirement of ESPRESSO, a well-designed integration API is also important since this allows CSPs to integrate and to use ESPRESSO easily without heavy modification of the architecture and implementation of their infrastructure. For instance, to provide an enhanced encryption service with a flexible critical level, the critical level should be one of API parameters along with data to be stored and user identification. Depending on the design, other parameters could be added. However, they should be carefully chosen since it may be difficult for CSPs to integrate ESPRESSO with redundant parameters.

3   System Architecture of ESPRESSO

In this section, we first present the detailed architecture and then describe the method to handle the flexibility and support multi-user scheme in ESPRESSO.

3.1   Architecture of ESPRESSO

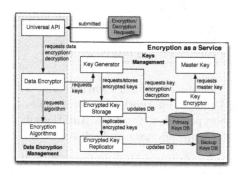

Fig. 1. ESPRESSO overall architecture

The overall architecture of ESPRESSO is depicted in Fig. 1 with two components: Data Encryption Management and Keys Management. The request flow is as follows. Universal API is the gate of ESPRESSO which can provide a wide range of interaction protocols allowing multiple CSPs to integrate ESPRESSO into their infrastructures. After receiving a request, Universal API delivers the request to Data Encryptor which is responsible for processing users' data using algorithms implemented in Encryption Algorithms. Data Encryptor requests encryption key from Keys Management through Key Generator which is the starting point of the Keys Management component. Key Generator retrieves the key stored in Encrypted Key Storage if it already exists, and sends it to Key Encryptor to decrypt using a master key. If the requested key does not exist in the database, that means the user is new on the system or the key for that specific critical level is not yet generated, Key Generator creates a new key and sends a key encryption request to Key Encryptor. The new key is then encrypted by the master key and sent back to Key Generator to store in Encrypted Key Storage. To assure the availability of encryption keys, encrypted keys are replicated and stored in Backup Keys DB.

3.2   Handling the Flexibility and Multi-user Scheme

To provide CSPs the flexibility in choosing a preferred encryption algorithm, ESPRESSO currently supports two algorithms: AES and Blowfish which are symmetric. By choosing symmetric algorithms, we eliminate the complexity of managing encryption key pairs which are supposed to be stored on different servers. Moreover, they are less intensive than asymmetric algorithms in terms of processing time. Additional algorithms can also be integrated into the system without breaking the architecture of ESPRESSO thanks to its agile design.

On the critical level of data, ESPRESSO provides three different critical levels by using three key lengths: 128, 192 and 256 bits for all supported encryption algorithms. The longer key length guarantees the higher critical level of data. A less than 128-bit key may be broken by the modern machine while a more than 256-bit key increases the latency of the service. Thus, each user can have up to three keys corresponding to three critical levels: the highest level uses 256-bit keys and the lowest level uses 128-bit keys, respectively. For a certain user, all the data with the same critical level are encrypted by the same key. Since a CSP

Table 1. Structure of the encryption keys table in MySQL

Field	Type	Description
key_id	Integer	Key identification: auto increment field
user_id	String	User identification
critical_level	Character	Critical level of user's data
key_string	String	Key string for encryption and decryption.

serves multiple users, each user is therefore identified by a user identification. We tie the user identification to the critical level and the encryption key by a tuple of $<$ user_id, critical_level, key_string $>$ in the encryption key database. Additionally, keys are generated on request of the CSP for a specific user and critical level.

4 Implementation of ESPRESSO

We use Python to implement ESPRESSO based on its broad adoption and efficiency. We implement in Universal API the Web Server Gateway Interface (WSGI) which allows CSPs to deploy ESPRESSO as a WSGI service. The implementation of Universal API handles the WSGI requests, i.e., extracting user_id, critical_level and data, and converts them to internal requests which are then forwarded to Data Encryptor. There are two functions in Data Encryptor: encrypt_data and decrypt_data. The encrypt_data function, which has three parameters: user_id, critical_level and data, prepares the encryption. It includes instructions for requesting the encryption key from Key Generator, initializing the encryption algorithm instance and finally invoking the execution of the encrypt_data function implemented in Encryption Algorithms. The algorithm selected by the CSP is saved in an INI configuration file with simple format, for example, [algorithm]name = AES. Instead of implementing all encryption algorithms by ourselves, we use a library namely PyCrypto [15] which provides the implementation of various algorithms such as AES, DES, RSA and ElGamal.

Since the critical_level parameter is needed to retrieve the encryption key for data decryption in the future; however, users may not remember which level was set for the data in the past, we include this parameter in the encrypted data. For a data retrieval request, the CSP gets the encrypted data from the storage server and passes it to ESPRESSO with the user_id parameter in a decryption request. Data Encryptor first extracts the critical_level parameter from the encrypted data and then invokes the decryption by calling the decrypt_data function.

To provide users a friendly manner to specify the data critical level, we decode three proposed critical levels by three letters: **A** stands for the high level, **B** stands for the medium level and **C** stands for the low level. Theses three symbolic letters hide the complex technical details of critical levels from users who are not expert in the security domain. The CSPs integrating ESPRESSO should provide a usage guideline to make their users aware of the trade-off between the strength and required processing time of each level, i.e., **A** is the strongest level but it requires longer time to complete the encryption.

Algorithm 1 Encryption and Decryption calls

Input: data, user_id and critical_level for an encryption; encrypted_data and user_id for
a decryption request; the ESPRESSO server address: server for both requests.
Output: Encrypted data for an encryption; plaintext data for a decryption request.
 1: connection = HTTPConnection(server); /*Create an HTTP/HTTPS connection*/
 2: connection.putrequest('EN', ''); /*'EN' for encryption and 'DE' for decryption*/
 3: **for** header in headers **do** /*Send all HTTP headers: user_id, critical_level*/
 4:     connection.putheader(header_name, header_value);
 5: **end for**
 6: **for** chunk in data **do** /*Send data by chunks*/
 7:     connection.send(chunk);
 8: **end for**
 9: response = connection.getresponse(); /*Waiting for response*/
10: Extract encrypted data or plaintext data from the response;
11: **return**

Encryption keys are generated by the Random library supported in Python. Each is a string including alphabet and numbers with length depending on the critical level. All keys are stored in a MySQL database whose the structure of the key table is shown in Table 1. Key Encryptor uses the same algorithm, i.e., AES or Blowfish, to encrypt the users' keys with a master key retrieved from Master Key. The implementation of Encrypted Key Storage and Encrypted Key Replicator handles the interaction with MySQL database, i.e., formulating the SQL query statements and executing the query.

5   Integration of ESPRESSO

We choose Swift [16] and Cumulus [17] to integrate ESPRESSO. These systems are open-source cloud platforms and they are widely used in both research community for experimental purpose and industry for commercial purpose. The integration involves determining a proper place in the source code of the storage systems where ESPRESSO is connected by using provided APIs and adding code instructions to realize that connection. The abstract pseudocode for encryption and decryption invocations from the storage systems is presented in Algorithm 1. Its detailed implementation depends on the target systems, programming language and supported library, e.g., Swift and Cumulus use Python while Eucalyptus uses Java. Generally, since ESPRESSO is implemented as a WSGI service, when a storage server requests for an encryption, a WSGI connection will be established (line 1). User's information and the data critical level are then passed by the connection header (lines 3 − 5). The data file is divided into chunks and sent to ESPRESSO (lines 6 − 8). When the data transmission is completed, ESPRESSO processes the data on its side while the storage server waits for the result (line 9) and continues the process after receiving data.

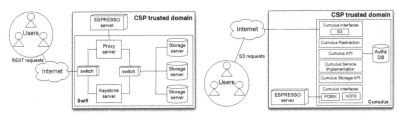

(a) With OpenStack/Swift.   (b) With Nimbus/Cumulus.

Fig. 2. Integration of ESPRESSO into cloud storage platforms

5.1   Integration of ESPRESSO into Swift

The integration of ESPRESSO into Swift is presented in Fig. 2a where we add the ESPRESSO server as a novel component of the Swift platform. ESPRESSO is deployed on a separate server rather than becoming an internal component of Swift. This avoids breaking down the Swift's code structure. Since the encryption and decryption happen only when users have downloading, uploading or updating requests which correspond to GET and PUT methods in the RESTful API supported by Swift, all of modifications were made to the swift/proxy/controllers/obj.py module in the proxy server at two functions: GET(self, req) and PUT(self, req).

On the user's side, this integration does not complicate the data management operation. Only the uploading and updating requests require one more parameter to be added: the data critical level. For instance, if users use cURL [18] to interact with Swift for data management, the data critical level will be added as a novel header: -H 'x-critical-level:A'.

5.2   Integration of ESPRESSO into Cumulus

ESPRESSO has also been similarly integrated into the Cumulus storage system. The encryption and decryption invocations, presented in Algorithm 1 are added in the cumulus/cb/pycb/cbRequest.py module at two classes: cbGetObject(cbRequest) and cbPutObject(cbRequest). Like Swift, the total number of code lines added is less than 50 for both methods. This assesses the easy and light adoption of ESPRESSO in any cloud storage platform.

Since Cumulus supports the Amazon's S3 REST protocol, many client libraries and tools, including s3cmd [19], boto [20] and jets3t [21] can be leveraged by Cumulus users. For instance, if user uses s3cmd, a novel header will be added to specify the data critical level: --add-header "critical-level: A".

With the integrated system, if users do not specify the critical level, ESPRESSO will automatically use the highest level, i.e., **A**, to encrypt the user's data.

6 Experiments and Performance Evaluation

6.1 Experiment Setup

The integrated storage systems were deployed using two dedicated physical servers on the same rack of the Communications & Networks Lab (CNL) at the National University of Singapore. Swift and Cumulus were installed on the server xx.xx.xx.64 and ESPRESSO was installed on the server xx.xx.xx.65. The servers are PowerEdge C6220 with Intel(R) Xeon(R) Processor E5-2640 2.50GHz, 24GB RAM. We used real data files which are downloaded from the Wikipedia archive [22]. The file size varies from several MB to 4GB that allows us to evaluate the efficiency of the encryption algorithm with different loads. Three following performance metrics were considered for evaluation:

- Latency of encryption algorithms: To show the efficiency of encryption algorithms, we measured the encryption time with different key lengths for the same algorithm. In addition, we compared the encryption time of two different algorithms with the same key length.
- Latency of the integrated system with and without ESPRESSO: To show the transparency of ESPRESSO, the total operation time (i.e., sum of the data uploading time from the client to the storage server and the data encryption time) of Swift with and without ESPRESSO were compared.
- Impact of network bandwidth: In this experiment, a remote client which uses the Internet backbone for transferring data was deployed. Two different network connections: WiFi and wired connection were applied.

For each experiment, we performed 5 times to measure the average and standard deviation values of performance metrics. The second and third experiments were performed on both systems. However, due to the space limit and to avoid the redundancy, only results on Swift are shown. A comparison of total operation time between Swift and Cumulus is given in the analysis of the third experiment.

6.2 Performance Analysis

Evaluation of Encryption Algorithms. Fig. 3a presents the encryption latency of the AES algorithm with respect to the data size. We executed AES with three different key lengths: 128, 192 and 256 bits. It is expected that with the same key length, the larger data volume is, the longer time is needed to complete the encryption. With the largest file at 4GB, the encryption time with 256-bit key is 93 seconds. Comparing the latency of AES with three key lengths, it is trivial that the longer key needs longer time to complete, however, it generates a more robust encryption, i.e., the data is more securely protected.

We also measured the encryption time of Blowfish and observed that there is the same behavior as AES. In Fig. 3b, we present the encryption time of AES and Blowfish with respect to the data size and with the same key length, 256 bits. The results show that Blowfish needs a longer time to complete the encryption for the same data compared to that of AES. Indeed, since Blowfish uses a 64-bit

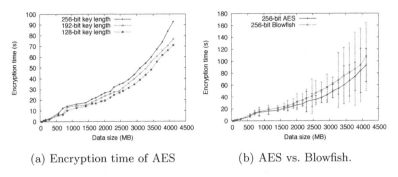

(a) Encryption time of AES   (b) AES vs. Blowfish.

Fig. 3. Performance of encryption algorithms

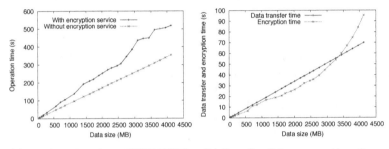

(a) With and without ESPRESSO.   (b) Details of the encryption time.

Fig. 4. Uploading time with/without ESPRESSO and details of encryption time

block size while AES uses a 128-bit block size, the number of blocks processed by Blowfish is doubled compared to that of AES. The processing transition between blocks leads to the overhead of Blowfish. The results also show the nature of the encryption algorithms that the decryption time is almost the same as the encryption time as expected. Thus, to avoid the redundancy, we do not present the results on decryption time here.

Integrated System Validation. To validate the integrated system, we run the Swift client on a machine located in the same LAN to reduce the data transfer time between the client and Swift. The encryption algorithm is AES and the critical level is **A**. Fig. 4a depicts the total operation time for uploading requests of Swift with and without ESPRESSO. In the case without ESPRESSO, the total operation time can be considered as the data transfer time from the client to the Swift server. It is expected that the total operation time of Swift with ESPRESSO is longer than that without ESPRESSO since an additional time is needed for data encryption. This overhead includes data transfer time from Swift to ESPRESSO, the encryption time and the transfer time from ESPRESSO back to Swift for resulted data. In the worst case, the total operation time increases 63.95%. The details of the encryption time overhead are presented in Fig. 4b. While the data transfer time between the Swift and ESPRESSO servers is small and not affected by other users since the servers are installed on the same rack,

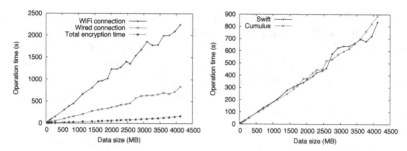

(a) Upload time from a distant client   (b) Swift vs. Cumulus performance.

Fig. 5. Total uploading time from a distant client to Swift and Cumulus

the encryption time dominates when the file size is large, i.e., larger than 3.5GB. Even though we assume 4GB files as the worst case scenario, which roughly corresponds to the total content of a single-sided DVD, one may have larger files to store. However, the results show that it is strongly discouraged to store large files to not significantly degrade the performance of the system.

Impact of Network Bandwidth In practice, users are not always located nearby the cloud. Therefore, the data transfer time from the user's location to the cloud is much larger than that presented in previous experiment. Indeed, we did the third experiment by running the client machine locating 3 kms from the Swift/Cumulus servers, using the Internet backbone for transferring data. In Fig. 5a, we present the total operation time of Swift for uploading requests when the client uses the WiFi and wired connection. The average uploading speed is 1.54 Mbps and 6.72 Mbps, respectively. The results show that the data transfer time from the client to the Swift server dominates in both connections. With the largest file with the WiFi connection, the total operation time is 37.45 mins while the encryption time overhead is only 2.75 mins, corresponding to 7.34% of the total operation time. From the point of view of a user who is sensitive with the latency, he may still not accept such overhead. However, considering the security aspect that the user's data is securely protected by CSPs, we believe that the cost represented by the time overhead is worth for such a security service. Fig. 5b presents the comparison of operation time between Swift and Cumulus when the remote client uses wired connection. The operation times of both systems are almost the same. While Swift needs longer time for replicating the data with 3 copies, Cumulus does not provide the replication service. However, this overhead on Swift is compromised by the fluctuation of the data transfer time.

7   Related Work

Most of literatures on data encryption have focused on providing a user-side encryption tool which allows the owner to share his data with different consumers. [23] proposed an Identity-Based Authentication scheme by which the owner can share his encrypted data stored in the cloud. In [5], YI Cloud, a framework for protecting the data privacy in the cloud, is presented. The framework includes two components: a client component which is deployed on the user's machine for encryption and key management, and a server component installed on Sector [24] for management of users and storage nodes. Both [5] and [23] did not provide the flexibility for providers and users as ESPRESSO did.

In [25], a progressive encryption system has been proposed based on Elliptic Curve Cryptography. The system allows the owner to share his encrypted data with other consumers without revealing the plaintext data to untrusted entities. The work did not present any real experiment but we believe that this approach involves an intensive computation, thus introduces high latency. Furthermore, [25] focused on the encryption algorithm and the sharing mechanism while we aim at providing an entire encryption service which can be adopted by any existing CSP. Similarly, [14] proposed a secure and scalable fine-grained data access control scheme for cloud computing by combining attribute-based encryption with techniques of proxy re-encryption and lazy re-encryption. Both [14] and [25] considered a different threat model where users do not trust any third party such as cloud providers. Hence, users must take full responsibility for the data encryption and key management on their local machines.

In [7], the authors presented PasS (Privacy as a Service), a set of security protocols for ensuring the privacy of data stored in the cloud. Although presenting a server-side encryption service, this work assumed that the encryption service is maintained by a third party that is trusted by users as well as CSPs. Instead of trusting the third party, CSPs can integrate ESPRESSO as a security component in their infrastructures. Thus, they can increase the reputation and help cloud users alleviate the security concerns with the third party.

8   Conclusion and Future Work

We proposed ESPRESSO, a standalone and transparent encryption service for cloud storage systems. It provides CSPs the flexibility of choosing their preferred encryption algorithm by supporting two algorithms: AES and Blowfish. With the flexible design, CSPs can easily integrate ESPRESSO without heavy modification and implementation of their infrastructures. ESPRESSO provides users three data critical levels which allow users to specify an appropriate level of their data. The integrated system does not require much effort from users to make their data protected. The experiments on the Swift and Cumulus storage systems show that the introduced encryption latency is negligible compared to the total operation time of a data management request. All these advantages assess the effectiveness of ESPRESSO to be integrated into any CSP on the production level. The work can be extended to support data-owner and data-consumer schemes. The access control will be used to handle access permission and an encryption key for each consumer. While we focused only on protecting the backup data in this paper, a secured computation could be considered since the data stored in the cloud can be also used for further computation. However, tackling secured computation properly would require a paper by its self to do justice to the issues involved. Thus, we address this issue in a future paper.

Acknowledgements. This work is supported by A*STAR SERC from the project entitled "Towards Designing Flexible, Cost Effective, Secured Service Provisioning Strategies for Heterogeneous Data Centres in a Cloud-of-Clouds infrastructure" (Grant No. 112 280 4009), and A*STAR TSRP from the project entitled "Secured Large Scale Shared Storage System" (DSI/11-200006).

References

1. IMEX: The Promise & Challenges of Cloud Storage. Technical report, IMEX Research (August 2010)
2. Tian, L.Q., Lin, C., Ni, Y.: Evaluation of User Behavior Trust in Cloud Computing. In: ICCASM 2010, Taiyuan, pp. 567–572 (October 2010)
3. Kamara, S., Lauter, K.: Cryptographic Cloud Storage. In: Sion, R., Curtmola, R., Dietrich, S., Kiayias, A., Miret, J.M., Sako, K., Sebé, F. (eds.) FC 2010 Workshops. LNCS, vol. 6054, pp. 136–149. Springer, Heidelberg (2010)
4. Factor, M., Hadas, D., Hamama, A., Har'el, N., Kolodner, E., Kurmus, A., Shulman-Peleg, A., Sorniotti, A.: Secure logical isolation for multi-tenancy in cloud storage. In: IEEE MSST 2013, Long Beach, CA, pp. 1–5 (May 2013)
5. Huang, Z., Li, Q., Zheng, D., Chen, K., Li, X.: YI Cloud: Improving User Privacy with Secret Key Recovery in Cloud Storage. In: IEEE SOSE 2011, Irvine, CA, pp. 268–272 (December 2011)
6. Hao, L., Han, D.: The study and design on secure-cloud storage system. In: ICECE 2011, Yichang, China, pp. 5126–5129 (September 2011)
7. Itani, W., Kayssi, A., Chehab, A.: Privacy as a Service: Privacy-aware Data Storage and Processing in Cloud Computing Architectures. In: IEEE DASC 2009, Chengdu, China, pp. 711–716 (December 2009)
8. Harrin, E.: Cloud Storage Vendors Offering Encryption as a Service. Technical report, Enterprise Networking Planet (February 2012)
9. Google, http://googlecloudplatform.blogspot.sg/2013/08/google-cloud-storage-now-provides.html
10. Amazon S3, http://docs.aws.amazon.com/AmazonS3/latest/dev/Welcome.html
11. Microsoft Azure (April 2014), http://www.windowsazure.com/en-us/
12. GoGrid, http://www.gogrid.com/
13. RackSpace, http://www.rackspace.com/
14. Yu, S., Wang, C., Ren, K., Lou, W.: Achieving secure, scalable, and fine-grained data access control in cloud computing. In: IEEE INFOCOM 2010, San Diego, CA, pp. 1–9 (March 2010)
15. Litzenberger, D.C.: PyCrypto (April 2014), https://www.dlitz.net/software/pycrypto
16. OpenStack (April 2014), http://swift.openstack.org/
17. Bresnahan, J., Keahey, K., LaBissoniere, D., Freeman, T.: Cumulus: An Open Source Storage Cloud for Science. In: ScienceCloud 2011, CA, pp. 25–32 (June 2011)
18. cURL, http://curl.haxx.se
19. s3cmd (April 2014), http://s3tools.org/s3cmd
20. boto (April 2014), http://code.google.com/p/boto

21. jets3t (April 2014), `http://jets3t.s3.amazonaws.com`
22. Wikipedia: Wikipedia archive (February 2014), `http://dumps.wikipedia.org`
23. Kang, L., Zhang, X.: Identity-based Authentication in Cloud Storage Sharing. In: MINES 2010, Nanjing, China, pp. 851–855 (November 2010)
24. Gu, Y., Grossman, R.L.: Sector and Sphere: The Design and Implementation of a High Performance Data Cloud. Philosophical Transactions of The Royal Society A: Mathematical Physical and Engineering Sciences 367 (1897), 2429–2445 (2009)
25. Zhao, G., Rong, C., Li, J., Zhang, F., Tang, Y.: Trusted Data Sharing over Untrusted Cloud Storage Providers. In: IEEE CloudCom 2010, Indianapolis, IN, pp. 97–103 (November 2010)

Adaptive CUSUM Algorithm to Detect Malicious Behaviors in Wireless Mesh Networks

Juliette Dromard[1], Rida Khatoun[2], and Lyes Khoukhi[1]

[1] University of Technology of Troyes, 12 rue Marie Curie 10010 Troyes, France
{dromardj,lyes.khoukhi}@utt.fr
[2] Telecom ParisTech 46 rue Barrault, 75013 Paris
rida.khatoun@telecom-paristech.fr

Abstract. Wireless mesh networks (WMNs) are very attractive networks as they are low cost and able to extend Internet rapidly in areas where other networks (e.g., Wi-Fi, MANETs, wired networks, 3G) cannot access due to their technical and/or economical limitations. However, these networks have to deal with security issues which prevent their deployment. In this paper, we propose a new reputation scheme which aims at preventing nodes from falsely detecting their neighbors as misbehaving due to packet loss over their links. The proposed reputation scheme is based on the fact that a link's packet loss ratio, when it is computed over a large quantity of observations, is quite stable over time. To detect misbehaving neighbors, a node, via its IDS, compares with the statistical method CUSUM (cumulative sum control chart) whether the distribution of packet loss rate observed for each of its neighbors follows the expected distribution or not. The validation of our solution shows that it allows to assign to nodes a trust value which reflects their real behavior.

Keywords: Wireless mesh networks, reputation computation, intrusion detection system.

1 Introduction

Wireless mesh networks (WMNs) have very attractive characteristics, they are low cost, easy to install and maintain. WMNs allow to cover white zones and to extend Internet to last miles, to hostile areas and to areas where the installation of cables is not economically viable. They are made up of fixed nodes (i.e., mesh routers (MR)) which form the backbone of the network and relay the data of mesh clients (MC) from MR to MR till reaching a gateway which sends them to the Internet.

However, the deployment of WMNs is limited by several security issues; this is due essentially to the characteristics of a WMN (e.g., the wireless nature of the channel, the multi-hop ad-hoc routing, the location of the MRs in public areas, etc.) [1] [2] [3]. The wireless nature of the channel allows any attacker situated in a mesh router's coverage zone to listen to the transmission of every packet

A. Sperotto et al. (Eds.): AIMS 2014, LNCS 8508, pp. 29–41, 2014.

that the MR forwards or sends. Furthermore, an attacker can easily scramble the data of the network by transmitting with a high power on the frequency used by the WMN. The attacker can also physically capture a MR as MRs are generally located in public areas, on a lamppost or on a bus stop [4] [2], for example. By capturing the routers, the attacker can retrieve the keys used for encryption, send false messages, drop packets, modify packets, and thus disrupts the network. The multi-hop nature of WMNs implies that every node may forward messages sent by other nodes. Thus, a WMN requires that every node collaborates in the routing process; hence, one compromised node can disrupt the whole network.

In order to overcome these security issues in WMNs, several security solutions based on cryptography schemes [5] [6] [7] have already been proposed. The amendment for mesh networking, the IEEE 802.11s, proposes also a security solution based on cryptography. Cryptographic schemes aim at preventing external nodes from entering the network as they don't possess the adequate cryptographic material to access the network. However, internal nodes can also misbehave and these solutions do not prevent such a situation. To detect internal misbehaving nodes in WMNs, researchers get interested in reputation schemes. In a reputation a scheme, every node monitors its neighbors via overhearing their transmissions, and, according to the outcomes of the monitoring, it assigns to each of them a reputation which is generally a value between 0 and 1 [8] [9] [10]. When the reputation value of a node is near to 0, the node is considered as misbehaving. In a reputation scheme, nodes generally monitor their neighbors by implementing the Watchdog IDS [11] [8] [10] [12]. The network interface card of a node which implements Watchdog is in promiscuous mode, thus, it can listen to every message sent in its covering zone even though it is not the destination of the message. A node can so check whether its neighbors correctly forward the message it sends to them or not, by overhearing their transmissions (see figure 1). In most reputation schemes based on Watchdog, a node assigns a reputation to each of its neighbors according to the number of packets it has correctly forwarded over the number of packets it has sent it. Then, a node interacts with a neighbor and forwards its packets according to its neighbor's reputation. The goal of reputation schemes is to isolate misbehaving nodes and/or to incite them to well-behave.

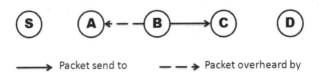

Packet send to   Packet overheard by

Fig. 1. Watchdog principle: Node A in a first step sends a packet to node B, B then, in a second step forwards this packet to node C. During this second step, node A overhears with the Watchdog IDS, whether node B forwards correctly to C the packet it has just sent to it.

However, a node's reputation can be distorted due to packet loss over the channel. Indeed, a node can consider that its neighbor has dropped its packet whereas the packet may, in fact, has been lost on the channel.

Furthermore, some experiments performed on real testbeds have shown that the packet loss rate on a WMN can be very high [13] [14] [15]. For example, the results of an experiment realized on a 38-urban wireless mesh network [15] have shown that most links pairs have intermediate delivery probabilities.

Thus, by not considering packet loss, Watchdog may launch many false positives, i.e., it may estimate that some nodes are misbehaving (i.e., drop packets), whereas in fact they are not (they just suffer from an important packet loss rate on their links). In consequence, reputation schemes which implement Watchdog may assign a bad reputation to a well-behaving node, due to packet loss over the channel. Thus, in these schemes a well-behaving node can be assigned a bad reputation and isolated unjustly from the network. In the rest of the paper, the term "bad node" refers to nodes which drops a certain percentage of packets and which can be either faulty, selfish or misbehaving whereas the term "good node" refers to node which does not drop any packet it receives.

In order to overcome this issue, we propose in this paper a new reputation scheme for WMNs:

- where every node integrates a reputation module made up of:
  - an IDS which aims at detecting bad nodes,
  - a computation reputation module which allows, based on the outcomes of the IDS, to assign a reputation to each node's neighbor .
- which has been validated with ns2 and the statistical R software [16]. The results of our validation shows that our system, contrary to most existing schemes, assigns to nodes a reputation which reflects their real behavior.

The rest of the paper is organized as follows. In the second section, we present a state of the art of the reputation systems in WMNs. Then, we introduce our packet loss rate model. Our IDS is proposed in the fourth section. In the fifth section, we present the computation reputation module of our solution. Then, we report the results of our evaluation, and finally, we conclude the paper.

2 Related Works

In the following, we present related works in the field of reputation systems. Most of these works were developed for MANETs. However, as a mesh network can be considered as a MANET with fix mesh routers, all these solutions can be easily implemented in mesh networks.

Pathrater [17] is a reputation system based on Watchdog for MANETs (Mobile Ad-hoc networks) which aims at avoiding misbehaving nodes on path flows. Every node in Pathrater associates to each of its neighbors a rating which is adjusted according to Watchdog outcomes. To select a path, a node calculates the metric of every path to the destination by averaging the ratings of every node along the path and selects the path which possesses the highest metric.

Pathrater needs that every node has an opinion about every other node in the network which is only possible if nodes are very mobile.

In [9], Jaydip Sen proposes a reputation system based on Watchdog in MANETs. A node reputation is computed with first hand information (i.e., information gathered via direct exchanges) and weighted second hand information (i.e., information gathered via indirect exchanges) which are combined with the node's previous reputation. The simulations show the efficiency of this solution to reflect a node's behavior through its reputation. However, the authors don't specify any punishment mechanism to avoid misbehaving nodes.

In [11], Yu Li presents a reputation system for WMNs using a multi-path routing protocol which aims at enforcing nodes' collaboration. Each node computes its neighbors' reputation while considering first hand evidences collected via Watchdog, the node's delay and the position of the node on the path. When a node's reputation is under a certain threshold, an alert is broadcasted and the node is punished; its packets are not any longer forwarded. The simulations show that this reputation system stimulates nodes' cooperation. However, this solution is not protected against bad mouthing , i.e., against nodes which send false accusations.

In [18], the authors proposed a Reputation-Aware Multi-hop routing Protocol (RAMP) in MANETs which relies on the routing algorithm DSR (Dynamic Source Routing)[19]. RAMP is based on direct observations collected via Watchdog and on indirect observations. Indirect observations are collected by the source of a flow during the route maintenance. Indeed, each node on the route path must acknowledge every packet of data received from the source. If the source does not receive any acknowledgement from a node in a Round Trip Time (RTT), it decreases the node's reputation; otherwise, it increases it. The nodes' reputation is adjusted according to the AIMD (Additive-Increase-Multiplicative-Decrease) algorithm. The evaluation of RAMP shows that it could achieve 10-15% less packet loss than some existing reputation-based schemes. However, RAMP may lead to an important increase of overhead as every node on a flow path must send an acknowledgement to the source each time it receives a packet of data.

In [20], the authors proposed a reputation system which aims at detecting malicious nodes in MANET. The originality of this work lies in a multi-dimensional trust based outlier detection and a gossip-based outlier detection algorithm. They have proposed multiple metrics in order to detect outliers such as the PMR (packet modification rate), the PDR (packet drop rate) and the RTS (request-to-send) flooding rate. Indeed, according to the way a node misbehaves, the countermeasures to apply may be different. The gossip-based outlier detection algorithm aims at identifying the top k outliers (the value of k must be a priori known). However, the authors do not propose any scheme to isolate misbehaving nodes and any method to fix the value of k.

[15] presents one of the major and most interesting studies of packet loss rate in a WMN. This article displays results obtained on an experimental 38-node urban 802.11b mesh network. They show that in WMNs, most pairs have intermediate

delivery probabilities. Thus, packet loss must be considered in Watchdog in order to prevent nodes from wrong accusations.

As we can observe, many reputation systems are based on Watchdog and do not consider packet loss and CSMA/CA unfairness [20] [21] [18] [15] [11] [9] [17]; thus, they may suffer from false negatives. In order to avoid this issue, we propose in what follows a reputation computation system based on an IDS which consider packet loss.

3   Packet Rate Not Overheard

In [15], the authors show that most links have intermediate loss rate. Furthermore, they point out that some links are bursty in terms of packet loss rate. However, they also show that "averaging over long time intervals (few seconds) smoothes out fluctuations" due to scattered burst; in other words, the packet loss rate, when computed over large intervals of times (few seconds), becomes quite stable over time. Thus, they display that "for most links, measuring a link loss rate over intervals as short as a few seconds is useful in predicting the near future. On the other hand, a small set of links (very bursty ones) varies substantially from one second to another". Furthermore, the authors in [22] have also shown via experiments on IEEE 802.11b wireless links that the packet loss rate on wireless links is quite stable. They assert that link qualities, at different times, are more or less similar and that the links'packet loss rate almost follow the same distribution, no matter the traffic is heavy or not. In order to prove this statement they performed the chi-square tests on observed data and found that the packet loss rates of links with the same length at different times follow the same distribution.

From the conclusions of these papers [22] [15], we model our network as a WMN where all links have a quite stable packet loss rate. Thus, the random variable which represents the packet loss rate of the directed link (i, j) denoted X_{ij}, is considered quite stable over time when it is computed over a quite large interval of time (few seconds) (see figure 2).

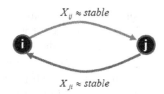

Fig. 2. Packet loss rate over links

In the following, the percentage of packets that j forwards and i overhears among the set of packets sent by node i to node j is termed "packet rate not overheard by i from j". Let us consider three nodes, node i, j and k and four

links between these nodes; links (i, j), (j, i), (k, j), (j, k) (see figure 3). To send
a packet to node k, node i sends it to node j which forwards it to k. As node
i monitors its neighbors, it can overhear j's communications. It can overhear
successfully j forwarding its packet, if the packet is not lost over both (i, j) and
(j, i), and is not dropped by j. Thus, the packet rate not overheard by i from j,
denoted X_{ij}^o, depends, when node j is a good node, only on the packet loss rate of
links (i, j) and (j, i). As the packet loss rate of these links is considered stable, the
packet rate not overheard by i from node j can be also considered as stable (see
figure 3). However, when j is a bad node, the packet rate not overheard depends
also on the percentage of packets that node j drops. Thus, the distribution of
packet rate not overheard by i from j is not the same depending on the node j
's behavior.

Fig. 3. Packet loss rate overheard from j by node i when j is a good node

4   Our Intrusion Detection System

Our detection intrusion system allows nodes to detect whether their neighbors
drop packets or not; this is achieved by monitoring changes in the packet rate not
overheard from each neighbor. Indeed, when a node misbehaves, it drops packets,
which generates an increase in the rate of packets that it does not forward and
so in the rate of packets that its neighbor does not overhear.

We assume that, every node i knows, for each of its neighbor j, the distribution
of the packet rate, denoted X_{ij}^o, it does not overhear j forwarding when this latter
is well-behaving and the standard deviation associated to this rate denoted σ_{ij}^o.
The value of these parameters can be extracted by performing tests on the
WMN's links before its deployment.

To detect changes in the packet rate not overheard, we have chosen the cumulative sum control charts (CUSUM) [23]. CUSUM is a sequential analysis technique which is used for monitoring detection changes. CUSUM detects changes
in the distribution by periodically computing two sums, the upper control limit
denoted C_z^+ and the lower control limit C_z^- which are the cumulative deviation
between the expected value and the observed value when the observed value is
respectively upper and lower than the expected one. When the upper control
limit or the lower control limit exceeds a certain threshold, CUSUM launches
an alert. CUSUM, in contrary to other methods of detection of change like the
Shewhart control charts, enables to detect small shifts [24].

Our IDS aims at detecting an increase in the mean of the random variable,
which means an increase in the packet rate not overheard. In our solution, each

time, a node i sends m packets to a neighbour j, it monitors the number of packets denoted n it does not overhear j forwarding and can then compute a realization x_z of the random variable X_{ij}^o (representing the packet rate not overheard by i from j) as follows :

$$x_z = \frac{n}{m}$$

Indeed, m must be large enough so that, this rate is computed on an interval of time superior to a few seconds. When the IDS of a node i gets a new realization x_z, it then computes the upper control limit C_z^+:

$$C_z^+ = max[0, x_z - (X_{ij}^o + K) + C_{i-1}^+] \quad and \, C_0^+ = 1 \qquad (1)$$

z represents the number of realizations, (i.e., the number of times it has already updated the upper control limit C_z^+), and K represents the reference value. More details about these parameters are given thereafter. Once, the IDS has updated the upper control limit, it checks whether it exceeds or not the decision interval H, i.e., if $C_z^+ \geqslant H$. If it does, the packet loss rate is assumed to have changed and node j is considered as misbehaving. To perform CUSUM, the values of the following parameters must be fixed:

- δ: it is the shift that the IDS wants to detect. This shift is expressed as a quantity of σ_{ij}^o. From this shift the out of control value of the packet rate not overheard is computed as follows: $X_t = X_{ij}^o \pm \sigma_{ij}^o \delta$
- K: it is the reference value. It is often chosen about halfway between the target value X_{ij}^o and the out of-control value X_t, in order to get good Average Run Length (ARL). The ARL is a measure of the performance of CUSUM.
- H: it is the decision interval. When the upper control limit or the lower control limit is above the decision interval H, we then consider that the process is out of control. It must be chosen so that we get a good ARL. There exists tables which allows, from the value of the parameter K, to choose the correspondent H in order to get a good ARL.

Thus, each time a node i gets a new realization x_z, it computes the upper control limit C_z^+ and checks whether this latter is above or not the decision interval H. If it is the case, then it assumes that the packet rate not overheard has changed and that j is misbehaving.

5   The Reputation Computation

Every node i stores about each of its neighbor j a reputation denoted R_{ij}. Once, a node i has performed CUSUM, it gets a value a_{ij} which is equal to 0 if CUSUM has launched an alert and 1 otherwise, and re-computes the value of R_{ij}. A new reputation R_{ij} is computed via the exponential moving average in order to consider older interactions:

$$R_{ij} = \beta R_{ij}^{old} + (1 - \beta)a_{ij} \qquad (2)$$

with R_{ij}^{old} the latest reputation which was computed and β the forgetting factor which value is situated between 0 and 1. The choice of the value of β depends on the network. The exponential moving average allows to get a smooth forgetting of node's old actions; the weighting for each older reputation decreases exponentially and never reaches zero. Thus, the value of a node's reputation is between 1 and 0; closer its reputation is to 1, the better the node's reputation is.

The reputation R_{ij} that a node i gets about a node j at the bootstrap, is set by the network administrator. It depends on the trust that the network administrator has then on the nodes. For example, if all these nodes have been established by a same company, then the administrator can have at the bootstrapping an entire confidence in the WMN's nodes and give then the maximum reputation; 1.

Every node only needs to store, for each of its neighbors, its current reputation and the last value of its upper control limit C_z^+. Thus, if a node has n neighbors, then it has only $2n$ values to store; the complexity storage of our solution is very low. Furthermore, each node re-evaluates its neighbors' reputation after a few seconds. To compute a node's reputation, the upper control limit must be re-evaluated (see equation 1), this latter must then be compared to the decision interval H and finally the node's reputation is obtained with formula 2. Thus, if a node has n neighbors, then it has only $3n$ operations to perform in a few seconds. Furthermore, as every node computes its neighbors' reputation with only local data, our solution does not trigger any overload and is scalable.

6   Evaluation of our Intrusion Detection System

The aim of this evaluation is to show that by considering packet loss over links, our solution assigns to nodes a reputation which represents more precisely their real behaviour. We compare our solution with the reputation system proposed in [9] via the event discrete network simulator ns2. In [9], the authors propose a reputation system based on Watchdog where each node assigns to its neighbour a reputation which considers the historical of its interactions and the percentage of packets that it overhears its neighbour forwarding. We have chosen to compare our approach with [9] as it is quite a generic solution of reputation system based on Watchdog.

Our solution has been evaluated with two different WMN's topologies; a mesh topology and a cross topology (see figures 4 and 5). They both possess one gateway which is represented by a red node on the figures. We introduce in each topology a bad node which drops a certain percentage p of packets of data it receives with success. The parameters of the simulation are presented in the table 6. In the following, we assume that the network's links have been chosen so that the packet loss rate is not inferior to 0.5 and do not belong to the few set of links which are very burst so that the packet loss rate is quite stable. Our solution can deal with packet loss rates over links superior to 0.5, however, a mesh network with very bad links would not be very efficient. In such a case,

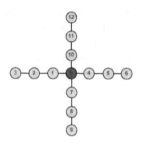

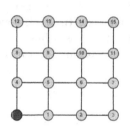

Fig. 4. Cross topology   **Fig. 5.** Mesh topology

only few packets would reach their destinations, so that we have decided to limit this rate to 0.5. However, our solution cannot deal with very bursty links as bursty links are most of the time quite unstable, so that we have chosen in our simulations to consider only links which are not very bursty. The packet loss rate of each link and the standard deviation associated to this rate are chosen according to a uniform normal law of parameters 0 and 0.5. Turning off links which burst is too important is indeed feasible as all the routers are, in WMNs, usually set up by a same entity. Thus, this entity can choose to turn off or on some links. According to [15], there is few very bursty links in WMNS, thus, turning off these links should not penalize much the WMN.

In the following, in order not to overload the figures, we have only represented the reputation of four nodes over times; three good nodes (node 1, 10 and 4) and one bade node (node 7).

Level	Parameter	Value
Signal propagation	Two-ray-ground model	
Packet loss rate	Mean of the rate	continuous uniform distribution of parameters 0 and 0.5
	Sandard deviation of the rate	continuous uniform distribution of parameters 0 and 0.5
Physical	Rate	54Mbit/s
	Frequency	$2,4GHz$
	PLCP preambule and header 's length	$20\mu s$
MAC	CSMA/CA	

Fig. 6. Values of the parameters used in our simulations

Figures 7 and 8 show the reputation of some mesh nodes in the WMN over time in the cross topology when the bad node drops 100% of the packets it receives with, respectively, the reputation system of [9] and ours. From these figures, we can notice that in existing solutions the reputation of good nodes depends on the value of the packet loss rate over their links and are not as high as they should be. Whereas in our solution good nodes possess the maximum trust which value is one. Both solutions give to the bad node a low trust which decreases quickly till 0. However, our solution takes longer to assign to the bad node a trust of 0 as it has to collect information during a few seconds about the node before assigning it a new trust value.

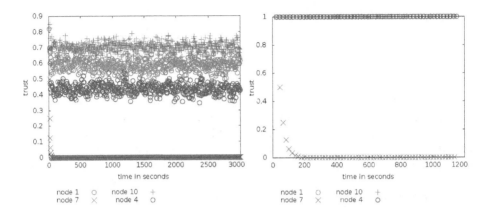

Fig. 7. The reference solution when $p = 100\%$ **Fig. 8.** Our solution when $p = 100\%$

Figures 9 and 10 show the reputation of some mesh nodes in the WMN over time in the cross topology, when the bad node drops 50 percent of the packets it receives with, respectively, the reputation system of [9] and our solution. From these figures, we can notice that with the reference solution, the reputation of good nodes depends on the value of the packet loss rate over their links. Whereas in our solution, good nodes possess the maximum trust. Both solutions give to the bad node a reputation with a low value. Our solution assigns to the bad node a lower reputation, however it takes quite a long time 200 seconds before the trust of node 7 decreases till the value 0. In the reference reputation system, we can notice that even though the reputation of the bad node is low, it is not very different from node 4 which packet loss rate over its links is important. Thus, our system allows to clearly identify the bad node whereas the reference solution cannot.

Figures 11 and 12 show the trust of some mesh nodes in the cross topology, when the bad node drops 20 percent of the packets it receives with, respectively, the reputation system of [9] and our solution. Our solution assigns to the bad node a low reputation; however, it takes quite a long time 500 seconds before the trust of node 7 reaches 0. With the reference reputation system, we can notice that the reputation of the bad node is quite high and even higher than some good nodes' reputation (node 4 and 1). Thus, when a bad node drops a little percentage of packets of data, the reference reputation system cannot identify it, whereas our solution is still able to; however, it takes quite a long time.

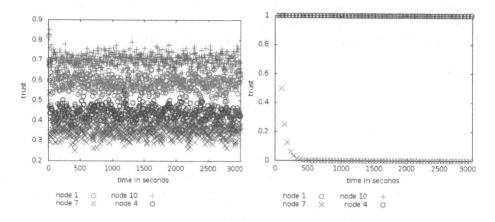

Fig. 9. The reference solution when $p = 50\%$

Fig. 10. Our solution when $p = 50\%$

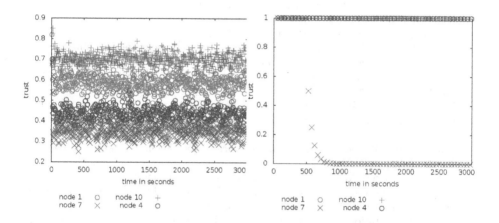

Fig. 11. The reference solution when $p = 20\%$

Fig. 12. Our solution when $p = 20\%$

7   Conclusion

In this article, we have proposed a new reputation system which considers packet loss rate in order to assign to nodes a reputation which reflects their behavior. Based on the fact that the packet loss rate over a link is quite stable over time, our solution allows to detect Greenhole and Blackhole by comparing the expected packet rate not overheard from a node with the observed one. If they differ, the node is assigned a bad reputation. To detect changes in the packet rate not overheard from a node, our solution applies the statistical method CUSUM. We have shown that our solution has a low resource and computational complexity, generates no overhead and is scalable. We have validated our solution via ns2 and compared it to an existing solution. The results have shown that our solution detects efficiently bad nodes even when they drop few packets.

References

1. Akyildiz, I.F., Wang, X., Wang, W.: Wireless mesh networks: a survey. Comput. Netw. ISDN Syst., 445–487 (2005)
2. Yi, P., Tong, T., Liu, N., Wu, Y., Ma, J.: Security in wireless mesh networks: Challenges and solutions. In: Sixth International Conference on Information Technology: New Generations, ITNG 2009, pp. 423–428 (2009)
3. Djahel, S., Begriche, Y., Nait-Abdesselam, F.: A bayesian statistical model to alleviate greediness in wireless mesh networks. In: 2010 IEEE Global Telecommunications Conference (GLOBECOM 2010), pp. 1–6 (2010)
4. Salem, N.B., Hubaux, J.P.: Securing wireless mesh networks. IEEE Wireless Communications, 50–55 (2006)
5. Hu, Y.C., Perrig, A., Johnson, D.B.: Ariadne: a secure on-demand routing protocol for ad hoc networks. Wirel. Netw., 21–38
6. IEEE standard for information technology-specific requirements part 11: Wireless lan medium access control (mac) and physical layer (phy) specifications amendment 10: Mesh networking. IEEE Std 802.11s-2011 (2011)
7. Wang, J., Jiang, N., Li, H., Niu, X., Yang, Y.: A simple authentication and key distribution protocol in wireless mobile networks. In: International Conference on Wireless Communications, Networking and Mobile Computing, WiCom 2007, pp. 2282–2285 (2007)
8. Yu, H., Shen, Z., Miao, C., Leung, C., Niyato, D.: A survey of trust and reputation management systems in wireless communications. Proceedings of the IEEE (October 2010)
9. Sen, J.: A distributed trust and reputation framework for mobile ad hoc networks. CoRR (2010)
10. Safaei, Z., Sabaei, M., Torgheh, F.: An efficient reputation-based mechanism to enforce cooperation in manets. In: Proceedings of the 4th International Conference on Communications and Information Technology (2010)
11. Li, Y.: A reputation system for wireless mesh network using multi-path routing protocol. In: Zhong, S., Dou, D., Wang, Y. (eds.) IPCCC. IEEE (2011)
12. Dromard, J., Khatoun, R., Khoukhi, L.: A watchdog extension scheme considering packet loss for a reputation system in wireless mesh network. In: 2013 20th International Conference on Telecommunications (ICT), pp. 1–5 (May 2013)
13. Reis, C., Mahajan, R., Rodrig, M., Wetherall, D., Zahorjan, J.: Measurement-based models of delivery and interference in static wireless networks. In: Proceedings of the 2006 Conference on Applications, Technologies, Architectures, and Protocols for Computer Communications, SIGCOMM 2006. ACM, New York (2006)
14. Maheshwari, R., Jain, S., Das, S.R.: A measurement study of interference modeling and scheduling in low-power wireless networks. In: Proceedings of the 6th ACM Conference on Embedded Network Sensor Systems, SenSys 2008, pp. 141–154. ACM, New York (2008)
15. Aguayo, D., Bicket, J., Biswas, S., Judd, G., Morris, R.: Link-level measurements from an 802.11b mesh network. In: Proceedings of the 2004 Conference on Applications, Technologies, Architectures, and Protocols for Computer Communications, pp. 121–132. ACM, New York (2004)

16. R Core Team: R: A Language and Environment for Statistical Computing. R Foundation for Statistical Computing, Vienna, Austria (2013)
17. Marti, S., Giuli, T.J., Lai, K., Baker, M.: Mitigating routing misbehavior in mobile ad hoc networks. In: Proceedings of the 6th Annual International Conference on Mobile Computing and Networking (2000)
18. Tan, H.: Ramp: a reputation-aware multi-hop routing protocol in wireless ad-hoc networks. In: Proceedings of the 4th International Symposium on Applied Sciences in Biomedical and Communication Technologies. ACM, New York (2011)
19. Johnson, D.B., Maltz, D.A.: Dynamic source routing in ad hoc wireless networks. In: Mobile Computing, pp. 153–181. Kluwer Academic Publishers (1996)
20. Li, W., Parker, J., Joshi, A.: Security through collaboration and trust in manets. Mobile Networks and Applications, 342–352 (2012)
21. Zaidi, Z., Landfeldt, B.: Monitoring assisted robust routing in wireless mesh networks. Mobile Networks and Applications, 54–66 (2008)
22. Jiang, H., Chen, S., Yang, Y., Jie, Z., Leung, H., Xu, J., Wang, L.: Estimation of packet loss rate at wireless link of vanet–rple. In: 2010 6th International Conference on Wireless Communications Networking and Mobile Computing (WiCOM), pp. 1–5 (September 2010)
23. Basseville, M., Nikiforov, I.V.: Detection of abrupt changes: theory and application. Prentice-Hall, Inc., Upper Saddle River (1993)
24. Montgomery, D.: Introduction to Statistical Quality Control, 3rd edn. John Wiley & Sons (1996)

Efficient Management of Virtualized Information-Centric Networks

Maxim Claeys[1], Steven Latré[2], and Filip De Turck[1]

[1] Department of Information Technology, Ghent University - iMinds
{maxim.claeys,filip.deturck}@intec.ugent.be
[2] Department of Mathematics and Computer Science, University of Antwerp - iMinds
steven.latre@uantwerpen.be

Abstract. The Internet has rapidly evolved from a network, connecting a couple of dozens of computers, to a network containing billions of devices. Furthermore, the current Internet is mostly used to deliver complex services with increasingly stringent Quality of Service (QoS) requirements. However, the underlying network model has remained the same, making the Internet not well suited to optimally support the current user trends and services. Currently, a lot of effort is being made in the area of network virtualization and Information-Centric Networking (ICN) to support the evolution towards the QoS constraint distribution of large amounts of information. Even though both directions offer a lot of opportunities, multiple important challenges have to be faced when managing the placement of content inside the network and guaranteeing delivery efficiency. These challenges are further increased when a combination of both trends is considered. This paper gives an overview of these challenges and how this PhD will deal with the mutual influences of network virtualization and ICN in an efficient way.

1 Introduction

Since its emergence in the 70's, the Internet has known a fenomenal growth. However, the fundamental principles have remained the same. In recent years, Internet usage has shifted to a variety of complex services that require the distribution of large amounts of information. These services include, amongst others, the delivery of Video on Demand (VoD) and popular social media like Twitter and Facebook. The delivery of these complex services is in strong contrast to the traditional usage of the Internet. It is the information itself, and no longer the communicating hosts, that plays a central role in the Internet. The source of the information is of minor importance to the end-user, as long as the delivery meets increasingly stringent Quality of Service (QoS) requirements.

These observations reveal multiple strong management challenges for the future Internet. In this area, two novel research directions can be identified. The development of Information-Centric Networking (ICN) architectures and algorithms [1], where the information is decoupled from its location at the network level, addresses the increasing importance of content distribution. This

A. Sperotto et al. (Eds.): AIMS 2014, LNCS 8508, pp. 42–46, 2014.

allows content to be duplicated everywhere in the network, enabling in-network caching [2]. Addressing individual data elements is in strong contrast to the current host-based IP addressing scheme.

On the other hand, a lot of research effort is being made in the area of network virtualization [3]. Just as the virtualization of computing resources enabled a lot of novel applications like cloud computing in data centers, network virtualization may offer similar perspectives in communication networks [4]. Network virtualization allows the differentiation of distinct services over a shared physical network. Furthermore, decoupling a service from a fixed physical location allows services to be dynamically configured and reconfigured. As these services are fully isolated, they can be managed individually. In this way, individual QoS requirements can be imposed.

Although both research areas offer a lot of new possibilities, multiple important challenges have to be dealt with. A first challenge can be found in ICN-based routing. Next to the fact that the number of data objects is a level of magnitude bigger than the number of end systems, multiple duplicates of data objects, spread across the network, further complicates the routing problem. Second, in-network caching can strongly benefit from efficient caching strategies. Advanced algorithms, considering pro-active content placement next to current reactive caching strategies, can strongly increase the delivery performance in the network. A third challenge can be found in finding the optimal resource allocation scheme in the virtualized network [5]. This challenge increases even further when reallocation in case of changing requirements or network conditions is considered.

2   Virtualized ICN Networks

This PhD research covers the design of an architecture and algorithms for the efficient management of virtualized information-centric networks. More specific, we focus on the elastic allocation of virtual network resources and on pro-active content placement. The remainder of this section will focus on the different algorithmic challenges of virtualized information-centric networks that will be addressed in this PhD.

2.1   Static Resource-Allocation and Content Placement

In this research phase, algorithms will be developed to calculate the optimal network configuration that meets the specified QoS requirements while minimizing the related costs. The resulting configuration will define both the content placement and the allocation of virtual network slices. This process is illustrated in Fig. 1. The system takes into account both the predicted requests and related QoS requirements for the service (A) and the physical network topology (B). Based on this input, the algorithm defines the optimal content placement in order to provide a cost-efficient service delivery and allocates the virtual network slices. The resulting solution satisfies both the service requirements and the physical resource capacities.

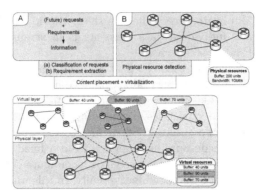

Fig. 1. Schematic overview of the static resource-allocation and content placement process

Both the allocation of virtual networks, taking into account physical resource capacities, and the content placement problem are known to be NP-hard [5,6]. Given the mutual influence between both problems, a combined approach is required. Because of the algorithmic complexity of the individual problems, an optimal solution can not be obtained in a scalable way. Therefore, we will have to reside to heuristic approaches. During this PhD, multiple algorithms will be developed, both using meta-heuristics and custom heuristics, tailored to the specific problem. For this purpose, multiple existing heuristics, both for the resource allocation problem (e.g. [7,8]) and the content placement problem (e.g. [9,10]), will be investigated in depth.

Even though we stated in the previous paragraph that an optimal solution can not be guaranteed in a scalable way, it will be very useful to model the problem as an Integer Linear Programming (ILP) problem. Using this formulation, an optimal solution can be calculated for problems of limited scale. These results can then be used as a benchmark to evaluate the developed heuristics.

2.2   Elastic Resource-Allocation and Content Placement

Given the high algorithmic complexity of the algorithms introduced in Section 2.1, the allocation of virtual network slices and the content placement can only be executed periodically in an off-line way on a relative large timescale. During the period in between two executions however, strong fluctuations in the request pattern can occur. Furthermore, requests for additional services can cause the optimal network configuration and content placement to change. For this reason, it is crucial to monitor the conditions and optimize the configuration on a short timescale if needed. In this way, virtual networks can be scaled in an elastic way by dynamically allocating more or less resources and moving content inside the network, based on the perceived requirements, analogous to virtual machines in cloud computing. It is important to note that these resources are not limited to traditional hardware resources like CPU and bandwidth capacity, but can additionally include higher level resources, e.g. the availability of specific protocols.

The elastic approach is illustrated in Fig. 2. It is important to note that, for reasons of clarity, the requirements are visualized in only one dimension. In reality however, the problem is more complex. As illustrated in this example, the allocated resources for the virtual network slice scale when the requirements change significantly. Furthermore, this reallocation could introduce a better content placement solution. In this way, the elastic network will be able to meet the QoS requirements at any time, while minimizing the related costs.

Requirements are very likely to fluctuate lightly during the monitoring period. However, small fluctuations do not necessarily cause the current configuration to be unsatisfactory. When the perceived requirements stay within a specific range, reconfigurations are not required. To detect consistent anomalous behaviour, anomaly detection techniques can be applied. Anomaly detection identifies patterns that do not correspond to the perceived normal behaviour. When such anomalies are detected, the resource allocation and content placement has to be reconfigured. A first step in this area has been taken with the implementation of a heuristic, dynamically adjusting the resource allocation of virtual networks using reinforcement learning [11]. In this way, the heuristic can adapt its behaviour based on the performance of previous decisions. Similar to the static case described in Section 2.1, this problem will be modelled as an ILP formulation to serve as a benchmark for the developed algorithms.

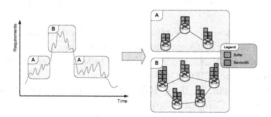

Fig. 2. Simplified schematic overview of the elastic scaling of virtual network slices, based on perceived requirements

3   Conclusion

For the Internet to efficiently deal with the delivery of current complex services, this paper proposed a combined approach to the problem of resource allocation in network virtualization and the information-centric content placement problem. A combined approach is crucial given the mutual influence between both problems. As a first step, heuristic approaches are proposed to define the optimal network configuration and content placement in a static way on a large time-scale. On a shorter time-scale, self-learning heuristics are proposed to adapt the network configuration and content placement to perceived fluctuations in the requests and requirements patterns. Using this approach, the elastic network is able to meet the QoS requirements in a cost-efficient way at any time.

Acknowledgements. Maxim Claeys is funded by grant of the Agency of Innovation by Science and Technology in Flanders (IWT). This work was partly funded by Flamingo, a Network of Excellence project (318488) supported by the European Commission under its Seventh Framework Programme.

References

1. Ahlgren, B., Dannewitz, C., Imbrenda, C., Kutscher, D., Ohlman, B.: A survey of information-centric networking. IEEE Communications Magazine 50, 26–36 (2012)
2. Psaras, I., Chai, W.K., Pavlou, G.: Probabilistic in-network caching for information-centric networks. In: ICN Workshop on Information-Centric Networking (2012)
3. Chowdhury, N.M.K., Boutaba, R.: A survey of network virtualization. Computer Networks 54, 862–876 (2010)
4. Khan, A., Zugenmaier, A., Jurca, D., Kellerer, W.: Network virtualization: a hypervisor for the internet? IEEE Communications Magazine 50, 136–143 (2012)
5. Haider, A., Potter, R., Nakao, A.: Challenges in resource allocation in network virtualization. In: 20th ITC Specialist Seminar (2009)
6. Sourlas, V., Flegkas, P., Paschos, G.S., Katsaros, D., Tassiulas, L.: Storage planning and replica assignment in content-centric publish/subscribe networks. Computer Networks 55, 4021–4032 (2011)
7. Balasubramaniam, S., Mineraud, J., Perry, P., Jennings, B., Murphy, L., Donnelly, W., Botvich, D.: Coordinating allocation of resources for multiple virtual iptv providers to maximize revenue. IEEE Transactions on Broadcasting 57, 826–839 (2011)
8. Leon-Garcia, A., Mason, L.: Virtual network resource management for next-generation networks. IEEE Communications Magazine 41, 102–109 (2003)
9. Qiu, L., Padmanabhan, V.N., Voelker, G.M.: On the placement of web server replicas. In: IEEE InfoComm. (2001)
10. Kangasharju, J., Roberts, J., Ross, K.W.: Object replication strategies in content distribution networks. Comput. Commun. 25, 376–383 (2002)
11. Mijumbi, R., Serrat, J., Gorricho, J.L., Claeys, M., De Turck, F., Latré, S.: Design and evaluation of learning algorithms for dynamic resource management in virtual networks. In: IFIP/IEEE Network Operations and Management Symposium (NOMS 2014), Krakow, Poland (May 2014)

Contributions to Efficient Resource Management in Virtual Networks

Rashid Mijumbi, Juan-Luis Gorricho, and Joan Serrat

Universitat Politècnica de Catalunya,
08034 Barcelona, Spain
{rashid,serrat}@tsc.upc.edu, juanluis@entel.upc.edu

Abstract. Network virtualisation is a promising technique for a better future Internet by allowing for network resource sharing. However, resource sharing requires that virtual nodes and links be embedded onto substrate nodes and links (virtual network embedding), and thereafter the allocated resources dynamically managed throughout the lifetime of the virtual network (dynamic resource allocation). Since the constrained virtual network embedding problem is NP–Hard, many existing approaches are not only static, but also make simplifying assumptions, most of which would not apply in practical environments. This PhD research proposes improvements to both virtual network embedding and dynamic resource allocation. The objective is to achieve an efficient utilisation of physical network resources. To this end, we propose a path generation-based approach for a one-shot, unsplittable flow virtual network embedding, and a reinforcement learning-based dynamic allocation of substrate network resources.

Keywords: Autonomic and self-management, Future Internet, Virtual Networks, Virtual Network Embedding, Dynamic Resource Allocation.

1 Introduction

Network Virtualisation [1] promises to allow infrastructure providers (InP) who own substrate networks (SN) to lease out chunks of their physical resources to service providers (SP) who use these resources to create virtual networks (VN), which can be used to provide end-to-end services to final users. A VN is composed of virtual links and nodes, which have to be embedded onto SN links and nodes respectively. One problem encountered in setting up a virtual network is the need for efficient management of SN resources. This problem can normally be divided into two steps; the first of which performs the embedding of virtual nodes and links onto substrate nodes and links respectively–also known as virtual network embedding (VNE)–and the second one involves dynamic resource allocation (DRA) throughout the lifetime of VNs, aimed at efficient resource utilisation.

VNE with constraints on virtual nodes and links (e.g. topology, node capacity and link bandwidth) reduces to the multi-way separator problem, which is known to be NP-Hard [2]. Therefore, several existing solutions that propose one-shot

A. Sperotto et al. (Eds.): AIMS 2014, LNCS 8508, pp. 47–51, 2014.

embedding such as [3] assume that all VN resource requirements are known a priori (offline case) and that the SN has unbounded resources, while others reduce the complexity further by assuming that the SN supports splitting of flows [4], and perform node and link embedding in two separate steps [5]. Even proposals that coordinate the two steps such as [2] still perform two separate embedding steps. Carrying out node and link embedding in two separate steps can lead to blocking or rejecting of resource requests at the link mapping stage and hence a sub-optimal substrate resource utilisation, which would negatively impact the revenue of InPs. The first part of this research (Section 2.1) proposes a *near optimal* solution to the unsplittable flow, one-shot VNE problem. This is achieved by formulating a mathematical program [6] of the VNE problem, and applying path generation [7] to allow for a faster, efficient solution. The objective is not only to reduce the time complexity of one-shot VNE, but also achieve comparatively good performance compared to two-step embedding proposals.

In addition, many current approaches [2]–[4] are static approaches (stop at the VNE step) without any considerations for possibilities of adjustments to the initial embedding, while those that propose dynamic solutions [8]–[11] do allocate a fixed amount of node and link resources to the VNs through out their life time. Overall, the number of dynamic solutions to VNE is limited [1]. Since network loading due to user traffic varies with time, allocating a fixed amount of resources based on peak loading could lead to an inefficient utilisation of overall SN resources, whereby, during periods when some virtual nodes and/or links are lightly loaded, substrate resources are still reserved for them, while possibly rejecting new requests for such resources. Once again, this would lead to inefficient resource utilisation and hence have a negative impact on the revenue of InPs, and could hinder the practical advancement of network virtualisation. Our second proposal (Section 2.2) follows a successful VNE, and involves the use of a decentralised multi-agent system (MAS) [12] which uses reinforcement learning (RL) [13] for life-cycle dynamic allocation of resources to all embedded VNs. The goal is to achieve efficient utilisation of overall SN resources, while ensuring that that the quality of service parameters such as packet drop rate (for virtual nodes) and delay (for virtual links) for the VNs are not affected.

2 Proposed Approaches: PaGe–VNE and RL–DRA

2.1 Path Generation-Based VNE (PaGe–VNE)

PaGe–VNE uses two mathematical programs. One is a path-based formulation of the one-shot VNE problem, also known as the primal problem, while the other is its corresponding dual problem. For given instances of the problem, both the primal and dual problems have approximately the same solution value. As shown in Fig. 1, for a given VN request, PaGe–VNE begins by obtaining an *initial solution* (composed of paths P_1 in an augmented substrate network [2]) to the primal problem using a VNE approach that performs node and link mapping in two *coordinated* stages. The coordination involves solving a mathematical program of the node mapping problem, which is biased by the virtual link demands

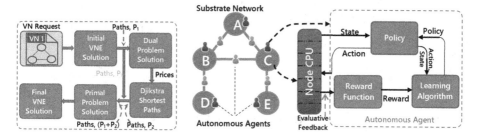

Fig. 1. PaGe–VNE   **Fig. 2.** RL–DRA

and substrate link capacities, and then the use *Dijkstra's* shortest path algorithm [14] for the link mapping stage. Since the initial solution involves node and link mapping in two separate stages, its computation takes much less time. However, the quality of the initial solution is not as good as would be obtained from performing a one-shot mapping. Therefore, PaGe–VNE's next step refines the initial solution, by using it as an input into the *dual problem*. This results into *prices* for the substrate network links and nodes. For every virtual link, these prices are then used to determine a *shortest path* from each of the possible substrate nodes at each of its ends using *Dijkstra's algorithm*. This set of paths, P_2–together with those obtained in the initial solution–are finally used to solve the primal problem and obtain a *final VNE solution*.

2.2   Reinforcement Learning-Based DRA (RL–DRA)

After VNE, we dynamically and opportunistically allocate resources to virtual nodes and links depending on the perceived need for them by virtual nodes and links. The opportunistic use of resources involves carefully taking advantage of unused virtual node and link resources to ensure that VN requests are not rejected when resources reserved to already embedded requests are idle. To this end, we use a distributed and dynamic approach (RL-DRA) shown in Fig. 2 to allocate resources to virtual nodes and links using RL. In RL-DRA, each substrate node or link is represented by an autonomous agent (AA). The node AAs manage node capacities while the link AAs manage link bandwidths. These AAs use a RL-based evaluative feedback mechanism to dynamically adjust the resources allocated to virtual nodes and links, ensuring that resources are not left under-utilised, and that enough resources are available to meet VN QoS needs. Specifically, at periodic intervals, each AA perceives the current level of utilisation of resources (*state*), and uses its *policy* to take an *action* (hence changing resource allocations). The AA then receives feedback which is an evaluation of the desirability of its action. This is achieved by defining a *reward function* which takes into account how efficient the AA's action lead to better resource utilisation and its effect on VN QoS, to calculate a scalar *reward* that is sent back to the agent. The AA then uses a *learning algorithm* (such as Q-Learning) to adjust its policy so as to maximise the reward it achieves in the long run.

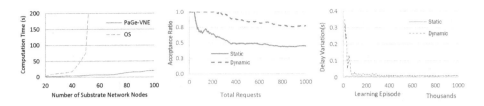

Fig. 3. Computation Time   **Fig. 4.** Acceptance Ratio   **Fig. 5.** Delay Variation

2.3   Obtained Results

Figs. 3–5 show *some* of the results from our proposals. In Fig. 3, PaGe–VNE has a significant computation time saving compared with a solution that determines an optimal solution (OS) of VNE while achieving almost the same VNE effciency (result not shown due to space restrictions). Fig. 4 confirms that RL-DRA leads to better substrate resource utilisation by accepting more VN requests than a static solution. Morever, as shown in 5, the better performance in RL-DRA is not at the expense of VN QoS, as the packet delay variation of the dynamic approach converges to that of the static one after the agent has learnt. We have written two papers [15], [16] as a result of these proposals. [15] is still under review while [16] has been accepted.

3   Conclusion and Future Work

This research is aimed at contributing to better resource management in network virtualisation. We have proposed a one-shot unsplittable flow VNE that improves solution computation time, and a distributed and dynamic approach that leads to better resource utilisation. However, some of the mathematical formulations used in PaGe–VNE can still become intractable for bigger problem instances. While a significant improvement in computation time is achieved compared to the optimal solution, and although in practice there are *high performance* tools [17] for efficiently solving such problems, more work can be done, for instance, by seeking a relaxation to the program which permits to solve it in polynomial time. In addition, implementing RL–DRA in real networks and in a multi-domain VN environment may raise more challenges since it may require a clear communication protocol (and a real management of this extra network load), negotiations and agreements between competing AAs that support inter-domain substrate paths. In future, we will study these issues and develop a prototype LAN where the AAs are based on a real AA development framework such as JADE [18].

Acknowledgments. This work is partly funded by Flamingo, a Network of Excellence project (318488) supported by the European Commission under its 7th FP, the EVANS project (PIRSES-GA-2010-269323), and TEC2012-38574-C02-02 from Ministerio de Economa y Competitividad.

References

1. Fischer, A., Botero, J., Beck, M., De Meer, H., Hesselbach, X.: Virtual Network Embedding: A survey. IEEE Communications Surveys Tutorials, 1–19 (2013)
2. Chowdhury, M., Rahman, M., Boutaba, R.: ViNEYard: Virtual Network Embedding Algorithms With Coordinated Node and Link Mapping. IEEE/ACM Transactions on Networking 20(1), 206–219 (2012)
3. Houidi, I., Louati, W., Zeghlache, D.: A Distributed Virtual Network Mapping Algorithm. In: IEEE International Conference on Communications, pp. 5634–5640 (2008)
4. Yu, M., Yi, Y., Rexford, J., Chiang, M.: Rethinking virtual network embedding: Substrate support for path splitting and migration. ACM/SIGCOMM Computer Communication Review 38(2), 17–29 (2008)
5. Zhu, Y., Ammar, M.: Algorithms for Assigning Substrate Network Resources to Virtual Network Components. In: Proceedings of IEEE INFOCOM, pp. 1–12 (2006)
6. Bradley, H., Magnanti: Applied Mathematical Programming. Addison-Wesley, (1977)
7. Barnhart, C., Johnson, E.L., Nemhauser, G.L., Savelsbergh, M.W., Vance, P.H.: Branch-and-price: Column generation for solving huge integer programs. Operations Research 46, 316–329 (1998)
8. Fan, J., Ammar, M.: Dynamic topology configuration in service overlay networks, A study of reconfiguration policies. In: Proc. IEEE INFOCOM (2006)
9. Rahman, M.R., Boutaba, R.: SVNE: Survivable Virtual Network Embedding Algorithms for Network Virtualisation. IEEE Transactions on Network and Service Management 10(2) (2013)
10. Fajjari, I., Aitsaadi, N., Pujolle, G., Zimmermann, H.: VNR algorithm: A greedy approach for virtual networks reconfigurations. In: IEEE Global Telecommunications Conference, pp. 1–5 (2011)
11. Gang, S., Yu, H., Vishal, A., Lemin, L.: A cost efficient framework and algorithm for embedding dynamic virtual network requests. Future Generation Computer Systems 29, 1265–1277 (2013)
12. Russell, S.J., Norvig, P.: Artificial Intelligence: A Modern Approach, 3rd edn. Prentice Hall, Englewood Cliffs (2010)
13. Sutton, S., Barto, G.: Reinforcement Learning: An Introduction. MIT Press, Cambridge (1998)
14. Cormen, T.H., Leiserson, C.E., Rivest, R.L., Stein, C.: Introduction to Algorithms, 3rd edn. MIT Press, Cambridge (2009)
15. Mijumbi, R., Serrat, J., Gorricho, J.L., Boutaba, R.: Path Generation-based Virtual Network Embedding. IEEE/ACM Transactions on Networking (Submitted) (under peer review)
16. Mijumbi, R., Gorricho, J.L., Serrat, J., Claeys, M., De Turck, F., Latré, S.: Design and Evaluation of Learning Algorithms for Dynamic Resource Management in Virtual Networks. In: IEEE/IFIP Network Operations and Management Symposium (NOMS), Krakow, Poland (2014) (accepted November 2013)
17. IBM ILOG CPLEX Optimizer (2014), http://www-01.ibm.com/software/integration/optimization/cplex-optimizer/about/ (visited January 08, 2014)
18. Bellifemine, F., Bergenti, F., Caire, G., Poggi, A.: Jade – A Java Agent Development Framework. In: Multi-Agent Programming. Multiagent Systems, Artificial Societies, and Simulated Organizations, vol. 15, pp. 125–147. Springer US (2005)

Management and Orchestration
of Virtualized Network Functions

Elisa Maini[1] and Antonio Manzalini[2]

[1] University of Naples Federico II, Via Claudio 21, 80125 Naples, Italy
[2] Telecom Italia Strategy - Future Centre, Via Reiss Romoli 274, 10148 Turin, Italy

Abstract. Software Defined Networking (SDN) and Network Function Virtualization (NFV) paradigms are driving a number of research activities aiming to develop virtual network infrastructures where Network Functions (NF) and services could be executed as applications in ensemble of virtual machines. This paper addresses the problem of managing and orchestrating said highly dynamic networks, where virtualized NFs and resources are created and destroyed depending on traffic demands, service requests, or other high-level governance goals such as the reduction of energy consumption.

1 Introduction

In the current networks most NFs (from layer 4 to layer 7) are provided by a number of middle-boxes. These nodes are based on closed software solutions running on specialized hardware representing a significant part of the Operational EXpenditures (OPEX) and CAPital EXpenditures (CAPEX) of network operators due to the management effort (e.g. for configuration) that they require [1], [2], [3], [4]. In principle, SDN and NFV are likely to offer the possibility to develop all NFs, e.g., middle-boxes, in open source software executed in standard hardware. If on one side, Future Networks will rely more and more on such software, which will, in turn, accelerate the pace of innovation and will reduce costs, on the other side, management and orchestration will be the true challenge. Automated operation processes (e.g. configuration of network and service equipment) could limit human intervention also wrong operations and a flexible and optimal provisioning of NFs and services could reduce equipment costs and allows postponing network investments. In this direction, SDN and NFV should be equipped with solid management and orchestration features, capable of automating networks and services operations. These paradigms will largely exploit virtualization technologies for sharing and aggregating resources, and for decoupling and isolating virtual network elements from the physical network. Further, the abstraction of virtualized network elements will enable and simplify the programmability of the network, increasing networking capabilities, allowing innovative service offerings: nevertheless this will increase also the overall management complexity of virtual NFs and virtual resources [7], [8]. In the following paper, we give an overview of the main research and challenges for the management and orchestration of virtualized NFs and, we provide an architectural

A. Sperotto et al. (Eds.): AIMS 2014, LNCS 8508, pp. 52–56, 2014.

solution for the placement of the virtual resources. As proof of these concepts, some preliminary results are provided.

2   Concepts and Technical Challenges

Each Virtual Network (VN) is viewed as a *managed network service* by the management software [5]. All managed network services are mapped to the available resources which allows users of the network service to access it, just like they would access a physical network service. For full operation of the managed network services, the management and orchestration needs to ensure that each VN has the following attributes:

- *separation*: network functions and the network infrastructure are kept separate. A VN of a service needs to be separated from the infrastructure used by an infrastructure provider, similarly to the manner in which a virtual compute environment is separated from the physical host;
- *isolation*: a VN of one service is isolated from all other VN services. Isolated VN services need to be offered side by side while sharing network resources of the infrastructure provider;
- *elasticity*: a VN can grow or shrink as necessary. A VN service needs to enable network elasticity;
- *federation*: a VN can span over more than one domain. An interchangeable VN service needs to be offered across local areas such that network service consumers would not be concerned by the area of the infrastructure location, the physical network used, or its configuration.

Based on the previous description, the management and orchestration component should:

a) *use adaptive and autonomic methods and systems* for automatic management NFs applied not only to the physical resources, but also virtual resources located inside the physical/virtual resources;
b) *optimize the allocation and orchestration of virtual resources* for dynamically instantiating, orchestrating and migrating multiple virtual machines across networks and service infrastructures.

To fulfill the latter, the next section provide a high-level description of a distributed orchestrator prototype.

3   Architecture and Experimental Results

The architecture depicted in Figure 1, is based on an orchestrator that ensures the *automatic placement of the virtual routers and the allocation of the network services* on them, supported by a monitoring system which collect and reports on behavior of the resources involved. The orchestrator manages the creation

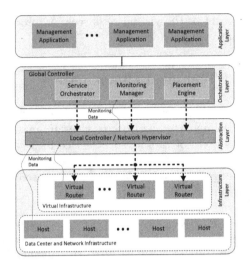

Fig. 1. Architecture overview

and removal of the virtual nodes, as well as configuring, monitoring, running and stopping software on them.

From an architectural viewpoint, NFs and services can be defined as a number of software components with their accompanying context together with configuration parameters. The provisioning of a service involves the creation of a IT infrastructure, followed by the installation of all necessary software components into the infrastructure, and finally configuring and starting those components. With SDN and NFV these processes can be simplified as the infrastructure provides a platform from which virtual machines can be run. SDNs can be directly manifested as virtual network topologies which need to be setup, have a managed lifecycle, and need to be shutdown - all under software control.

The architecture involves a *Global Controller*, in other words a distributed management infrastructure that has centralized functionality and it is responsible for the setup, configuration, optimization, and shutdown of the network entities. It takes input from various *Management Applications* regarding various requirements (e.g. network resources or response time) and then configures the network nodes through a set of *Local Controllers*. In order to manage the challenging and dynamic infrastructures of virtual networks there needs to be a monitoring system (*Monitoring Manager*) which can collect and report on the behavior of both the physical resources (e.g. cpu usage, memory usage) and the virtual resources (e.g. utilization level of the virtual links). These monitoring data items are sent to the Global Controller so that it can use the monitoring information in order to make decisions regarding network strategies. In particular, it may decide to add new nodes in order to fulfil the high-level policies and goals which are network operator requirements. In this way, the virtual network topology changes dynamically according to the network virtual resources usage.

The *Placement Engine* is the component in charge of performing the actual placement of the virtual routers according to the initial topology and the usage of the virtual network elements. This is an important feature because, when we configure a network, considering some initial information, some of these parameters may change during the course of the system's operation and a reconfiguration may be required to maintain optimized collection of information. The decision of the Placement Engine is encoded in an algorithm which can be rather simple, such as counting the number of virtual routers on a host, or it can be based on a set of constraints (e.g. the usage of the virtual links) and policies that represent the network properties. Also, the Placement Engine may be able to utilize or share some algorithmic elements from computer cloud placement algorithms such as [9] and [10].

Figure 2 provides some experimental results achieved using the Very Lighweight Network and Service Platform (VLSP) testbed [6]. It shows the number of virtual routers allocated on each host (shown on the *y-axis*) versus the time of the experimental run (shown on the *x-axis*). The hosts: host 1, host 2 and host 3 are represented by blue, green and yellow lines respectively. Here, we present two different placement algorithms: the algorithm used in Figure 2(a) is a kind of load balancing algorithm as it tries to get a similar number of routers on each host. The algorithm used in Figure 2(b) tries to determine the host that is *least busy* in terms of virtual network traffic. More details are explained in [11].

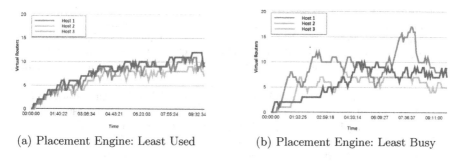

(a) Placement Engine: Least Used   (b) Placement Engine: Least Busy

Fig. 2. Behaviour of different placement algorithms

4   Conclusion and Prespectives

In this paper, we have argued the main research directions for the management and orchestration of virtualized NFs and services in Future Networks and provided an architectural description of our orchestrator prototype. The results presented here demonstrate that different embedded algorithms in each of the Placement Engines give very different placement strategies for the virtual routers. In future work will be considered other placement algortitms, which we expect to get more complex and to encapsulate multiple metrics.

References

1. Manzalini, A., Minerva, R., Dekel, E., Tock, Y., Kaemfer, E., Tavernier, W., Casier, K., Verbrugge, S., Colle, D., Collegati, F., Campi, A., Cerroni, W., Vilalta, R., Munoz, R., Casellas, R., Martinez, R., Mazzocca, N., Maini, E.: Manifesto of Edge ICT Fabric. In: Proceedings of 17th International Conference on Intelligence in Next Generation Networks (ICIN), Venice, Italy, October 15-16 (2013)
2. Manzalini, A., Saracco, R.: Software Networks at the Edge: a shift of paradigm. In: IEEE Software Defined Networks for Future Networks and Services (SDN4FNS), Trento, Italy, November 11-13 (2013)
3. Manzalini, A., Minerva, R., Callegati, F., Cerroni, W.: Clouds of Virtual Machines at the Edge. IEEE Com. Mag. Future Carriers Networks (July 2013)
4. Manzalini, A., Deussen, P.H., Nechifor, S., et al.: Self-optimized Cognitive Network of Networks. Oxford Journals The Computer Journal 54(2), 189–196 (2010)
5. Clayman, S., Clegg, R., Mamatas, L., Pavlou, G., Galis, A.: Monitoring Aggregation and Filtering for Efficient Management of Virtual Networks. In: 7th International Conference on Network and Service Management (CNSM), Paris (October 2011)
6. Clayman, S.: User Space Routing, Open Source Software, http://clayfour.ee.ucl.ac.uk/usr/
7. Galis, A., Clayman, S., Mamatas, L., Rubio-Loyola, J., Manzalini, A., Kuklinski, S., Serrat, J., Zahariadis, T.: Softwarization of Future Networks and Services - Programmable Enabled Networks as Next Generation Software Defined Networks. In: IEEE Software Defined Networks for Future Networks and Services (SDN4FNS), Trento, Italy, November 11-13 (2013)
8. Galis, A., Rubio-Loyola, J., Clayman, S., Mamatas, L., Kukliński, S., Serrat, J., Zahariadis, T.: Software Enabled Future Internet - Challenges in Orchestrating the Future Internet. In: Pesch, D., Timm-Giel, A., Calvo, R.A., Wenning, B.-L., Pentikousis, K. (eds.) Monami. LNICST, vol. 125, pp. 228–244. Springer, Heidelberg (2013)
9. Breitgand, D., Epstein, A.: SLA-aware Placement of Multi-Virtual Machine Elastic Services in Compute Clouds. In: IFIP/IEEE International Symposium on Integrated Network Management (IM 2011), Dublin, Ireland, May 23-27 (2011)
10. Breitgand, D., Epstein, A.: Improving Consolidation of Virtual Machines with Risk-aware Bandwidth Oversubscription in Compute Clouds. In: ACM/IEEE INFOCOM 2012, Track II (2012)
11. Clayman, S., Maini, E., Galis, A., Manzalini, A., Mazzocca, N.: The Dynamical Placement of Virtual Network Functions. In: 1st IEEE/IFIP International Workshop on SDN Management and Orchestration, SDNMO 2014 (to appear, 2014)

Towards Incentivizing ISPs to Mitigate Botnets

Qasim Lone, Giovane C.M. Moura, and Michel Van Eeten

Economics of Cybersecurity Group
Faculty of Technology, Policy and Management
Delft University of Technology
Delft, The Netherlands
{q.b.lone,g.c.moreiramoura,m.j.g.vaneeten}@tudelft.nl

Abstract. ISPs form a centralized point to control botnet infections. However, they do not have enough incentives to invest in mitigation of botnets. In this paper, we propose an approach based on comparative metrics to incentivize ISPs to mitigate botnets. This research is still in its initial phase and will contribute to a Ph.D. thesis after four years.

1 Introduction

A botnet is network of compromised machines, controlled by a botmaster, which is used to carry out attacks [1]. Some of the common attacks botnets in which partake include spam, phishing, distributed denial-of-service (DDoS), credential theft, and click fraud. These attacks incur significant financial losses; for instance, it is estimated that spam causes losses of US$ 20 billion [2] yearly, only in the United States.

Previous studies have shown that most of the malicious hosts are concentrated in a small number of Internet Service Providers (ISP). Van Eeten *et al.* [3] found that 50 ISPs account for around half of all spamming IP addresses worldwide. In another study, Moura [4] found that 20 Autonomous Systems (AS), out of 42,201, were responsible for 50% of all spamming IP addresses. Similar trends were also found in [5–7].

Taking these observations into account, ISPs would then form a centralized control point and, this concentration in a small number of ISPs would make it easier for them to mitigate botnets. There are a number of steps ISPs can take to reduce infected machines in their networks, including quarantining, providing links to antivirus software, and notifying customers about infections in their computers. However, there is little evidence that ISPs are taking many concrete actions. For example, in [3], Van Eeten *et al.* found that only 10% of infected customers were notified by their Dutch ISPs.

2 Research Problem

Such a low rate of ISPs actions can be due to several reasons, such as, content filtering may violate user's privacy of the customers according to the legislation of

A. Sperotto et al. (Eds.): AIMS 2014, LNCS 8508, pp. 57–62, 2014.

some of the countries [8]. However, one of the prime reasons is *lack of incentives* for ISPs to invest in mitigation of botnets [3]: if the market for Internet access is characterized by price competition, ISPs would be strongly discouraged to invest more in botnet mitigation than their competitors, *i.e.*, they would be disincentivised to contact and quarantine more infected customers than their competitors.

We do not really know to what extent individual providers actually and effectively fight botnets. This information asymmetry impedes the functioning of markets and may even result in market failure. It weakens the incentives to invest in mitigation, because users and other stakeholders cannot tell good performing providers from bad ones. In order to improve incentive structure of ISPs, analytical models based on game theory can be utilized to explore and evaluate relative security performance of ISPs. Various studies [9–11] based on empirical data suggest that metrics can be an effective way to measure cyber security performance. In this research our focus is to develop comparative metrics to evaluate ISPs efforts to mitigate botnets. The proposed research problem leads to the following research questions.

1. What kind of network measurement data is required to statistically account for botnet population in the networks of ISPs ?
2. How to turn the measurements into comparative relative metrics for ISPs performance in botnet mitigation ?
3. How can these metrics contribute to evaluate and incentivizing botnet mitigation by ISPs ?

3   Approach

Research question 1, from previous section, focuses on types of measurement data we can use to statistically estimate botnet population in ISP. We will obtain access to data which is collected by various collaborators of the project. There are two types of measurement data for botnets: data which is collected *outside* or *inside* botnets.

The first type of data is obtained by observing direct attacks from infected machines, for example, machines taking part in spam or participating in DDoS attack. It is collected using various approaches, including, honeypots, spam traps, intrusion detection system, sinkholes. This type of data helps capture wide range of botnets. However, captured data might have false positives and false negatives, due to limitation in detection capabilities of these systems. We already have access to DShiled and Spam trap from this category of datasets.

In the second type of measurement, data is obtained by taking over command and control centers (C&C) of botnets. The advantage of this approach is that we have accurate data but the downside is that measurements are only limited to a single botnet, such data is not representative of the total population. We have access to ZeroAccess, Conficker and Zeus botnet data sets, which were collected by taking over the respective botnet.

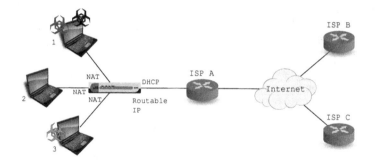

Fig. 1. Relationship between ISPs, botnet and home users

Hence, a detailed study will be performed on available data sources keeping in view advantages and limitations of these sources, so that we can statistically estimate the presence of botnet in the networks of ISPs.

The goal of research question 2 is to extract botnet metrics from network measurement data collected in research question 1. The developed metrics need to be consistent, normalized (for *e.g.* by number of customers per ISP), easily understandable by customers, and validated [12], *i.e.* to prove that they in fact capture the behavior they are supposed to capture.

To create such metrics, there are many challenges to overcome for example, consider measuring botnet presence in the networks of ISPs. To illustrate this, consider Figure 1. In this Figure, we see that a subscriber of ISP A is using a home router (with DHCP and NAT) to connect three laptops to the Internet. Laptop 1 has two malware instances running, while laptop 3 has one and laptop 2 has none. There are three bots which are operating from two different laptops and are hiding behind a single public routable IP address.

This exemplifies how complex it is to count botnet presence in ISP networks, and how IP addresses do not correspond to the number of botted computers [13]. To show how the number of IP addresses may significantly differ from the actual number of hosts, we have analyzed the variation on the number of IP addresses of 1,064 RIPE Atlas probes [14][1], over a 1 year period. As can be seen, there is a significant variation among the probes and, on average, each probe had 24 IP addresses (1:24). In another study, Stone-Gross *et al.* [15] hijacked the Torpig botnet for 10 days, and found that on average, each bot had (1:7) IP addresses, varying significantly according to ISP and country.

Some of the major challenges in developing these metrics include, bot counting, partial view, false positives/ negatives, and relative potency of botnets. Therefore, in research question 2, we will carry out a detailed literature review and various types of networks measurements to develop these metrics.

---

[1] Atlas probes are small hardware devices distributed all over the world and used to measure Internet connectivity and reachability, developed and maintained by the *Réseaux IP Européens* Network Coordination Centre (RIPE NCC).

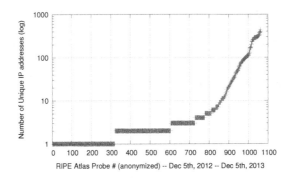

Fig. 2. Number of unique IP addresses per RIPE probe

In research question 3, we will investigate how the developed comparative metrics can be utilized to maximize economic incentives of ISPs. Tang *et al.* [9] found a total of 16% reduction in spam after spam rankings were published on a website. Similarly, there are yearly/quarterly reports published by various security companies [16–19] on security measurements. However, these studies are usually too limited to certain type of infection, do not rank ISPs based on performance or are not transparent on how these rankings were developed. Hence our goal in research question 3, will to not only to publish these rankings frequently, but to also make them accessible and understandable for majority of Internet consumers.

4   Final Considerations

As discussed in Section 1, malicious hosts are concentrated in small number of ISPs, which makes it easier to mitigate botnets. However, ISPs have limited incentives to invest in botnet mitigation. The effectiveness of mitigation measures cannot be established without accurate and reliable reputation metrics [9]. Without such metrics, there is only anecdotal evidence that cannot be reliably interpreted. Additionally, we can also evaluate effectiveness of mitigation strategies relative to each other. This Ph.D. research aims at designing comparative metrics to incentivize ISPs to take countermeasures for botnet mitigation. The goals of this work should be achieved within a period of four years, as part of Ph.D. thesis.

Acknowledgments. This work was partly funded by the Advanced Cyber Defense Centre *(ACDC)* project (#325188), which is supported by the European Commission under its ICT Policy Support Programme as part of the Competitiveness and Innovation Framework (CIP-PSP).

References

1. Gu, G., Perdisci, R., Zhang, J., Lee, W., et al.: Botminer: Clustering analysis of network traffic for protocol-and structure-independent botnet detection. In: USENIX Security Symposium, pp. 139–154 (2008)
2. Rao, J.M., Reiley, D.H.: The economics of spam. The Journal of Economic Perspectives 26(3), 87–110 (2012)
3. van Eeten, M., Bauer, J.M., Asghari, H., Tabatabaie, S., Rand, D.: The Role of Internet Service Providers in Botnet Mitigation: An Empirical Analysis Based on Spam Data. In: WEIS 2010: Ninth Workshop on the Economics of Information Security (2010)
4. Moura, G.C.M.: Internet Bad Neighborhoods. Ph.D. dissertation, University of Twente, Enschede, The Netherlands (March 2013), http://dx.doi.org/10.3990/1.9789036534604
5. Collins, M.P., Shimeall, T.J., Faber, S., Janies, J., Weaver, R., De Shon, M., Kadane, J.: Using Uncleanliness to Predict Future Botnet Addresses. In: Proceedings of the 7th ACM SIGCOMM Conference on Internet Measurement, IMC 2007, pp. 93–104. ACM, New York (2007)
6. Ramachandran, A., Feamster, N.: Understanding the Network-level Behavior of Spammers. In: Proceedings of the 2006 Conference on Applications, Technologies, Architectures, and Protocols for Computer Communications, SIGCOMM 2006, pp. 291–302. ACM, New York (2006)
7. van Wanrooij, W., Pras, A.: Filtering Spam from Bad Neighborhoods. International Journal of Network Management 20(6), 433–444 (2010)
8. Huston, G.: Opinion: The ISP – The Uncommon Carrier. The Internet Protocol Journal 5(3), 23–27 (2002), http://www.cisco.com/web/about/ac123/ac147/archived_issues/ipj_5-3/uncommon_carrier.html
9. Tang, Q., Linden, L., Quarterman, J., Whinston, A.: Improving internet security through social information and social comparison: A field quasi-experiment. In: WEIS 2013: Twelfth Workshop on the Economics of Information Security (2013)
10. Baker, W.H., Rees, L.P., Tippett, P.S.: Necessary measures: Metric-driven information security risk assessment and decision making. Commun. ACM 50(10), 101–106 (2007), http://doi.acm.org/10.1145/1290958.1290969
11. Rees, L.P., Deane, J.K., Rakes, T.R., Baker, W.H.: Decision support for cybersecurity risk planning. Decision Support Systems 51(3), 493–505 (2011), http://www.sciencedirect.com/science/article/pii/S0167923611000728
12. Kaner, C., Bond, W.P.: Software engineering metrics: What do they measure and how do we know? In: METRICS 2004. IEEE CS. Press (2004)
13. Fabian, M., Terzis, M.: My botnet is bigger than yours (maybe, better than yours): Why size estimates remain challenging. In: Proceedings of the 1st USENIX Workshop on Hot Topics in Understanding Botnets, Cambridge, USA (2007)
14. RIPE_NCC, "RIPE Atlas", https://atlas.ripe.net
15. Stone-Gross, B., Cova, M., Cavallaro, L., Gilbert, B., Szydlowski, M., Kemmerer, R., Kruegel, C., Vigna, G.: Your botnet is my botnet: analysis of a botnet takeover. In: Proceedings of the 16th ACM Conference on Computer and Communications Security, pp. 635–647. ACM (2009)
16. Microsoft, Microsoft Security Intelligence Report, http://www.microsoft.com/security/sir/default.aspx

17. McAfee, McAfee Threats Report, http://www.mcafee.com/us/resources/
    reports/rp-quarterly-threat-q1-2013.pdf
18. TrendMicro, Security Research and Threat Analysis,
    http://www.trendmicro.com/us/security-intelligence/
    research-and-analysis/index.html
19. European Union Agency for Network and Information Security, Cybersecurity
    cooperation - Defending the digital frontline, http://www.enisa.europa.eu/
    activities/Resilience-and-CIIP/critical-applications/botnets/botnets-
    measurement-detection-disinfection-and-defence/at_download/fullReport

Enhancing Network Security:
Host Trustworthiness Estimation

Tomáš Jirsík and Pavel Čeleda

Institute of Computer Science,
Masaryk University, Brno, Czech Republic
{jirsik,celeda}@ics.muni.cz

Abstract. Network connected devices has become inherent part of our lives. These devices have come to be more and more mobile and are target of various malware attacks. An inability to guarantee or check proper security settings of such devices poses a serious risk to network security. In this paper we propose a novel concept of flow based host trustworthiness estimation. The estimated trustworthiness determines a level of the risk to the network security the host posses. This concept enables network operators to identify a potential dangerous host in their network and take an appropriate precautions. Models used for trustworthiness estimation are based on scoring either single events or host characteristics. In order to be able to estimate trustworthiness of a host even in large scale networks, the data used for estimation are reduced only to extended network flows. The research is in its initial phase and will conclude with Ph.D. thesis in three years.

Keywords: network flow, host, model, trustworthiness, scoring.

1 Introduction

The development of mobile devices capable of internet connection increases the diversity of hosts connected to a network. The current trend is to grant almost anybody a permission to bring and connect own device. The access is granted even to devices, whose security status is unknown. The unsecured device can then unintentionally serve as an entry point for an attacker. Moreover, it is hard, or even impossible to reach the devices physically in order to check their proper settings. Remote access to them is also undesirable due to privacy issues.

Given the circumstances described above, the network operators need a way, how to asses a level of risk they undertake when they let a device connect into their network. The level of the risk the device poses can be represented by the concept of trustworthiness. The more trustworthy operators find the device, the lower risk the device poses to the inner security of the network. Based on the trustworthiness estimation the operators can consequently take adequate measures when allowing the device to connect to the network like a deployment of extended security precautions.

As in the case of security settings, it is not efficient to collect data needed for trustworthiness estimation directly from the devices, especially in the large scale

A. Sperotto et al. (Eds.): AIMS 2014, LNCS 8508, pp. 63–68, 2014.
© IFIP International Federation for Information Processing 2014

networks. A better way is to employ passive network monitoring. Monitoring devices like FlowMon [8], nProbe [14] and YAF [7] are capable of collecting aggregated representation of all connections in the network, called network flows. This mean of monitoring enables us to monitor all devices even in high speed networks. Based on acquired flow data we can then estimate *host trustworthiness*. By the term *host* we understand a device connected into the network.

Naturally, we do not intend to estimate the trustworthiness of all hosts in the Internet, we want to focus on hosts located within the monitored network. We stand for the concept of cleaning our house *(network)* first [6]. This approach also ensures sufficient data from flow network monitoring to determine the potentially malicious hosts. The results of our approach will have impact on network monitoring management and reduces amount of resources needed for maintaining network security.

The aim of this paper is to propose a concept for a host trustworthiness estimation as a topic of prospective Ph.D. thesis. In the Section 2 we discuss problem and possible pitfalls of this approach. Section 3 states research questions based on previous discussion and describes proposed approach to problem solution. Section 4 presents final considerations.

2   Problem Disscussion

The aim of this paper is to asses an estimate of host trustworthiness. The estimate should indicate a potentially danger host and must employ flow based monitoring to be able to monitor whole traffic. Using analogy to financial sector and credit scoring [17], we can regard the estimate as a measure, which represents a *trustworthiness of a host*. The greater risk to the network security the host poses, the lower is its trustworthiness. Features chosen to estimate the measure of trustworthiness should properly represent host behavior. There are papers [5,12] and surveys [9,3] which discuss flow-based host behavior classification. The authors classify host behavior into several categories based on predefined features observation. Nevertheless, they do not classify host in terms of security nor use any model to asses individual host trustworthiness.

Considering the fact that we intend to use only flow data, there are certain issues arising that need to be solved in order to be able to estimate the trustworthiness:

1. Host Identification. In the flow data, a host is identified by IP address. Using a MAC address for host identification is meaningless in this case since the monitoring devices collecting flow data are usually located at routers therefore they do not know the MAC address of the host. They know only MAC address of adjacent router. In order to be able to properly collect all hosts characteristics, *the host must be represented unambiguously*. An IP address can serve as unique host identificator in static addressed networks. In dynamic addressed networks, though, a host obtains a different IP address anytime it connects to the network. Therefore a host cannot be unambiguously identified via its IP address and we need to find a different approach to the host identification.

2. Per Host Characteristics. Flow records were originally developed for network monitoring and they represent a network traffic from the connection point of view. Also measured characteristics reflects this original purpose: majority of them are counted *per flow*. However, a host monitoring requires a rearrangement of the flow records. They should be stored in a *per host* manner. This shift opens possibilities for definition of new host based characteristics obtained from network traffic. Further, we need to develop a suitable type of model for trustworthiness estimation and identify which characteristics should be used as model variables.

We believe it to be a promising approach to focus on the flow monitoring from the host point of view. Solving the above mentioned issues enables us to estimate the host trustworthiness and identify risk. Moreover the results can be used for optimization of privileges granting or improved allocation of resources for traffic monitoring.

3   Research Questions and Proposed Approach

The goal of this research is *to estimate a host trustworthiness based only on flow information*. Apart from necessary engineering task, which includes a development of tools for storing, processing and querying flow data in host based format, we identify following research questions based on previously described problems and state proposed approach to each question:

1. *Is it possible to unambiguously identify a host employing only flow information?*

Solving research question 1 is crucial to further collection of host characteristics. We intend to identify a set of host specific flow elements, among others OS type, port distribution. We can also employ elements from application layer, e.g., User Agent in HTTP protocol. To the best of our knowledge, there is a lack of literature on flow-based host identification. There is literature on user identification [13] and on means for passive OS fingerprinting or NAT detection [11,1], though. Further, we consider to implement some results of host classification research, such as detecting type of the host [9]. A combination of these elements should be specific enough to provide us a unique host identification. In case we find an unambiguous host identification impossible, we imply a set of assumptions on the host in order to be able model host trustworthiness.

2. *How can the trustworthiness of a host be estimated? What features should be used for the estimation?*

Regarding the research question 2, the first step is to define trustworthiness, then we select monitored features. The selection of monitored features is dependent on the type of model used for estimation. So far, we considered implementation of two types of models. First, inspired by credit scoring, we propose a model based on scoring host behavior. An example of features representing host behavior is shown in [5]. The features are going to be scored based on their potential security risk and the total score for a particular host is going to be computed. The second model is similar to previous one, just instead of scoring flow features we score flow events. The flow event is an abstraction of sequence of related flows. Typical example of such an event is a visit to a web site - a single event, visiting a web site, generates many flows as additional contents of the website, e.g. banners, are downloaded. Identification of the events is a challenging task since we need to discover relations between particular flows in order to group them into a single event [4].

3. *What methodology should be used to evaluate proposed models for host trustworthiness estimation?*

Answering research question 3 is essential for evaluation of proposed models. Since it is almost impossible to find the ground truth in real-world measured data [15], usual means of model evaluation based on false/true positive/negative rates, like receiver operating characteristic [2], are inapplicable. There exist datasets, which contain labeled traces and we could distill ground truth from them [16]. Many of them are rather old, though, and they do not represent real world traffic properly [2]. To find the ground truth, we are developing a cloud-based security research testbed [10] that is designed for controlled simulation of network attacks. Using this testbed, we intend to carry out controlled experiments that enable us to measure a very-close-to-real-world data. Based on this data we evaluate the models by classical methods of model evaluations. We plan to asses the performance of method for unambiguous host identification in a similar way.

4   Conclusion

To enhance network security we have proposed a concept of host trustworthiness estimation. Since our research is in its early stage, we present a description of the problem and state research questions. Further, we briefly introduce intended approach to the problem. So far, we have developed necessary tools for collecting data and flow information extension, e.g., HTTP monitoring [18], and we have implemented the testbed for the model evaluation [10].

We are painfully aware of privacy issues arising and we want to take strict precautions. We intend to give an proper attention to this area and by no means we do not link a user identity to a host to maintain the privacy of the users.

The main purpose of this proposed research is to asses a security risk the host poses. Nevertheless, results of the research are not limited only to network security management. They can be used to design special tailored services, optimization of the quality of the services or for traffic shaping.

Acknowledgments. This material is based upon work supported by Cybernetic Proving Ground project (VG20132015103) funded by the Ministry of the Interior of the Czech Republic.

References

1. Abt, S., Dietz, C., Baier, H., Petrović, S.: Passive Remote Source NAT Detection Using Behavior Statistics Derived from NetFlow. In: Doyen, G., Waldburger, M., Čeleda, P., Sperotto, A., Stiller, B. (eds.) AIMS 2013. LNCS, vol. 7943, pp. 148–159. Springer, Heidelberg (2013),
   http://dx.doi.org/10.1007/978-3-642-38998-6_18
2. Bhuyan, M., Bhattacharyya, D., Kalita, J.: Network anomaly detection: Methods, systems and tools. IEEE Communications Surveys Tutorials PP(99), 1–34 (2013)
3. Callado, A.C., Kamienski, C.A., Szabo, G., Gero, B.P., Kelner, J., Fernandes, S.F.L., Sadok, D.F.H.: A survey on internet traffic identification. IEEE Communications Surveys and Tutorials 11(3), 37–52 (2009)
4. Caracas, A., Kind, A., Gantenbein, D., Fussenegger, S., Dechouniotis, D.: Mining semantic relations using NetFlow. In: 3rd IEEE/IFIP International Workshop on Business-driven IT Management, BDIM 2008, pp. 110–111 (2008)
5. Dewaele, G., Himura, Y., Borgnat, P., Fukuda, K., Abry, P., Michel, O., Fontugne, R., Cho, K., Esaki, H.: Unsupervised host behavior classification from connection patterns. Int. J. Netw. Manag. 20(5), 317–337 (2010),
   http://dx.doi.org/10.1002/nem.750
6. François, J., Moura, G.C.M., Pras, A.: Cleaning your house first: Shifting the paradigm on how to secure networks. In: Chrisment, I., Couch, A., Badonnel, R., Waldburger, M. (eds.) AIMS 2011. LNCS, vol. 6734, pp. 1–12. Springer, Heidelberg (2011), http://dl.acm.org/citation.cfm?id=2022216.2022218
7. Inacio, C.M., Trammell, B.: YAF: Yet Another Flowmeter. In: Proceedings of the 24th International Conference on Large Installation System Administration, LISA 2010, pp. 1–16. USENIX Association, Berkeley (2010),
   http://dl.acm.org/citation.cfm?id=1924976.1924987
8. INVEA-TECH: FlowMon Exporter – Community Program (2013), http://www.invea-tech.com (cited January 23, 2014)
9. Kim, H., Claffy, K., Fomenkov, M., Barman, D., Faloutsos, M., Lee, K.: Internet traffic classification demystified: Myths, caveats, and the best practices. In: Proceedings of the 2008 ACM CoNEXT Conference, CoNEXT 2008, pp. 11:1–11:12. ACM, New York (2008), http://doi.acm.org/10.1145/1544012.1544023
10. Kouřil, D., Rebok, T., Jirsík, T., Čegan, J., Drašar, M., Vizváry, M., Vykopal, J.: Cloud-based Testbed for Simulation of Cyber Attacks. In: Proceedings of the 2014 IEEE Network Operations and Management Symposium, NOMS 20124 (to appear, 2014)
11. Krmicek, V., Vykopal, J., Krejci, R.: Netflow based system for nat detection. In: Proceedings of the 5th International Student Workshop on Emerging Networking Experiments and Technologies, Co-Next Student Workshop 2009, pp. 23–24. ACM, New York (2009), http://doi.acm.org/10.1145/1658997.1659010
12. McHugh, J., McLeod, R., Nagaonkar, V.: Passive network forensics: Behavioural classification of network hosts based on connection patterns. SIGOPS Oper. Syst. Rev. 42(3), 99–111 (2008), http://doi.acm.org/10.1145/1368506.1368520
13. Melnikov, N., Schönwälder, J.: Cybermetrics: User identification through network flow analysis. In: Stiller, B., De Turck, F. (eds.) AIMS 2010. LNCS, vol. 6155, pp. 167–170. Springer, Heidelberg (2010),
   http://dx.doi.org/10.1007/978-3-642-13986-4_24
14. ntop: nProbe (2014), http://www.ntop.org/products/nprobe/ (cited January 23, 2014)

15. Ringberg, H., Roughan, M., Rexford, J.: The need for simulation in evaluating anomaly detectors. SIGCOMM Comput. Commun. Rev. 38(1), 55–59 (2008), http://doi.acm.org/10.1145/1341431.1341443

16. Stolfo, S., Fan, W., Lee, W., Prodromidis, A., Chan, P.: Cost-based modeling for fraud and intrusion detection: results from the jam project. In: Proceedings of the DARPA Information Survivability Conference and Exposition, DISCEX 2000, vol. 2, pp. 130–144 (2000)

17. Thomas, L.C., Crook, J., Edelman, D.: Credit Scoring and Its Applications. Society for Industrial and Applied Mathematics, Philadelphia (2002)

18. Velan, P., Jirsík, T., Čeleda, P.: Design and Evaluation of HTTP Protocol Parsers for IPFIX Measurement. In: Bauschert, T. (ed.) EUNICE 2013. LNCS, vol. 8115, pp. 136–147. Springer, Heidelberg (2013)

Outsourcing Mobile Security in the Cloud

Gaëtan Hurel, Rémi Badonnel, Abdelkader Lahmadi, and Olivier Festor

Université de Lorraine, LORIA, UMR 7503, France
INRIA Grand Est - Nancy, France

Abstract. In order to prevent attacks against smartphones and tablets, dedicated security applications are deployed on the mobile devices themselves. However, these applications may have a significant impact on the device resources. Users may be tempted to uninstall or disable them with the objective of increasing battery lifetime and avoiding configuration operations and updates. In this paper, we propose a new approach for outsourcing mobile security functions as cloud-based services. The outsourced functions are dynamically activated, configured and composed using software-defined networking and virtualization capabilities. We detail also preliminary results and point out future research efforts.

1 Introduction

The large-scale deployment of smartphones and tablets [1][2] has led to new security attacks. Because mobile devices are used for a wide range of applications (e.g. call, sms, web, work, banking), they often carry significant amounts of sensitive information that may be stolen. Mobile application markets act as an important threat vector since controls performed on submitted applications are not often available or too weak to detect potential hidden malwares [11]. The problem gets worse as end users do not systematically activate mobile security applications because they do not want to reduce the battery lifetime of their device. In that context, we propose a new approach for outsourcing mobile security so that mobile devices could benefit from remote security functions deployed in cloud infrastructures, therefore minimizing local resource consumption and user involvement [9]. In addition, moving security functions from end-user devices to cloud servers could significantly reduce the overall time spent on associated management tasks (e.g. updates and configurations) and related risks (e.g. misconfigurations). For that purpose, we define a cloud-based architecture able to integrate a large set of security functions for mobile devices. This architecture aims at outsourcing such functions in the cloud and dynamically deploying and combining them using Software-Defined Networking (SDN) and virtualization technologies such as Network Function Virtualization (NFV). Our main goal is to investigate to what extent mobile security can be efficiently outsourced in the cloud, and to evaluate the potential benefits such a strategy can introduce. The remainder of the paper is organized as follows. Related work is discussed in Section 2. We describe our proposed approach for cloud-based mobile security using SDN and virtualization in Section 3. Section 4 details preliminary results, while conclusions and future work are given in Section 5.

A. Sperotto et al. (Eds.): AIMS 2014, LNCS 8508, pp. 69–73, 2014.

2 Related Work

Several cloud-based approaches have already been proposed in the literature in order to provide security solutions for mobile devices. Some solutions exploit cloning methods using virtualization to execute security checks, such as Portokalidis et al. [12] and Kim et al. [8]. Some others directly outsource security functions of the mobile devices. Kilinc et al. [7] introduce a cloud-based applications firewall for Android devices, while Oberheide et al. [10] present a cloud-based antivirus for mobile devices of different platforms. More recently, Jin et al. [6] have focused on an SDN-based appliance to detect mobile malwares using traffic analysis performed at the network controller level. In [13], Sherry et al. explore a new design to efficiently and transparently outsource enterprise middleboxes in the cloud using virtualization. Although their work is not dedicated to mobile security, it confirms the potentiality of using the cloud capabilities to outsource security functions. We can observe that most of existing solutions are only partial as they focus on specific instances of the whole security threats set. In addition, they show a lack of flexibility and contextualization regarding how and when to use them. Our solution differs in two main points, namely (i) the way to choose relevant security functions for mobile devices according to their context and current risks, and (ii) the way to outsource, activate and dynamically compose those security functions using SDN and virtualization technologies.

3 Mobile Security as a Service

We propose a new strategy for delivering composable and dynamic security functions for mobile devices, as a transparent service in the cloud. In comparison with traditional on-device models, security is no more performed through a relatively static heap of functions which are executed on mobile devices. Instead, it is *mainly* based on a set of security functions hosted in the cloud and dynamically composable depending on the current context and risk level. Following the cloud terminology, our solution can be classified as a *Mobile Security as a Service (MSaaS)* strategy. The rationale behind moving security functions in the cloud is that setting up a large number of applications and maintaining them to entirely cover the security threats set is a difficult and overwhelming task, even for expert users. Furthermore, users' requirements regarding security of their devices and more generally mobile security threats may vary significantly over time and depending on the context. Our approach aims at addressing these resource consumption, dynamicity, and maintenance constraints. Cloud computing provides the necessary resources and elasticity for efficiently deploying security functions. In particular, we strongly believe that SDN and virtualization technologies can be exploited for facilitating the dynamic composition and transparent deployment of these functions in the cloud. Security functions will be set up as standard cloud services or by leveraging the NFV paradigm, where Virtualized Network Functions (VNF) are deployed on commodity hardware and particularly designed to ease service chaining.

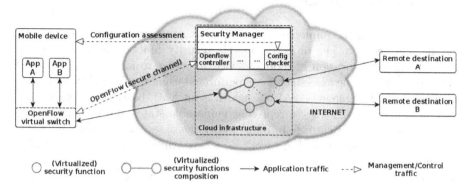

Fig. 1. Our cloud-based mobile security architecture

The proposed solution is depicted in Figure 1 and involves three distinct entities, namely (i) the mobile device which has several running applications and an integrated OpenFlow-based virtual switch, (ii) the security manager which is hosted by a cloud provider and manages security functions using specific modules (e.g. OpenFlow controller), and (iii) the remote destinations interacting with the mobile device. When an application wants to communicate with a remote destination, all the messages from and to that application are handled by the virtual switch of the device. At the beginning of the communication, the switch may probe an OpenFlow controller configured by the security manager in order to know how to route the related messages for applying security treatments on them. Depending on the risks and context, the manager activates the appropriate security functions and design a customized security composition in a proactive or reactive manner. By pushing the necessary OpenFlow rules within the cloud provider network, the controller then links those security functions to finalize the given composition building and notifies the switch. This one finally makes all the incoming and outgoing messages pass through that composition before reaching the final destination. Therefore, most of the security checks are applied *in the cloud* instead of *on the devices*. Security compositions are designed by the manager according to several factors such as the originating application, the remote destination and the network properties. For example, a mobile application requiring access to the enterprise intranet would need to use a security composition including at least an anti-malware and a data leakage prevention mechanism. On the other hand, a well-known gaming application should deserve less requirements from a security point of view, and some tradeoffs regarding whether or not to use on-device mechanisms could be considered in order to prevent unnecessary communication delay for example. The features are not limited to traffic analysis - the security manager can host additional security functions such as a configuration checker capable of controlling the proper configuration of the mobile devices. Using our approach, most of the security intelligence will be moved at the security manager level, potentially minimizing users involvement.

4   Preliminary Results

We have worked on the implementation of a first security function for our out-sourcing architecture. The objective of this security function is to analyze in the cloud the configuration of mobile devices in order to identify their poten-tial vulnerabilities. The assessments are performed using the Open Vulnerability and Assessment Language (OVAL)[3], which is an XML-based language widely used to standardize the way to represent vulnerable states and to perform as-sociated assessments. Before fully outsourcing the assessment engine, we have first designed an assessment framework [5] where Android devices periodically fetch vulnerability definitions from a remote server and perform associated local assessments to detect vulnerable states. The solution shows good accuracy re-garding vulnerability detection but involves significant usage of resources on the mobile devices during self-assessments. This observation has led us to completely outsource the assessment engine as security function in the cloud [4]. In this new design, mobile assessments are moved in the cloud to the remote server, which implements a probabilistic assessment model in order to distribute vulnerability evaluations across time. This new version consumes about 75% less resources on Android devices, while maintaining the same or even better accuracy regarding vulnerability detection. The reduction in usage of resources on the devices can be explained by two main reasons, namely (i) outsourcing assessments in the cloud offloads most of the work to the remote server, and (ii) the cloud is capable of hosting our probabilistic model in order to calculate partial assessments during each assessment period. The information collected about vulnerable configura-tions can then be exploited by the security manager in order to activate specific treatments for traffic targeting vulnerable devices.

5   Conclusions and Perspectives

The cloud paradigm offers new perspectives to support security functions for mobiles devices. Currently, mobile security is a major issue despite existing ap-plications, and this trend is likely to continue during the next years. As on-device architectural models show several limits including resource usage on the devices side, we propose a new strategy for decoupling and outsourcing security in the cloud and for achieving stronger and pervasive protection of mobile systems. In parallel, leveraging virtualization technologies and software-defined networking may particularly improve transparency and dynamicity with respect to deploy-ment, chaining and composition of security functions. As future work, we plan to pursue our investigation on composition mechanisms and their exploitability for our solution. We are also interested in leveraging data gathering and shar-ing methods between security functions amongst cloud infrastructures to build large datasets. Such datasets could be useful to extract valuable information about mobile threats and attacks trends for example. In that context, we plan to explore correlation mechanisms and machine learning algorithms by taking advantage of the huge computation capacities offered by the cloud.

Acknowledgments. This work was partly funded by Flamingo, a Network of Excellence project (ICT-318488) supported by the European Commission under its Seventh Framework Program.

References

1. IDC Forecasts Worldwide Tablet Shipments to Surpass Portable PC Shipments in 2013, Total PC Shipments in 2015, http://www.idc.com/ getdoc.jsp?containerId=prUS24129713 (last visited in February 2014)
2. More Smartphones Were Shipped in Q1 2013 Than Feature Phones, An Industry First According to IDC, http://www.idc.com/getdoc.jsp?containerId= prUS24085413 (last visited in February 2014)
3. The Open Vulnerability and Assessment Language (OVAL), http://oval.mitre.org/ (last visited in February 2014)
4. Barrère, M., Hurel, G., Badonnel, R., Festor, O.: A Probabilistic Cost-efficient Approach for Mobile Security Assessment. In: Proceedings of the 9th IFIP/IEEE International Conference on Network and Service Management, CNSM 2013 (2013)
5. Barrère, M., Hurel, G., Badonnel, R., Festor, O.: Ovaldroid: An OVAL-based vulnerability assessment framework for Android. In: Proceedings of the 13th IFIP/IEEE International Symposium on Integrated Network Management (IM 2013), pp. 1074–1075 (2013)
6. Jin, R., Wang, B.: Malware Detection for Mobile Devices Using Software-Defined Networking. In: Proceedings of the 2nd GENI Research and Educational Experiment Workshop (GREE 2013), pp. 81–88 (2013)
7. Kilinc, C., Booth, T., Andersson, K.: WallDroid: Cloud Assisted Virtualized Application Specific Firewalls for the Android OS. In: Proceedings of the 11th IEEE International Conference on Trust, Security and Privacy in Computing and Communications (TrustCom 2012), pp. 877–883 (2012)
8. Kim, T., Choi, Y., Han, S., Chung, J.Y., Hyun, J., Li, J., Hong, J.W.: Monitoring and Detecting Abnormal Behavior in Mobile Cloud Infrastructure. In: Proceedings of the 12th IEEE/IFIP Network Operations and Management Symposium (NOMS 2012), pp. 1303–1310 (2012)
9. Li, Q., Clark, G.: Mobile security: A look ahead. IEEE Security and Privacy 11(1), 78–81 (2013)
10. Oberheide, J., Veeraraghavan, K., Cooke, E., Flinn, J., Jahanian, F.: Virtualized In-Cloud Security Services for Mobile Devices. In: Proceedings of the 1st Workshop on Virtualization in Mobile Computing (MobiVirt 2008), pp. 31–35 (2008)
11. Percoco, N., Schulte, S.: Adventures in BouncerLand: Failures of Automated Malware Detection within Mobile Application Markets. In: Black Hat USA 2012 (2012), http://media.blackhat.com/ (last visited in February 2014)
12. Portokalidis, G., Homburg, P., Anagnostakis, K., Bos, H.: Paranoid Android: Versatile Protection for Smartphones. In: Proceedings of the 26th Annual Computer Security Applications Conference (ACSAC 2010), pp. 347–356 (2010)
13. Sherry, J., Hasan, S., Scott, C., Krishnamurthy, A., Ratnasamy, S., Sekar, V.: Making Middleboxes Someone else's Problem: Network Processing As a Cloud Service. In: Proceedings of the ACM SIGCOMM 2012 Conference on Applications, Technologies, Architectures, and Protocols for Computer Communication, pp. 13–24. ACM (2012)

Characterizing and Mitigating
the DDoS-as-a-Service Phenomenon

José Jair Santanna and Anna Sperotto

Design and Analysis of Communication Systems (DACS)
University of Twente
Enschede, The Netherlands
{j.j.santanna,a.sperotto}@utwente.nl

Abstract. Distributed Denial of Service (DDoS) attacks are an increasing threat on the Internet. Until a few years ago, these types of attacks were only launched by people with advanced knowledge of computer networks. However, nowadays the ability to launch attacks have been offered as a service to everyone, even to those without any advanced knowledge. *Booters* are online tools that offer *DDoS-as-a-Service*. Some of them advertise, for less than U$ 5, up to 25 Gbps of DDoS traffic, which is more than enough to make most hosts and services on the Internet unavailable. Booters are increasing in popularity and they have shown the success of attacks against third party services, such as government websites; however, there are few mitigation proposals. In addition, existing literature in this area provides only a partial understanding of the threat, for example by analyzing only a few aspects of one specific Booter. In this paper, we propose mitigation solutions against DDoS-as-a-Service that will be achieved after an extensive characterization of Booters. Early results show 59 different Booters, which some of them do not deliver what is offered. This research is still in its initial phase and will contribute to a Ph.D. thesis after four years.

1 Introduction

On March 2013, a Distributed Denial of Service (DDoS) attack almost broke the Internet [1]. The attacker was able to control up to 300 gigabits per second (Gbps) of network traffic and exhaust the communication resources of several hosts and networks, by misusing several services on Internet. Historically, DDoS attacks can be launched only by using advanced technical skills of the attackers, such as computer programming and specific knowledge of computer networks. These skills allow attackers to control several hosts and services with vulnerabilities on the Internet and perform attacks.

However, nowadays, a phenomenon is becoming popular: DDoS attacks are offered as a service (i.e., *DDoS-as-a-Service*), allowing everyone, even those without any kind of advanced knowledge, to launch attacks. Referred to on the Internet as *Booters*, these online tools offer several types of DDoS attacks, with different firepower (network throughput), often by charging low prices, such as

A. Sperotto et al. (Eds.): AIMS 2014, LNCS 8508, pp. 74–78, 2014.

25 Gbps for U\$ 5. In addition, *Booters* provide extra services which reduce even more the knowledge needed for customers to perform attacks, such as a *Skype resolver* that discovers the IP address based on the name account of a Skype user.

Booters have gaining in popularity on the Internet and have been used to perform DDoS attacks against several third party services, such as government websites [2], personal websites [3], and game servers [4]. Although increasingly popular [5], the existing literature brings only a partial understanding of the threat [6] [7] [8] [9], for example by analyzing the characteristics of only a single *Booter*, even though a survey of the offered services had allowed us to identify 59 *Booters* (as shown in Section 3).

DDoS-as-a-Service is not a new type of DDoS attack, but several existing types of DDoS attacks. To mitigate just one specific type of DDoS attack is a great challenge. To mitigate several different types, as Booters offer, poses an even greater challenge. In this research we aim to provide an extensive characterization of *Booters* and propose mitigation solutions against DDoS-as-a-Service. In addition, this research will contribute to the understanding of different types of DDoS attacks found nowadays, and characterize the changes in cyber-attack communities.

The remainder of this paper is organized as follows. Section 2 will discuss the research questions, followed by a description of our proposed approach. After that, closing this paper, we provide early results of our research in Section 3.

2   Goal, Research Questions, and Approach

The goal of our research is **to characterize and mitigate the *DDoS-as-a-Service* phenomenon**. To pursue this goal, we have defined the following research questions (RQ) as the basis of our research:

- **RQ$_A$**: How to characterize the DDoS-as-a-Service phenomenon?
- **RQ$_B$**: How to mitigate the DDoS-as-a-Service phenomenon?

By considering Booters as the front-end to access and launch DDoS-as-a-Service, our approach to address both characterization and mitigation research questions is based on investigating each element of the Booters business case (depicted in Fig. 1), and the interaction between them. The Booter business case is composed of the Booter *Customer*, the *Booter* itself, and the *Target* system. Each arrow in the Figs. 1a and 1b represents a step of our approach, which are described in the next sub-sections.

2.1   Characterization Steps

In the context of characterization steps we identify the following research questions.

- **RQ$_{A.1}$: How popular Booters are and which services they offer?** This research question is the basis to achieve a thorough understanding about the Customer's point of view. In this way, we aim to bring awareness about often

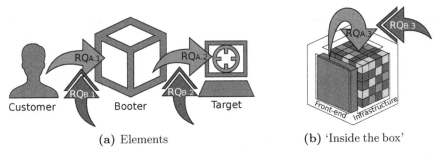

(a) Elements   (b) 'Inside the box'

Fig. 1. Booters business case

Booters have been accessed are and to survey all the key characteristics of Booters. By addressing this research question, we will estimate the size of the threat Booters pose on the Internet.

- RQ$_{A.2}$: What are the characteristics of DDoS attacks launched by Booters? The goal of this research question is to investigate the damage that Booters are able to generate against target systems. Furthermore, we want to compare what is offered to customers (i.e., RQ$_{A.1}$) with what they actually deliver. Finally, and a requisite to achieve the next research question, we want to characterize the infrastructure used to perform attacks.

- RQ$_{A.3}$: How do Booters control infrastructures that perform attacks? In general, Booters are a 'closed box' that advertise themselves by using private infrastructure to perform attacks. However, some works [6] [10] have shown that those infrastructures are composed of several misused hosts and services. Therefore, in this research question we characterize the behavior inside the Booter's box, by investigating the connection between the front-end, in general a Booter's website, and the back-end, composed by the infrastructure that performs attacks, as depicted in the Fig. 1b.

2.2 Mitigation Steps

In the context of mitigation steps we identify the following research questions.

- RQ$_{B.1}$: How to mitigate DDoS-as-a-Service at the customer level? Booters often advertise themselves as stress testers, i.e., tools that stress-test the performance of networks and services, to avoid legal implications. This situation would apply only if the Booter would allow traffic to be sent only to the infrastructure of the customer. However, most Booters recommend to customers not to attack their own infrastructure. Therefore, this research question is the basis to propose solutions to mitigate the '*misbehavior*' of Booters' customer. One way to achieve this is to work in collaboration with exponents of the law to propose countermeasure against Booters and malicious customers.

- RQ$_{B.2}$: How to mitigate DDoS-as-a-Service at the target level? The goal of this research question is to serve as the base to achieve solutions able to cope with different types of DDoS attacks. To do so, we will use the characteristics of DDoS attacks launched by Booters (i.e., $RQ_{A.2}$) to propose specific mitigation solutions against their damaging effects.

- $RQ_{B.3}$: How to mitigate DDoS-as-a-Service at the point where the infrastructure is controlled? Conventional approaches to mitigate DDoS attack aims to find the Command-and-Control (C&C) infrastructure, which is generally hidden behind spoofed IP addresses and several layers of C&C. Nevertheless, once $RQ_{A.3}$ has been addressed, we are able to propose automated solutions to mitigate DDoS attacks at the command and control level.

In summary, the steps presented in this Section, especially in the characterization part, will be achieved based on analysis of large-scale network measurements. To collect this data, we count on global measurements, provided by RIPE Atlas [11], Hurricane Electric [12], and Alexa [13], for example. In addition, we count on collaborations already established, to support our studies and deploy mitigation solutions developed during this research, such as: *SURFnet* [14], CERT.at [15], and the partners of the FLAMINGO Network of Excellence [16]. It should be noted that the steps described in this Section can be addressed out of the presented order.

3   Early Results and Final Considerations

We have developed a crawler that uses Google's Custom Search [17] to find information related to the DDoS-as-a-Service phenomenon, such as blogs, videos, reports, and websites. We have used the following keywords: 'booter', 'ddoser', 'stresser', 'ddos-as-a-service', and 'ddos-for-hire'. Through our crawler and manual classifications, we found 59 Booters since October 2013. Among them, we have identified 34 Booters that are continuously reachable, while the other 25 appeared to be at times offline during the measurement period. The reachable Booters offer the most common DDoS attacks observed nowadays [18], which include: SYN floods, DNS amplification attacks, and attacks based on HTTP GET. In addition, experiments, performed against a dummy target at the University of Twente, seem to indicate that Booters do not always deliver what they advertise. For example, Rebel-security [19] offers 3 Gbps of attack traffic while we measured only 1 Gbps. Even worse, some Booters, such as Olympus Stresser [20] and Vdoss [21], charge money to deliver just a handful of ICMP packets, while was ordered amplification attacks based on UDP.

This research is still in its initial phase and the main goal of this work – as described previously – must be achieved within a period of four years, as the core of a Ph.D. research program.

Acknowledgments. This research is funded by FLAMINGO, a Network of Excellence project (318488) supported by the European Commission under its Seventh Framework Programme.

References

1. Prince, M.: The DDoS That Almost Broke the Internet,
   `http://blog.cloudflare.com/the-ddos-that-almost-broke-the-internet`
   (accessed on April 7, 2014)
2. Karami, M., McCoy, D.: Understanding the Emerging Threat of DDoS-as-a-Service. In: Proceedings of the 6th UNSENIX Workshop on Large-Scale Exploits and Emergent Threats. LEET 2013 (2013)
3. Krebs, B.: The World Has No Room for Cowards,
   `http://krebsonsecurity.com/2013/03/the-world-has-no-room-for-cowards`
   (accessed on April 7, 2014.)
4. Prolexic: Multiplayer Video Gaming Attacks, `http://www.prolexic.com/`
   `knowledge-center-white-paper-series-gaming-reflection-attacks-`
   `drdos-ddos` (accessed on April 7, 2014)
5. Lackery, J.: A New Twist on Denial of Service: DDoS as a Service,
   `http://blogs.cisco.com/security/a_new_twist_on_denial_of_`
   `service_ddos_as_a_service/` (accessed on April 7, 2014)
6. Prolexic: Threat: DDoS Booter Shell Scripts, `http://www.prolexic.com/`
   `knowledge-center-ddos-threat-advisories-booter-shell-scripts.html` (accessed on April 7, 2014)
7. Prolexic: Quarterly Global DDoS Attack Report Q3, `http://www.prolexic.com/`
   `knowledge-center-ddos-attack-report-2013-q3.html` (accessed on April 7, 2014)
8. Goncharov, M.: Russian Underground 101, `http://blog.trendmicro.com/`
   `trendlabs-security-intelligence/a-look-into-the-russian-underground/`
   (accessed on April 7, 2014)
9. Krebs, B.: Ragebooter: Legit DDoS Service, or Fed Backdoor,
   `http://krebsonsecurity.com/2013/05/ragebooter-legit-ddos-`
   `service-or-fed-backdoor/` (accessed on April 7, 2014)
10. Santanna, J.J.: DDoS as a Service, `http://www.ietf.org/proceedings/`
    `interim/2013/10/14/nmrg/slides/slides-interim-2013-nmrg-1-11.pdf`
    (accessed on April 7, 2014)
11. Atlas, R.: Ripe Atlas website, `https://atlas.ripe.net` (accessed on April 7, 2014)
12. Hurricane Electric: Hurricane Electric - BGP Toolkit Home, `http://bgp.he.net`
    (accessed on April 7, 2014)
13. Alexa: Alexa website, `http://www.alexa.com` (accessed on April 7, 2014)
14. SURFNet: SURFNet website, `http://www.surf.nl` (accessed on April 7, 2014)
15. CERT.at: Computer Emergency Response Team Austria website,
    `http://www.cert.at` (accessed on April 7, 2014)
16. FLAMINGO: FLAMINGO website, `http://www.fp7-flamingo.eu` (accessed on April 7, 2014)
17. Google: Google's Custom Search, `https://developers.google.com/`
    `custom-search/`(accessed on April 7, 2014)
18. Arbor Networks: Worldwide Infrastructure Security Report - Volume IX,
    `http://www.arbornetworks.com/resources/infrastructure-security-report`
    (accessed on April 7, 2014)
19. Rebel-security: Rebel Security's Website, `http://rebel-security.com` (accessed on April 7, 2014)
20. Olympus Stresser: Olympus Stresser's Website, `http://olympusstresser.org` (accessed on April 7, 2014)
21. VDoSs: VDoSs' Website, `http://vdoss.net` (accessed on April 7, 2014)

Characterisation of the Kelihos.B Botnet*

Max Kerkers, José Jair Santanna, and Anna Sperotto

Design and Analysis of Communication Systems (DACS)
University of Twente
Enschede, The Netherlands
m.kerkers@student.utwente.nl, {j.j.santanna,a.sperotto}@utwente.nl

Abstract. Botnets are organized networks of infected computers that are used for malicious purposes. An example is Kelihos.B, a botnet of the Kelihos family used primarily for mining bitcoins, sending spam and stealing bitcoin wallets. A large part of the Kelihos.B botnet was sinkholed in early 2012 and since then bots are sending requests to controlled servers. In this paper, we analyze and characterize the behavior of Kelihos.B. Our analysis is based on the log file of the bot request logged at the sinkhole from March 2012 to early November 2013. We investigate both the overall characteristics of the botnets, as well as on its evolution over time since the time of the sinkholing. Our results indicate that, although this trend is decreasing, there are possibly still newly infected bots even more than a year from the original sinkholing.

Keywords: Botnet, Kelihos.B, Hlux2, Characterisation, Sinkhole.

1 Introduction

Botnets are one of the modern threats to society. A botnet consists of several malware-infected computers (bots) that are controlled by the owners of the botnet. Botnets have for example been used to send spam or to launch distributed denial of service (DDoS) attacks [1]. One of such botnets is Kelihos.B, which was primarily used for mining bitcoins, sending spam and stealing bitcoin wallets [2].

The Kelihos.B botnet was sinkholed on the 21st of March 2012 by security experts from Kaspersky, CrowdStrike, and SURFnet, among others [2]. Sinkholing is the operation of re-directing C&C requests to a set of controlled servers by reverse-engineering the botnet C&C mechanisms. As these controlled servers will not send any jobs to the bots, the botnet is in practice disrupted [4]. Since then, the sinkholing servers have collected large numbers of data from the bots that are still active, although ineffective.

The goal of this paper is to characterize the Kelihos.B botnet. This characterization will contribute to the better understanding of the evolution over a

---

* It should be noted that an initial version of this paper has been presented at the 20th Twente Student Conference on Information Technology, as for requirement of the Bachelor degree in Computer Science. However, the conference was an internal event of the University of Twente, of which the proceedings have not officially been published by any publisher [3].

A. Sperotto et al. (Eds.): AIMS 2014, LNCS 8508, pp. 79–91, 2014.

period of one year and nine months of a sinkholed botnet (from March 2012 to November 2013). Our analysis confirms and updates preliminary results on the Kelihos.B botnet that have been carried on days after the sinkholing [2,4] or in occasion of other sinkholing operations [5]. However, the analysis presented in this paper vastly extends previous results and sheds new light on aspects that are not considered in literature. First, we analyze the long term behavior of the hosts contacting the sinkhole, which is only hinted at [5]. Second, we identify the presence, still today, of newly infected hosts from different the Autonomous Systems, which indicates that the infection vector for this Botnet is still partially active. Last, we analyze the temporal behavior of hosts in different continents, which highlights the presence of a clear day-night pattern and implies a certain type of infected hosts.

This paper is structured as follow. In the Section 2 we provide background information about the structure of the botnet and the sinkholing operation. Then the considered dataset and analysis methodology are described in Section 3. In Section 4, the analysis results are provided. Finally, we conclude in Section 5.

2   Background

A botnet is a collection of hosts, called bots, which are infected with malicious software. Bots are typically controlled by one or more Command & Control servers (C&Cs), which belongs to the owner of the botnet and are used to send bots tasks they have to execute [1].

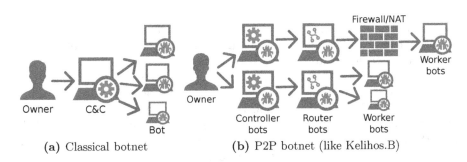

(a) Classical botnet   **(b)** P2P botnet (like Kelihos.B)

Fig. 1. Botnet architectures

In a classical botnet, as shown in Figure 1a, the C&C server is centralized and it has knowledge about the addresses of every bot in the botnet. Despite the simplicity of structuring these botnets, a central C&C server is also a single point of failure, since only the central server has to be disabled to shutdown the botnet. Recently, botnets based on a peer-to-peer (P2P) infrastructure have become more common. Examples are the Zeus (P2P variant) [6], Sality [7] and Kelihos.B, the botnet considered in this paper. An exemplified architecture of a

P2P botnets is shown in Figure 1b. In these botnets, the bots themselves will propagate C&C instructions, and the presence of a centralized C&C server is therefore not needed anymore. When a host is infected and becomes a bot, it will contact a hit-list of trusted hosts from which to request further information and instructions. This process is called bootstrapping.

Kelihos.B is not the first version of the Kelihos botnet to be sinkholed. The first Kelihos botnet (or Hlux) was shutdown by a sinkhole operation in September 2011 [8]. The Kelihos family consisted of three types of bots: controllers, routers and workers, indicated in Figure 1b. The controllers are the bots that are operated by the owners of the botnet and where the instructions originate. The router bots have a list of other bots in the network and their goal is to redistribute the instructions they receive from the controllers. Finally the workers are the bots that execute these instructions. Bots that are located behind firewalls or NATs and therefore cannot be reached from outside are always put themselves in worker mode. Examples of possible instructions these workers can execute include sending spam, participating in distributed denial of service attacks and updating itself to a newer version. These instructions are called jobs. When a bot wants to obtain new instructions it sends a job request to a set of predefined routers. When the bot wants to obtain an update of the list of other bots in the network, it sends a bootstrap request to exchange their lists of routers. Bots that are new in the network always contain a list of several router bots to obtain more router addresses from.

Kelihos.B, a new slightly altered version of Kelihos, was discovered merely weeks after the first sinkholing. Kelihos.B had mostly the same functionality as the original Kelihos botnet. However the botnets also showed some differences, such as: the use of encrypted communication protocol and a new set of encrypted keys. In addition, according [9] and [2], Kelihos.B was used for different purposes, such as to intercept passwords, stealing bitcoin wallets, sending spam and performing DDoS attacks. The family of Kelihos botnets targets Windows-based hosts and it mainly spread via social networks, in particular via a so-called Facebook worm that allures users to download a photo album [10]. At the time of writing this paper it is known that Kelihos has mutated again into a new version that shows the additional feature of stealing Internet browsers passwords [11,12] and was sinkholed in 2013.

In Section 3 the dataset of the sinkholed Kelihos.B botnet is described.

3   Dataset and Analysis Methodology

The dataset consists of log files from the controlled sinkholing server from the National Research and Education Network of the Netherlands, SURFnet. The log files contain a record for each request to the server done by a bot. Figure 2 is an example of what those records look like. As can be seen each request is logged together with a human readable timestamp of when the request was received, followed by whether it was a bootstrap request or a job request, from which IP-address and port the request originated. Furthermore, job requests also contain the version of the bot from which the request originates and the operating system of the infected host.

```
[2012-03-21 17:40:27.48661] bootstrap request from x.x.x.x:3810
[2012-03-21 17:40:27.58262] job request from y.y.y.y:2924 - 376ae8[...],
    v126 "plus001", os info: 5.1.2600, platform 2
```

Fig. 2. Examples of log entries (IP-addresses are anonymized)

The dataset spans over a period of one year and nine months, from March 21, 2012 until November 7, 2013. In total, the dataset contains almost 594 million of requests. Therefore this data first had to be aggregated and structured such that it would be easier to analyze.

The logs have been augmented with additional information, such as geolocation data as the originating country and continent of the request, and routing data, i.e., the originating autonomous system. For determining the country from which the IP-addresses originate the MaxMind [13] database was used. In this database the country in which IP-addresses are located can be found. Then, for determining in what continent the country was located the incf.countryutils [14] module was used. This contains a list of which countries are in which continents. For determining the autonomous systems the PyASN module [15] was used. This module uses BGP RIB data from the first of January 2013 to determine which autonomous system an IP-address is in.

The augmented dataset allows us to investigate the following characteristics:

– Types of requests (bootstrap or job);
– IP-addresses and the information derived from those, such as Autonomous System numbers and Geo-location information;
– Port numbers;
– Operating systems (for job requests);
– Bot versions (for job requests);

Our analysis methodology is structured along two main aspects. First, we analyze the dataset as a whole, therefore presenting an *overall analysis* of the main data characteristics (Sec. 4.1). Second, we show a *temporal analysis* of the data, in which we highlight how the sinkholed botnet is evolving over time (Sec. 4.2).

4   Analysis Results

This section presents the outcome of our analysis. First, we present the overall characterization of the Keilhos.B network in Section 4.1; then, in Section 4.2, we proceed to describe how the botnet has evolved over time in the considered period.

4.1   Overall analysis

The dataset shows that in total 3.7M unique IP-addresses have contacted the sinkhole with 593.4 M requests. Of those, 81.5% were bootstrap requests and 18.5% were job requests. This seems to indicate that the maintenance of the botnet infrastructure, achieved by acquiring bootstrap information, is prevalent comparing with requests for new jobs. This behavior is also ensuring that the botnet, once sinkholed, is continuously controlled, even if new hosts will be infected and became part of the botnet. However, we are not able to quantify if the sinkholing operation has in a way altered the bot behavior, for example causing a larger number of bootstrap requests.

The analysis of the geographical characteristic of the hosts contacting the sinkhole shows that a large fraction of the infected population was located in Poland. This holds both if we consider the percentage of requests received by the sinkhole (Table 1a), as well as the percentage of involved IP addresses (Table 1b). However, Table 1a and Table 1b also indicate that, although several countries appear in the top 10 countries in both the percentage of sent request as well as the percentage of involved IP addresses, there is not a direct correlation between the two lists. Examples are given by the United States, which generate 6.97% of the requests (41.3 M requests), but only hosts 2.24% of the IP addresses (83K IP addresses); or Hungary, which generated 3.66% of the requests (21M requests), but does not appear in the top 10 most active countries in term of IP addresses.

Table 1. Geographical distribution of request and IP addresses

(a) Requests per country

Country	Request[%]
Poland	34.13%
United States	6.97%
Turkey	6.85%
Hungary	3.66%
Mexico	3.38%
Argentina	3.24%
Spain	3.06%
Romania	3.04%
Bulgaria	2.22%
Vietnam	2.02%
Others	31.13%

(b) IPs per country

Country	IP[%]
Poland	24.85%
Turkey	11.08%
Thailand	4.76%
India	4.74%
Mexico	4.50%
Egypt	4.04%
Vietnam	3.98%
Pakistan	3.56%
Argentina	2.48%
United States	2.24%
Others	33.75%

To better understand how many requests each IP address performs towards the sinkhole, Figure 3 shows the cumulative distribution function of the number of requests per IP address. From the figure, we derive that 17% of the IP addresses (0.63M IP addresses) have only sent a single request to the server. In addition, 90% of the IP addresses (3.3M) appear up to 135 times in the logs.

Table 2. Top 10 of Autonomous Systems in percentage of requests

AS	Name	Requests (%)
5617	TPNET Telekomunikacja Polska S.A.	7.28%
9121	TTNET Turk Telekomunikasyon Anonim Sirketi	5.09%
6830	LGI-UPC Liberty Global Operations B.V.	3.78%
29314	VECTRANET-AS VECTRA S.A.	3.23%
21021	MULTIMEDIA-AS Multimedia Polska S.A.	3.20%
12741	INTERNETIA-AS Netia SA	2.50%
7922	COMCAST-7922 - Comcast Cable Communications, Inc.	2.00%
8151	Uninet S.A. de C.V.	1.91%
8048	CANTV Servicios, Venezuela	1.61%
10481	Prima S.A.	1.36%
Others		68.03%

The remaining 10% of the distribution shows a long tail, where a handful of IP addresses are responsible for up to 2M requests. The most active IP address is located in Montenegro and it created 0.35% of all the requests in the dataset (2M requests).

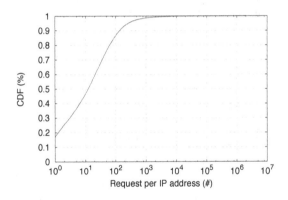

Fig. 3. Cumulative distribution function of the number of requests per IP-addresses

The total number of unique Autonomous Systems (AS) in the dataset is 7629. Also considering ASes, it is easy to see that Poland dominates the top 10 list of most active ASes in terms of requests. As Table 2 shows, the AS where most requests originate from is AS5617 (TPNET Telekomunikacja Polska S.A.), with a share of 7.3% requests (43.3M requests). With a share of 5.1% (30.2 M requests), the second largest origin of requests is the AS9121 from Turkey.

Figure 4 shows the cumulative distribution function of the source ports from which the requests originate. The ports that are by far used most are in the range 1024 – 5000, used in 70% of the requests. In only less than 1% of the requests, the bots used to communicate a port in the restricted range (smaller

Table 3. Bot information

(a) Bot version

Version	Requests [%]
121	1.47
122	1.12
125	22.65
126	72.93
Other	1.83

(b) Operating Systems

Operating System	Requests [%]
Windows XP + Windows Server 2003	87,73%
Windows Vista + Windows Server 2008	2,10%
Windows 7 + Windows Server 2008 R2	10,17%

than 1024). The ports in the ranges 5000 – 50000 and larger than 50000 are both equally used in are used in 15% of the requests.

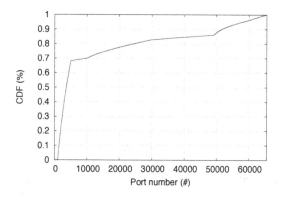

Fig. 4. Cumulative distribution function of originating ports of requests

The two most occurring bot versions are the version 126 with 72.9% and the version 125 with 22.7%. All the other versions combined have a share of less than 5%. This can be seen in Table 2a. As will be seen in the next section these percentages remain close to this values over time.

Finally, our analysis indicates that all requests originate from computers running the Windows operating system. As can be seen in Table 2b almost 88% of the job requests originate from computers running Windows XP (or Windows Server 2003), while the other infected hosts run other operating systems in the Windows family.

4.2   Temporal Analysis

In Figure 5 we show the time series of the number of requests per hour received by the sinkhole. The figure shows ranges where data are missing, due to some corrupted logs in the dataset. The overall trend indicated by Figure 5 is an almost exponential decrease in the number of requests per hour, with a more stable tendency towards the last months of this measurement. In November 2013, the sinkhole received between 3000 and 12000 request per hour.

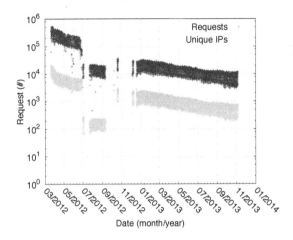

Fig. 5. Total number of requests and IP addresses per hour

Similarly, Figure 6 shows the amount of new IPs per hour over the dataset. If we exclude the initial phase, where the faster decrease is due to the beginning of our measurement period, Figure 6 indicates that the number of new IPs contacting the sinkhole decreases almost exponentially. For example, from the first week of January 2013 to the first week of November 2013, the number of new IP addresses per day decreases from an average of 123 to an average of 48. The number of new IP addresses can indicate both the presence of newly infected hosts, as well as old infections that may belong to networks with dynamic IP allocation (DHCP). In Table 4 we show the number of new Autonomous Systems that appear in the dataset, grouped per quarters. Please note that the first quarter of 2012 only covers the days from the 21st of March to the 31st of March, and the last quarter of 2013 covers the first of October to the 7th of November. Table 4 clearly indicates, for the all duration of the considered dataset, IPs belonging to new ASes have progressively contacted the sinkhole, therefore supporting the theory that the Kelihos.B botnet is still evolving.

As shown in Figure 7 three periods can be identified in which the distribution of job requests is around the same percentage. From the 21st of March until the 29th of June 2012 this average percentage is 13.7%, while from the 20th of December 2012 this average percentage is 32.0%. In the period between the 29th of June 2012 and the 20th of December 2012 there are some gaps due to the earlier described corrupted data. Except for those gaps there is a remarkably high average percentage of job requests of 64.1%.

In Figure 8 we have investigated the possible relationship between the requests and the continent where they originate. Figure 8a presents the average number

Table 4. Number of new autonomous systems per quarter of the year

Year	Quarter	Number of new ASes
2012	1*	4628
2012	2	2805
2012	3	5
2012	4	62
2013	1	69
2013	2	33
2013	3	21
2013	4*	6

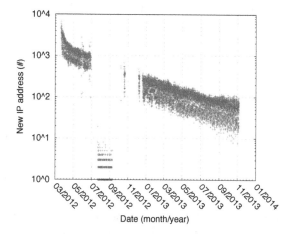

Fig. 6. Number of new IP-addresses per hour over time

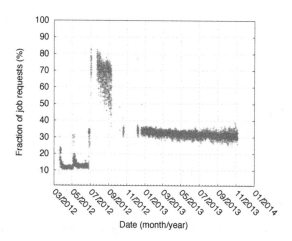

Fig. 7. Percentage of job requests per hour

of requests per hour for the continent of origin of a request, normalized by the average number of requests per continents. Similarly, Figure 8b shows the average number of IP-addresses per hour per continent. The normalization allows a direct comparison of the temporal trend of the requests and IP address per hour between different continents. A value of 100% indicates a number of requests or IP addresses equal to the average number. The times in the figures correspond to the times in the dataset as described in Section 3. Although a partition of the dataset in continents is only a simplification of approximating time zones, the results in Figure 8 already indicates that each continent shows a clear day/night pattern. This seems to suggest that the population of infected hosts in the dataset is biased towards laptop and workstations. This observation is also supported by the fact that 87.2% of the infected hosts run Windows XP, as shown in Table 2b.

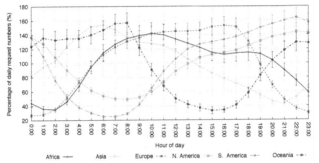

(a) Average number of requests per hour of the day normalised by the average number of requests per continent

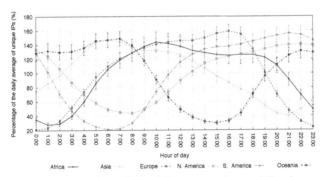

(b) Average number of IP-addresses per hour of the day per continent normalised by the average number op IP-addresses per continent

Fig. 8. Geographical request and host distribution per hour of day

Finally, we have investigated the distribution of the bot version and the operative system of the infected hosts over time. In Figure 9 the development of the version distribution can be seen. All versions follow the exponential decrease of the total number of requests. Interestingly enough, all versions were already present at the time of the sinkholing, and they are persistent over the entire dataset. Also, they percentage with respect to the number of request per hour tends to remain stable. The only notable exceptions are versions 126 and 128, which seem to fade faster just after the sinkholing.

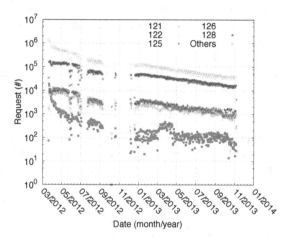

Fig. 9. Number of requests from version number of bots per day

There is no significant change in the distribution of operating systems over time. However, there seems to be a small increase in the share of operating systems running Windows XP. This can be seen in Figure 10.

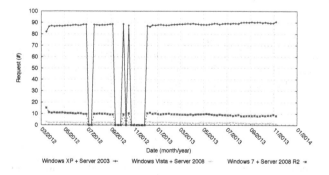

Fig. 10. Percentage of used operating systems for requests per week

5   Conclusions

In this paper we have investigated the peer-to-peer botnet Kelihos.B. The botnet was sinkholed in early 2012. Using the requests to the sinkholing server we were able to determine what the characteristics of this botnet are. This was accomplished by first analyzing the overall behavior of the botnet in a time-independent fashion and then analyzing the behavior over time to obtain knowledge about how the botnet evolved over time.

In overall, most requests and IP-addresses originate from Poland, although the distribution of IP addresses per country indicate that there is not a one-to-one match between the number of requests and the number of active IP addresses. A telling example is the United States, which is the second most active country per number of requests, but rank only in 10th position per number of active hosts. Overall, 90% of the other IP-addresses have sent less than 135 requests, but the distribution of the number of requests per IP address has a long tail, and a single IP address, located in Montenegro, was able to generate more than 2M requests. Furthermore the AS5617 TPNET Telekomunikacja Polska S.A., which is located in Poland, is the autonomous system from which most requests originate. Finally most bots run version 126 of the botnet software and most bots run on Windows XP.

With respect to the temporal botnet behavior, we can see that the number of requests shows a decreasing trend, although it recently tends to stabilize. On the other hand, the number of new IP addresses contacting the sinkhole seems to constantly decrease over time. The analysis of the requests per continent shows that hosts in different continent follows a day-night pattern. Combined with the observations relative to the operative system of the bots, we can confirm that Kelihos.B primarily targeted personal computer. When considering the distribution of the bot versions and operating systems, our analysis shows that the distributions over time remain the same for the duration of the monitoring period. Also, our results indicate that the bots are still fairly active and the combined analysis of newly appearing IP addresses from different ASes indicates that the infection vector is sill active.

Acknowledgments. The authors would like to thank Rogier Spoor (SURFnet) for providing the data used in this research and information about the sinkholing. This research is funded by FLAMINGO, a Network of Excellence project (318488) supported by the European Commission under its Seventh Framework Programme.

References

1. Elliott, C.: Botnets: To what extent are they a threat to information security? Information Security Technical Report 15(3), 79–103 (2010)
2. Ortloff, S.: FAQ: Disabling the new Hlux/Kelihos Botnet (2012),
   http://www.securelist.com/en/blog/208193438/
   FAQ_Disabling_the_new_Hlux_Kelihos_Botnet (accessed April 2014)

3. Kerkers, M.: Characterisation of the Kelihos.B Botnet. In: 20th Twente Student Conference on IT, University of Twente (2014)
4. Werner, T.: P2P Botnet Kelihos.B with 100.000 Nodes Sinkholed (2012), http://www.crowdstrike.com/blog/p2p-botnet-kelihosb-100000-nodes-sinkholed/index.html (accessed April 2014)
5. Stefan Ortloff: Sinkholing the Hlux/Kelihos botnet - what happened? (August 2013), https://www.securelist.com/en/blog/208214147/Sinkholing_the_Hlux_Kelihos_botnet_what_happened (accessed April 2014)
6. Binsalleeh, H., Ormerod, T., Boukhtouta, A., Sinha, P., Youssef, A., Debbabi, M., Wang, L.: On the analysis of the Zeus botnet crimeware toolkit. In: 8th Annual International Conference on Privacy Security and Trust (PST), pp. 31–38. IEEE (2010)
7. Rossow, C., Andriesse, D., Werner, T., Stone-Gross, B., Plohmann, D., Dietrich, C.J., Bos, H.: SoK: P2PWNED-Modeling and Evaluating the Resilience of Peer-to-Peer Botnets. In: IEEE Symposium on Security and Privacy (SP), pp. 97–111. IEEE (2013)
8. Werner, T.: Botnet Shutdown Success Story: How Kaspersky Lab Disabled the Hlux/Kelihos Botnet (2011), http://www.securelist.com/en/blog/208193137/Botnet_Shutdown_Success_Story_How_Kaspersky_Lab_Disabled_the_Hlux_Kelihos_Botnet (accessed April 2014)
9. Knowles, R., Stevens, A.: How Kaspersky Lab and CrowdStrike Dismantled the Second Hlux/Kelihos Botnet: Success Story (2012), http://www.kaspersky.com/about/news/virus/2012/How_Kaspersky_Lab_and_CrowdStrike_Dismantled_the_Second_Hlux_Kelihos_Botnet_Success_Story (accessed April 2014)
10. Raff, A.: Kelihos. B is still live and social (March 2012), https://www.seculert.com/blog/2012/03/kelihosb-is-still-live-and-social.html (accessed April 2014)
11. Adamov, A.: A Modification of Kelihos Looks for Passwords Stored in Internet Browsers (March 2013), http://www.lavasoft.com/mylavasoft/malware-descriptions/blog/a-modification-of-kelihos-looks-for-passwords-stored-in-internet-browsers (accessed April 2014)
12. Adamov, A.: Update on Kelihos Botnet (August 2013), http://www.lavasoft.com/mylavasoft/malware-descriptions/blog/update-on-kelihos-botnet-august-2013 (accessed April 2014)
13. MaxMind: MaxMind GeoIP Database (2013), http://www.maxmind.com/en/geolocation_landing (accessed April 2014)
14. Ritz, R.: incf.countryutils (2009), https://pypi.python.org/pypi/incf.countryutils (accessed April 2014)
15. Asghari, H.: PyASN 1.2 (March 2010), https://code.google.com/p/pyasn/downloads/detail?name=PyASN-1.2.zip (accessed April 2014)

A Study of RPL DODAG Version Attacks

Anthéa Mayzaud[1], Anuj Sehgal[2], Rémi Badonnel[1],
Isabelle Chrisment[1], and Jürgen Schönwälder[2]

[1] TELECOM Nancy, Université de Lorraine, LORIA UMR 7503,
Inria Nancy-Grand Est, Villers-lès-Nancy, 54600 France
{anthea.mayzaud,remi.badonnel}@inria.fr, isabelle.chrisment@loria.fr
[2] Computer Science, Jacobs University Bremen,
Campus Ring 1, 28759 Bremen, Germany
{s.anuj,j.schoenwaelder}@jacobs-university.de

Abstract. The IETF designed the Routing Protocol for Low power and Lossy Networks (RPL) as a candidate for use in constrained networks. Keeping in mind the different requirements of such networks, the protocol was designed to support multiple routing topologies, called DODAGs, constructed using different objective functions, so as to optimize routing based on divergent metrics. A DODAG versioning system is incorporated into RPL in order to ensure that the topology does not become stale and that loops are not formed over time. However, an attacker can exploit this versioning system to gain an advantage in the topology and also acquire children that would be forced to route packets via this node. In this paper we present a study of possible attacks that exploit the DODAG version system. The impact on overhead, delivery ratio, end-to-end delay, rank inconsistencies and loops is studied.

1   Introduction

The emergence of low-cost low-power resource constrained nodes capable of wireless networking enables new applications ranging from a smart electricity grid to mobile health solutions. Such constrained network devices could be integrated with the existing Internet infrastructure, so that they may utilize software services already available coupled with the nodes control and data-gathering capabilities.

Lacking any form of multi-hop routing, most networks of such resource constrained devices rely on a router being present on the local link. The Routing Protocol for Low-power Lossy Networks (RPL) was designed by the IETF [1] to fit within resource constraints of embedded devices. RPL not only forms loop-free routing topologies but also optimizes these for application specific goals, e.g. energy conservation, by using metrics available to a device. However, the features that enable RPL to provide this level of flexibility could also be manipulated by malicious nodes to cause harm to the network.

Some of these attacks can be mitigated by using the security mechanisms proposed by RPL, however, important details like key-management are left-out by the current standard [2] and cryptographic algorithms are not only complex

A. Sperotto et al. (Eds.): AIMS 2014, LNCS 8508, pp. 92–104, 2014.

to implement unless there is dedicated cryptographic hardware support, but also consume significant resources on constrained devices [3]. An evaluation of several popular RPL implementations[1] reveals that none of them support secure RPL operation. This makes attacks on RPL quite a possibility.

One attack that can misuse an internal RPL process, normally used for ensuring a loop and error free topology, is the version number attack. A malicious node modifies the version number associated with a topology, thereby forcing a rebuild of the entire routing tree. Since the version number is included in control messages by parents, there is no established mechanism for ensuring the integrity of the reported version number. A forced rebuild can cause increased overhead, depletion of energy reserves, channel availability issues and even loops in the routing topology. An attacker can also become the parent of its neighbors, thereby snooping on or modifying packets routed via itself. This paper studies the effects that a version number attack can have upon an RPL network.

The paper is organized as follows. An overview of related work is presented in Section 2, followed by an overview of the RPL protocol in Section 3. The version number attack is detailed in Section 4 and the experimental setup used for evaluating the impact of this attack is provided in Section 5. Results of the study are discussed in Section 6 before drawing conclusions in Section 7.

2 Related Work

The IETF RoLL working group performed a security threat analysis for RPL [8]. This study identified potential security issues in RPL networks and proposed countermeasures to address them. The identified threats were partly classified into four categories: (1) authentication, (2) confidentiality, (3) integrity and (4) availability. The version number attack considered here could be categorized as an integrity threat, i.e. an unauthorized modification attack. The IETF security threat study does not, however, provide an assessment of the seriousness of such attacks, which is the goal of this study.

In recent years, several studies on attacks in RPL networks have also been performed. For instance, authors of [9] investigated consequences of black-hole attacks in RPL networks and how they can be detected using specific measurable metrics. Others works such as [10] or [11] explored several attacks against RPL, including sink-hole and worm-hole. However, these are attacks that could be addressed by enabling the secure mode of RPL operation as well.

Version number attacks have also been suggested previously [12,13], but their effects have not been analyzed to understand whether it would be prudent to mitigate such attacks or not. The Version Number and Rank Authentication (VeRA) [13] approach provides integrity of version numbers and ranks advertised in control messages via hash and signature operations. Their approach is not only shown to be faulty by the authors of [14], but another mechanism called TRAIL that uses the root as a trust anchor and monotonically increases node

---

[1] Contiki 2.6 [4], TinyOS 2.1.2 [5], RIOT 2013.08 [6] and SimpleRPL 1.0 [7] for Linux were evaluated during the course of this study.

ranks is also proposed by them. Considering that both approaches require maintaining state information that is likely to diminish already constrained computing resources, it is interesting that the impact of version number attacks on RPL networks was not analyzed before. As such, this study aims to quantify the consequences a version number attack can have on a network.

3   The RPL Protocol

RPL forms loop-free topologies termed Destination Oriented Directed Acyclic Graphs (DODAGs), which organize nodes into a hierarchical structure of a single root, children and further descendants. Objective functions are used by RPL to optimize the topology based on predefined goals, e.g. energy consumption, hop-count or link quality. Multiple instances of RPL, each being an execution of RPL with a specific objective function, can be run within a network, each with its own DODAGs [1]. While a node may be a member of multiple instances, it can only join a single DODAG in an instance at any point in time.

An RPL DODAG is created and maintained by the use of the following control messages: (1) DODAG Information Solicitation (DIS), (2) DODAG Information Object (DIO) and (3) Destination Advertisement Object (DAO). A node wishing to join a network begins by broadcasting DIS messages. These solicit DIO messages, which contain information, like node ID and objective code point, about the DODAG. Since DIO messages are also periodically broadcast, a node may choose to just wait till it receives one from its neighborhood. The rate at which these DIO messages are broadcast is determined by the trickle algorithm [15]. Essentially, the longer a DODAG has been stable, the fewer the number of DIO transmissions.

A node determines its rank in the DODAG by calculating it from the objective code point specified in a received DIO message. If multiple DIO messages from several neighbors are received, then the neighbor that provides the best rank is chosen as the parent. This approach forms upwards routes, i.e. towards the root. The DAO message, which contains all routable prefixes, is sent up the tree to form downwards routes [1]. Each node receiving the DAO message aggregates the prefixes and propagates it further upwards, thereby making downwards routes available to parents.

Loops are avoided by ignoring messages, which arrived from a descendant, traveling downwards. Furthermore, nodes are normally only permitted to change their parents in case of improvements in rank. Any movement in the topology that results in worse ranks is prohibited, unless it occurs during a loop avoidance measure or when the root creates a new version. Even with built-in methods to avoid loops, it is possible for a loop or rank inconsistencies to occur in some situations. There are a few methods provided by RPL to rectify such situations.

The *data path validation* mechanism is used to detect rank related inconsistencies. Special flags, to indicate expected direction of the packet ('*O*' flag) and rank errors detected while forwarding ('*R*' flag), are carried in the RPL IPv6 header options [16] of multi-hop data packets. A rank inconsistency

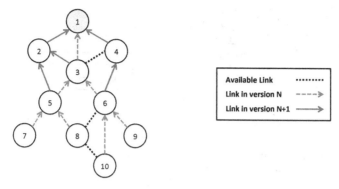

Fig. 1. New DODAG iteration. In red solid arrow, the new DODAG is being built, in blue dashed arrow the old topology is shown. Since the blue graph is an older version of the DODAG, nodes in the new version cannot send packets over blue links. But, packets can be sent from old to new iteration, i.e. from blue to red.

occurs when there is a mismatch in the direction indicated by the 'O' flag [1]. The 'R' flag is set on such a packet and it is forwarded. A loop is detected when a packet with an inappropriate 'O' flag and the 'R' flag enabled is received. This packet is dropped and the trickle timer used for controlling DIO transmissions is reset [15].

Nodes disappearing from a network due to lack of battery power or poor link conditions is more likely to occur in low-power lossy networks than loops in an RPL network [17]. To deal with such situations, RPL provides the global and local repair mechanisms. When the *global repair* mechanism is used, it initiates a rebuild of the entire DODAG by incrementing the version number of the DODAG [1]. The version number is carried in the DIO message; each receiving node compares its existing version number against the one received from its parent and in case the received version is higher, it must ignore its current rank information, reset trickle timers and initiate a new procedure to join the DODAG. Amounting to a reconstruction of a new DODAG, this global repair mechanism guarantees a loop free topology, however, it is also quite costly.

To avoid rebuilding the entire DODAG when a parent node disappears, two *local repair* mechanisms are also provided [1]. The first allows nodes to temporarily route through neighbors of the same rank, while the other approach is to switch parents. These approaches may be used in combination as well to avoid any loss of connectivity.

4   Version Number Attack

The version number is used by the root to control the global repair process of RPL and to ensure that all nodes in the DODAG are up-to-date with the routing state. Every DIO message carries the version number so that in case receiving nodes are part of an outdated DODAG version, they can join the new DODAG by recalculating their rank and then updating their stored version number.

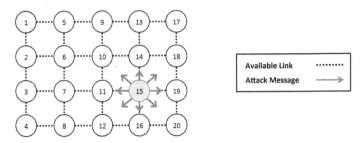

Fig. 2. The grid topology used for performing experimental evaluation of the version number attack. The location of the attacker is varied from nodes 2 to 20.

An older value of the version advertised in DIO messages indicates that the node did not migrate to the new version of the DODAG. Such a node should not be considered a preferred parent by other nodes. While the global rebuild process is ongoing, it is possible for two versions of a DODAG to temporarily coexist. To avoid loops data packets are permitted to transit from the old version to the new one but not the other way, as shown in Figure 1. This is because the old version is no longer a DAG and loop free topologies cannot be guaranteed in this situation.

To avoid possible inconsistencies in the network, the version number should be propagated unchanged through the DODAG. However, there is no mechanism in RPL to check if the integrity of the version number is maintained in received DIO messages. A malicious node may change this field in its own DIO messages to harm the network. Nodes receiving a malicious DIO, with a new version number, will reset their own trickle timer, update the version in their own records and advertise this new version through DIO messages to their neighborhood as well. This can cause the illegitimate version number to propagate through the network.

Such manipulation of the version number in the DIO packets does not only cause an unnecessary rebuild of the whole DODAG but it also generates loops in the topology. This can negatively impact energy reserves of the nodes, routing of data packets and channel availability.

5   Experimental Setup

The Contiki 2.6 operating system [4] was used to perform an evaluation of the version number attack. Contiki is appropriate for this study because not only does it provide an RPL implementation that works on multiple platforms, but also allows the emulation of some common platforms within the Cooja simulator [18].

The default RPL implementation of Contiki does not support the complete data path validation mechanism. While it uses 'O' flags to detect possible rank inconsistencies, it does not set the 'R' flag or drop packets with this flag. Furthermore, the trickle timers are also not reset the way they should be. Since this mechanism is used to repair inconsistencies and loops, both of which are

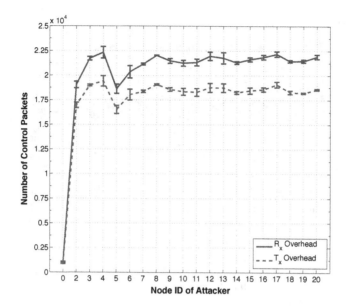

Fig. 3. The incoming and outgoing control packet (DIS, DIO, DAO) overhead for every location of the attacker. (Node ID 0 indicates no attacker; the error bars show the standard deviation between the five simulation runs.)

expected to be created by the version number attack, the Contiki implementation was modified to include it. Another motivation behind this was to study the impact of the version attack on RPL while any mitigation approaches described by the standard are functioning.

The TelosB mote with the ContikiMAC RDC was used as the development platform since its resources, while limited, are enough for the Contiki RPL implementation to function. Rather than building a topology of actual nodes the TelosB binary was used in Cooja, which uses MSPSim to emulate the MSP430 architecture and the performance of a MSP430F1611 microcontroller used by the TelosB. This allows us to test a relatively large topology size under multiple scenarios. The effect of the lossy IEEE 802.15.4 is also minimized allowing us to study the behavior of RPL, rather than its interaction with the channel.

A grid topology of 20 nodes using the UDGM radio model [18], shown in Figure 2, was setup for all experiments in Cooja. Across all experiments, node 1 is the DODAG root and also the sink to which all other nodes send messages every twenty seconds. The attacker is designed to constantly send incorrect version numbers, which are greater than the root's by one. This scenario is adopted because it allows relocation of the attacker to multiple positions easily, making it possible to study the consequences of the attack from different locations and neighborhood scenarios within a network. A random back-off of up to six seconds is also added to this periodic transmission time on all nodes so that packet collisions are avoided when possible. The nodes are placed at a regular distance

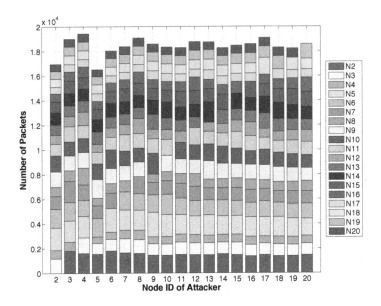

Fig. 4. The per node outgoing packet overhead (DIS, DIO, DAO), for every location of the attacker

of 30m from their vertical and horizontal neighbors. The transmission strength is set such that packets are received successfully by nodes within a 30m radius and the signal causes interference with other nodes for a radius of 60m. This ensures that every node only has vertical and horizontal neighbors reachable during the simulation, thereby adding predictability and ease of analysis to the results.

Each simulation lasts for a lifetime of fifty minutes. One simulation was executed without any attacker in the network so as to obtain a baseline for comparisons against. Further nineteen simulations are also run, with the location of the attacker being fixed to one of nodes 2 to 20, such that at least one simulation with the attacker located at every node between 2 and 20 is executed. Moving the position of the attacker in the network allows us to study the impact that the position of an attacker and the size of neighborhood have upon the behavior of the RPL network. This entire set of twenty simulations is repeated five times to obtain some statistical significance in order to ensure dependability. Attacks start after five minutes of simulation time, so that the network has enough time to settle and a stable RPL topology emerges.

The following metrics are used to perform this study: (1) *Packet overhead*, which is the total number of RPL control packets, i.e. DIS, DIO and DAO message, transmitted (outgoing overhead) and received (incoming overhead) in the network. As such, in the no attacker scenario these are the messages necessary to form and maintain an RPL DODAG. (2) *Delivery ratio*, which is the number of data packets successfully delivered to the sink (node 1) compared to the total number of data packets generated by all nodes in the network. (3) *Average*

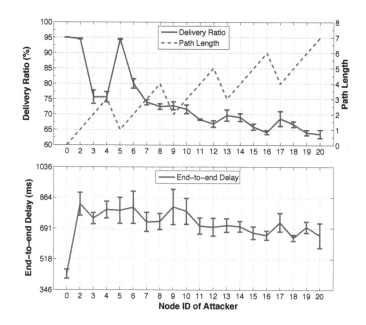

Fig. 5. The total delivery ratio and end-to-end delay for every location of the attacker. Path length, i.e. the hop count, to the attacker from root is also shown. (Node ID 0 indicates no attacker; the error bars show the standard deviation between the five simulation runs.)

end-to-end delay, which is the average amount of time it takes for all packets, from every node in the network, to be successfully delivered to the sink. Lost and dropped packets are not considered in this calculation. (4) *Inconsistencies*, which are the number of packets detected by a node that are destined for a descendant but also arrive from a child or vice versa. (5) *Loops*, which are the number of packets detected by a node that not only indicated an inconsistency but also have the 'R' flag enabled, i.e. a possible loop was previously detected on this path.

6   Results

The average incoming and outgoing packet overhead experienced by the entire network, for each location of the attacker, is shown in Figure 3. The incoming and outgoing overhead when there is no attacker (attacker ID 0 in the figure), both are about 1250 packets, which can be considered reasonable for a network of 20 nodes that functions for 50 minutes. However, as soon as an attacker is introduced, the overhead can increase by up to 18 times in the network. At first glance it appears that the overhead increases as the attacker moves into regions where it has more neighbors. Closer inspection of Figure 3 reveals that mostly nodes in the bottom row of the topology (4, 8, 12, 16 and 20) produce

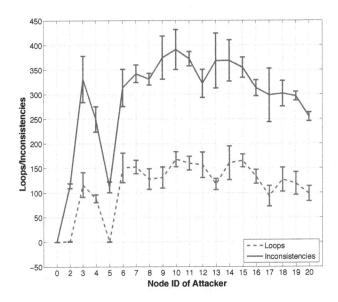

Fig. 6. The total number of loops and inconsistencies in the network, for every location of the attacker. (Node ID 0 indicates no attacker; the error bars show the standard deviation between the five simulation runs.)

localized maximums in their column of the topology. Since each of these nodes end up towards the tail-end of their section of the DODAG, it also implies that the further away a node is from the root, the more damage it can do because this provides it an opportunity to spread the damage further. The location of nodes 2 and 5 produces a topology that is analogous to each other, thereby leading to results that are similar in both their cases. As such, not only the number of neighbors, but also the distance from the root impacts the level of increase in the overhead.

Since the position of the attacker can impact the overhead, it is interesting to also investigate which nodes a particular position of the attacker can effect. Only the per node outgoing packet overhead is plotted in Figure 4, because the incoming and outgoing packet overhead is closely related. While it is intuitive to assume that the largest increase in overhead would be contributed by nodes neighboring the attacker, because these are most likely to form loops, the results from Figure 4 indicate otherwise. The version number attack, by design, is propagated across all neighbors, even if they are not relatives of the current node. This causes a significant increase in control packets to cascade all across the network, leading to the observed results. As such, a version number attack is worse than many others because it does not only impact the attacker's neighborhood but also the entire network.

This increased overhead decreases channel availability, thereby impacting delivery ratio. The delivery ratio, averaged over five runs, for the entire network,

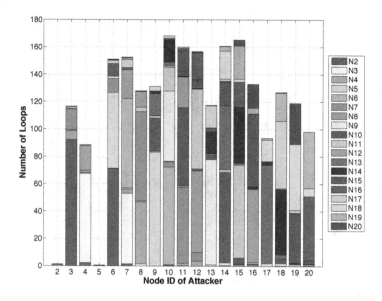

Fig. 7. The total number of loops detected per node, for every location of the attacker

with respect to the location of the attacker, is shown in Figure 5. It is immediately apparent that the version number attack can have a significant impact on delivery ratio, with it being reduced by up to about 30%. More interestingly, a similar pattern can be seen in the effect on delivery ratio, as was on the overhead. As such, the path length of the location of the attacker is also shown in Figure 5. This makes it clear that there is a strong correlation between the distance of the attacker from the root and the effect of the version number attack on delivery ratio. A good example of this is that the delivery ratio when the attacker is located on nodes 2 and 5 is exactly the same, and they both also have a path length of 1 to the root. In fact, the correlation between the delivery ratio and path length can be seen across all positions of the attacker, with the attacker located at the bottom of the topology in Figure 2, i.e. farthest from the root, leading to worst impact on delivery ratio.

The end-to-end delay is also a good measure of a network's performance. The average end-to-end delay for different attacker locations can also be seen in Figure 5. Any packet that was not delivered did not contribute towards calculation of the end-to-end delay. As with other metrics, it is obvious that an attack significantly impacts end-to-end delay, by almost doubling it as against no attack within the network. Unlike overhead and delivery ratio, there is no strong correlation between location of the attacker and the delay. This is because the delay is effected by a number of things, such as the channel availability, number of loops, possible alternate routes, neighborhood density, etc. The large number of factors that can influence this also cause a high variation in the delay results across the set of simulations, as is also evident from Figure 5.

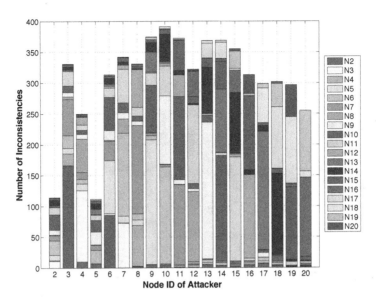

Fig. 8. The total number of inconsistencies detected per node, for every location of the attacker

Since the version number attack creates loops (packets encountered with the 'R' flag) and rank inconsistencies (packets that mismatch actual direction and have 'O' flag set) in the network, it is important to also understand how these are effected. The number of such inconsistencies the network can be seen in Figure 6. The pattern of rank inconsistencies and loops are closely related because loops are a form of rank inconsistency and also counted into it. Unlike before, attacker locations farthest from the root generally lead to the least number of inconsistencies and loops in the network. On the other hand, attacker locations closest to the root, but with most amount of neighbors lead to the highest number of inconsistencies and loops. For example, nodes 3 and 6 create more inconsistencies than nodes 2 and 5, which are closer to the root node. This is because both nodes 2 and 5 have fewer neighbors than nodes 3 and 6. As such, the number of loops are closely related to the number of neighbors an attacker has and increases with proximity to the root. Closer proximity to the root likely has this behavior because it forces a rebuild from the root faster as well, causing this to cascade into the rest of the DODAG before a new attack cycle can begin.

This interesting relationship of inconsistencies and loops with the location of the attacker means that it would be useful to understand where in the network most of this effect is centered. As such the number of loops and inconsistencies per node are plotted in Figures 7 and 8 respectively. It is immediately apparent from these plots that as the location of the attacker shifts towards higher node IDs, the loops and inconsistencies also shift the area of impact towards them. Closer analysis reveals that while there might be some loops created in nodes that are farther away from the attacker, the majority of them are located within the direct neighborhood. In fact, the bulk of these loops and inconsistencies are detected by the parent, and alternate parents, of the attackers. This is because most of the packets will be routed towards the preferred parent, or the alternate parent in case of the preferred parent being unavailable. The next highest quantity of loops and inconsistencies is detected at the children of the attackers. For example, when the attacker is located at node 11, the highest number of loops and inconsistencies are detected by parent nodes 7 and 10. The children, nodes 12 and 15, account for the majority of the rest of these anomalous situations.

7   Conclusions

A study was performed to quantify the effects of version number manipulation attacks within RPL networks. Through simulations it was discovered that control overhead can increase by up to 18 times, thereby impacting energy consumption and channel availability. This in turn can reduce the delivery ratio of packets by up to 30% and nearly double the end-to-end delay in a network. A strong correlation between the position of the attacker and the effect on the network was also observed. An attacker located as far away from the root as possible causes the highest increase in overhead, and similarly a higher path length between the attacker to the root also causes the higher packet loss. It was also discovered that loops and rank inconsistencies created by the attack are generally located around the neighborhood of the attacker, with parents or alternate parents experiencing the maximum loops, followed by the descendants.

Such impact caused by the version number attack makes it important to develop mechanisms that can be used to mitigate it, especially since the integrity of the version field in the DIO message is not verified even in secure operation mode of RPL. However, since RPL is likely to be used in low-power lossy networks comprised mostly of constrained devices, these mitigation strategies should be as simple as possible.

Acknowledgments. This work was partly funded by Flamingo, a Network of Excellence project (ICT-318488) supported by the European Commission under its Seventh Framework Program.

References

1. Winter, T., Thubert, P., Brandt, A., Hui, J., Kelsey, R., Levis, P., Pister, K., Struik, R., Vasseur, J., Alexander, R.: RPL: IPv6 Routing Protocol for Low-Power and Lossy Networks. IETF RFC 6550 (March 2012)
2. Seeber, S., Sehgal, A., Stelte, B., Rodosek, G.D., Schönwälder, J.: Towards A Trust Computing Architecture for RPL in Cyber Physical Systems. In: IFIP/IEEE International Conference on Network and Service Management (CNSM), Zürich, Switzerland (October 2013)

3. Sehgal, A., Perelman, V., Kuryla, S., Schönwälder, J.: Management of Resource Constrained Devices in the Internet of Things. IEEE Communications Magazine 50(12), 144–149 (2012)

4. Dunkels, A., Gronvall, B., Voigt, T.: Contiki - a Lightweight and Flexible Operating System for Tiny Networked Sensors. In: 29th Annual IEEE International Conference on Local Computer Networks (LCN), Tampa, FL (November 2004)

5. Ko, J., Dawson-Haggerty, S., Gnawali, O., Culler, D., Terzis, A.: Evaluating the Performance of RPL and 6LoWPAN in TinyOS. In: Workshop on Extending the Internet to Low Power and Lossy Networks (IP+SN), Chicago, IL (April 2011)

6. Baccelli, E., Hahm, O., Günes, M., Wählisch, M., Schmidt, T.C.: RIOT OS: Towards an OS for the Internet of Things. In: 32nd IEEE INFOCOM Poster Session, Turin, Italy (April 2013)

7. Cheneau, T.: SimpleRPL (February 2014), https://github.com/tcheneau/simpleRPL

8. Tsao, T., Alexander, R., Dohler, M., Daza, V., Lozano, A., Richardson, M.: A Security Threat Analysis for Routing Protocol for Low-power and Lossy Networks (RPL). IETF Internet Draft <draft-ietf-roll-security-threats-06> (December 2013)

9. Chugh, K., Aboubaker, L., Loo, J.: Case Study of a Black Hole Attack on LoWPAN-RPL. In: Proc. of the Sixth International Conference on Emerging Security Information, Systems and Technologies (SECURWARE), Rome, Italy, pp. 157–162 (August 2012)

10. Weekly, K., Pister, K.: Evaluating Sinkhole Defense Techniques in RPL Networks. In: 20th IEEE International Conference on Network Protocols (ICNP), Austin, TX, pp. 1–6 (November 2012)

11. Wallgren, L., Raza, S., Voigt, T.: Routing Attacks and Countermeasures in the RPL-Based Internet of Things. International Journal of Distributed Sensor Networks 13(794326) (2013)

12. Landsmann, M., Perrey, H., Ugus, O., Wählisch, M., Schmidt, T.: Topology Authentication in RPL. In: 32nd IEEE INFOCOM Poster Session, Turin, Italy (April 2013)

13. Dvir, A., Holczer, T., Buttyan, L.: VeRA - Version Number and Rank Authentication in RPL. In: 8th IEEE International Conference on Mobile Adhoc and Sensor Systems (MASS), Hangzhou, China, pp. 709–714 (October 2011)

14. Perrey, H., Landsmann, M., Ugus, O., Wählisch, M., Schmidt, T.: TRAIL: Topology Authentication in RPL. arXiv preprint arXiv:1312.0984 (2013)

15. Levis, P.A., Patel, N., Culler, D., Shenker, S.: Trickle: A Self Regulating Algorithm for Code Propagation and Maintenance in Wireless Sensor Networks. In: 1st Symposium on Networked Systems Design and Implementation (NSDI), San Francisco, CA (March 2004)

16. Hui, J., Vasseur, J.: The Routing Protocol for Low-Power and Lossy Networks (RPL) Option for Carrying RPL Information in Data-Plane Datagrams. IETF RFC 6553 (March 2012)

17. Korte, K.D., Sehgal, A., Schönwälder, J.: A Study of the RPL Repair Process Using ContikiRPL. In: Sadre, R., Novotný, J., Čeleda, P., Waldburger, M., Stiller, B. (eds.) AIMS 2012. LNCS, vol. 7279, pp. 50–61. Springer, Heidelberg (2012)

18. Osterlind, F., Dunkels, A., Eriksson, J., Finne, N., Voigt, T.: Cross-Level Sensor Network Simulation with COOJA. In: 31st IEEE Conference on Local Computer Networks (LCN), Tampa, FL, pp. 641–648 (November 2006)

Toward a Source Detection of Botclouds: A PCA-Based Approach

Hammi Badis[1], Guillaume Doyen[1], and Rida Khatoun[2]

[1] Université de Technologie de Troyes, ERA ICD UMR CNRS 6281
[2] Telecom ParisTech, France
{badis.hammi,guillaume.doyen}@utt.fr, rida.khatoun@telecom-paristech.fr

Abstract. Cloud computing security is often focused on data and users security and protection against external intrusions. However, it exists an area of cloud security that is often overlooked and that can have disastrous consequences: the conversion of cloud computing into an attack vector. Beyond a legitimate usage, the numerous advantages of cloud computing are exploited by attackers. Botnets supporting Distributed Denial of Service (DDoS) attacks are among the greatest beneficiaries of this malicious use. In this paper, we propose a novel source-based detection approach that aims at detecting the abnormal virtual machines behavior. The originality of our approach resides in (1) relying only on the system's metrics of virtual machines and (2) considering a source-based detection. Our approach is based on Principal Component Analysis to detect anomalies that can be signs of botcloud's behavior supporting DDoS flooding attacks. We also present the results of the evaluation of our detection algorithm.

1 Introduction

For the last few years, cloud computing has gained and is still gaining momentum. The reason lies in the numerous benefits it offers to its users, such as a fast deployment of services, a substantial reduction of both infrastructure and operation costs, a fair pay-per-use system, and all of this, while ensuring large scalability.

However, beyond the legitimate usage of these advantages, the latter are also exploited by malicious users, in order to use the cloud as a support for their attacks toward any third party connected to the Internet. Such a phenomenon represents a major issue since it strongly increases the power of distributed massive attacks while involving the responsibility of cloud service providers. The greatest beneficiaries of this cloud conversion into an attack support are botnets, which are called in this case botclouds. Indeed, a botcloud can be setup on demand and at very large scale without requiring a long dissemination phase nor expensive deployment costs. Botnets are primarily used to launch Distributed Denial of Service (DDoS) attacks which are considered among of the most dangerous ones. For instance, an experimental study [1] has shown how the cloud could be at the source of many attacks. To that aim, for five of the most famous

A. Sperotto et al. (Eds.): AIMS 2014, LNCS 8508, pp. 105–117, 2014.

cloud service providers (CSP), the authors rent some virtual machines (VM), deployed and executed different attacks (e.g., DDoS, shellcode, malware traffic, malformed traffic, etc.) during a 21-day period. However, they did not encounter any reaction nor countermeasure from any of the cloud service providers. In the same issue, a group of researchers [2] have investigated how the cloud could be used to build a large botcloud, where they realized large DDoS flooding and click fraud attacks.

In this context, our goal is to develop a source-based detection system to protect the cloud infrastructure from being a support for DDoS attacks. Such a goal is highly challenging since it induces the detection of distributed and weak footprint malicious operations at their source in a highly heterogeneous and dynamic environment. The originality of our work resides in (1) the consideration of system metrics in the detection of flooding denial of service attacks by considering (2) a source-based detection. Indeed, due to the impossibility to master the infected personal computers that arrange botnets, current DDoS and botnets detection solutions are solely based on a network approach and located at the target side [3]. However, the complete control of the attack support by the CSP, enables the consideration of system metrics that can facilitate botclouds detection and the consideration of a source-based detection approach which, to the best of our knowledge, have never been studied to date.

In this paper, we propose a novel method of using Principal Component Analysis (PCA) for Botclouds' supporting DDoS detection. We present the results of the validation of our approach through a simulation tool that relies on real traces that we obtained through *in situ* experimentations.

This paper is organized as follows: Section 2 gives an overview of the related works. Then, Section 3 describes the approach we propose for the detection of botclouds leveraging DDoS flooding attacks. Section 4 discusses the evaluation results. Conclusion and future work are given in Section 5.

2   Related Works

2.1   Host Based IDS

In [4], the authors presented an Unsupervised Behavior Learning (UBL) system for predicting performance anomalies in virtualized cloud systems. UBL is a host-based IDS, implemented at the hypervisor level which uses a set of continuous VM behavior learning modules to capture the patterns of normal operations of VMs relying on system metrics (CPU, MEM, TX, RX). To that aim, it leverages Self Organizing Map (SOM), an unsupervised learning method, to predict anomalies by looking at early deviations from the normal system behaviors. This work is related to ours since, it considers the same metrics as our system. However, the limit of UBL relies in monitoring computer activities on a single host. Thus, it does not enable the building of a global view of intrusions and is not effective in detecting fast-spreading attacks such as DDoS ones. Unlike [4], our approach relies on a signature-based approach implemented at the source hosts which do not need a learning phases such as in UBL.

2.2   Collaborative IDS

DDoS attacks represent large-scale coordinated attacks. Thus, in order to detect them efficiently, we need to combine the evidences of suspicious network or host activity from multiple distributed hosts and networks. To overcome the problem of IDS isolation, Collaborative Intrusion Detection Systems (CIDS) have been proposed to correlate suspicious evidence between different IDSs, thus improving the efficiency of intrusion detection. Several CIDSs have been proposed in the last few years. [5] represents a collaborative system that detects DDoS flooding attacks as far as possible from the victim host. It relies on a distributed architecture composed of multiple Intrusion Protection Systems forming overlay networks of protection rings around subscribed customers. [6] is a proposed gossip-based collaborative system of host based IDSs, which use distributed probabilistic inference to detect network intrusions. The system relies on a fully distributed architecture. [7] proposes a CIDS that uses the Chord DHT (Distributed Hash Table) system to organize IDSs into a P2P network. Each IDS shares its blacklist with others through a fully distributed P2P overlay. If a suspicious IP is reported more than a threshold N, then all the IDSs which reported it will be notified. The system relies only on IP addresses in the identification of potential intruders. Thus, it is not effective against worms having a low spreading degree (less than N). In [8], the authors proposed a hierarchical CIDS based on dependency. Participating hosts are clustered into cooperating regions and a Markov model is used to aggregate the alerts collected from the local hosts within the region. Then, sequential hypothesis testing is applied globally to correlate findings across regions.

2.3   Source-Based IDS

Source-based detection approaches represent a very promising solution to detect large scale attacks and to avoid their side-effect damages. To the best of our knowledge, the sole attempt to design and implement a source-based DDoS detection system is presented in *D-WARD* [9]. In the latter, the authors proposed a DDoS defense mechanism that autonomously detects and stops attacks originating from the networks they monitor, thus avoiding them from being involved in these attacks. Attacks are detected by the constant monitoring of two-way traffic flows between the network and Internet and a periodic comparison with normal flow models. However, the limitation of this solution is the large number of independent network administrative domains that must deploy it in order to be efficient.

2.4   Our Previous Work

In [10] and [11], we presented the results of an intensive measurement campaign we conducted in the aim of featuring and understanding a botcloud in its execution environment. We considered the case of a public CSP, providing an Infrastructure as a Service (IaaS), such as Amazon EC2. We reproduced the case where a malicious user rents several virtual machines to host a bot-cloud intended to support DDoS attacks. The botcloud was implemented over Hybrid_V1.0 botnet[1]. We have realized transport layer DDoS flooding attacks (TCP SYN and UDP flooding). Indeed, the popularity of these attacks is due to their high effectiveness against any kind of service since there is no need to identify and exploit any particular flaws of victims' services. From a timeline perspective, all the experiments we conducted are composed of three phases, each lasting one hour. These are: (1) a first phase of normal state, where the botcloud is deployed, active but does not attack; (2) a second phase of attack toward a third party and finally (3) a third phase where the attack is stopped and the system comes back to normal. We have performed our experimentation over Planet-Lab [12] which relies on the LXC[2] project for virtualization. We used PlanetLab to face the need of an execution environment in which several tenants execute legitimate services while we are able to deploy and control a modified safe version of a botcloud. In order to maintain the privacy of the ten-ant's activity [13], we have limited the measurements to the sole metrics that are commonly available at the hypervisor level, thus operating in a black box way. As a result, the metrics we collect are: CPU (%), memory (MEM (KB/s)), bandwidth sent (TX (Kb/s)) and bandwidth received (RX (Kb/s)). The mon-itoring of tenants (slices) was performed every minute, through the Slicestat[3] service. Over the all measurement campaign, and beyond the results we present here, we have collected about 18 GBytes of log files.

In [10], we have highlighted, over a PCA [14], the correlations between the different collected system metrics of a botcloud. Indeed, in the case of UDP flood attack, CPU and TX metrics are positively and strongly correlated and both are negatively and strongly correlated with RX metric. Concerning the case of TCP SYN flood attack, there is a strong and positive correlation between the TX and RX metrics and both are strongly and negatively correlated with the CPU metric. In the second part of the work, we have detected and separated the attack phase from the idle one, for the two study-cases, namely, botclouds supporting UDP flood and TCP SYN flood attacks. We have also confirmed the hypothesis of the strong similarity of bots' behaviors.

In [11], we have shown, using PCA, that from a system perspective, whatever the attack rate, the contribution of metrics in modeling the botcloud's behavior is almost constant. In addition, the factorial space defined by the eigenvectors' matrix and which defines the botcloud's activity is also, almost constant. These results have led us to define the generic factorial space that represents the ac-tivity of a botcloud supporting a DDoS flooding attack. In this paper, we use this factorial space for the detection of botcloud's activity against legitimate workload.

---

[1] http://security-sh3ll.blogspot.com/2010/01/hybrid-botnet-system-v10-released.html

[2] https://linuxcontainers.org

[3] http://codeen.cs.princeton.edu/slicestat/

3   A Source Approach Based on a PCA

In this section, we describe the approach we propose for a source-based detection of botclouds leveraging DDoS flooding attacks. First, we give an overview on PCA, the statistical method we used in our detection process. Then, we detail the steps of our detection approach. Table 1 describes the different notations used in the next sections.

Table 1. Notations table

X^k	The kth $[n \times p]$ Data matrix	x_{ij}^k	The jth variable of the kth $[n \times p]$ Data matrix at time i
e_{it}^k	The ith eigenvector of tenant k calculated at time t	w	Size of time monitoring window
M_t^k	$[p \times p]$ Eigenvectors matrix of tenant k calculated at time t	W_t^k	$[w \times p]$ Data matrix of last activity belonging to tenant k at t time
λ_{it}^k	The ith eigenvalue of tenant k calculated at time t	W_{ij}^k	The jth variable of W^k at time i
p	Number of variables of a matrix	S_t^k	normalized matrix of W_t^k
n	Number of rows of a matrix	S_{ij}^k	The jth variable of S^k at time i
t	Time index	C_t^k	Covariance matrix of tenant k calculated at time t
m	Number of chosen Principal Components	vm_{ij}^{vk}	The jth variable of vth virtual machine belonging to tenant k at time i
k	Tenant's number	V^k	Number of VMs belonging to a tenant k
d_t^k	Decision made for tenant k at time t	v	VM's number
D_t^k	Dissimilarity value of M_t^k and R	R	Reference factorial space for a DDoS attack
H	Threshold	σ	Standard deviation

3.1   Principal Component Analysis

PCA [14] is a descriptive statistical method belonging to the factorial category. It is aimed at easing the exploration and analysis of high-dimensional vectors of input data by reducing their dimensions and enabling the extraction of features. Given a data matrix X^k of n observations, also called individuals, composed of p variables, the PCA explains the variance-covariance structure of the set of variables through a few new variables, called principal components or factors, which are functions of the original variables. Principal components represent linear combinations of the p variables with important properties: the computed principal components, which are in general 2 or 3, respectively have the highest variances so that they best represent the data in a reduced dimension space and highlight their linear relations. Also, components are uncorrelated and the total variance of all the principal components equals the total variance of the original variables. More precisely, the principal components are computed by firstly, solving the eigenvalue problem of the variance-covariance matrix described by Equation 1

$$Ce_i = \lambda_i e_i \qquad (1)$$

where C represents the variance-covariance matrix, λ_i $(i = 1, 2, \ldots, p)$ are the corresponding eigenvalues and e_i represents their corresponding eigenvectors. Secondly, computing the first m eigenvectors $(e_1, e_2, \ldots, e_m)$ which correspond to the m largest eigenvalues $(\lambda_1, \lambda_2, \ldots, \lambda_m)$ where $(m < p)$.

Many works such as [15] and [16], rely on PCA in network intrusion detection. The authors in [15], have showed how PCA can be used for real-time anomaly detection. The authors in [16] have confirmed that a detection mechanism based on PCA can be suitable for large amounts of real time data.

As we need to detect attacks in a highly heterogeneous and dynamic workload, using PCA fits perfectly our study context, since it does not require any distribution model assumption on the data while many statistical based intrusion detection methods assume a normal or at least known distribution model.

3.2   Problem Modeling and Detection Algorithm

The first step of the detection process, consists in data monitoring and collection, which is done for all VMs, belonging to all tenants. Especially, the metrics we consider are CPU (%), memory (MEM (KB/s)), bandwidth sent (TX (Kb/s)) and bandwidth received (RX (Kb/s)). Most data sets contain one or a few unusual observations [15]. When an observation is different from the majority of the data or don't assume the same statistical distribution model, it is considered as an outlier. The authors in [17], demonstrated that PCA is very sensitive to outlier data. Since we are interested in the global behavior of a tenant and not a particular VM, as a first filter for outlier data, we use an arithmetic average. That way, the detection algorithm uses, for each tenant, a data matrix X^k that represents the arithmetic average of the global activity of tenant k as input. An entry x_{ij}^k represents the average calculated on all the ith rows corresponding to the jth variable (column) of all the VMs $vm_{ij}^{vk}(v = 1, 2, \ldots, V_k)$, belonging to tenant k, as explained by Equation 2. Using the arithmetic average has no influence on our study. In fact, we have demonstrated in [10] that the behavior of a simple bot (VM) is very close to that of the global botcloud, due to the strong correlation of the different bots.

$$x_{ij}^k = \frac{1}{V^k} \sum_{v=1}^{V^k} vm_{ij}^{vk} \qquad (2)$$

Our detection algorithm always relies on the previous activity of the tenant, and detects any new changes in its behavior. We represent this previous activity by a sliding window of time which we name W_t^k.

$$W_t^k = \begin{bmatrix} x_{(t-w)\,1}^k & \cdots & x_{(t-w)\,p}^k \\ \vdots & \ddots & \vdots \\ x_{t\,1}^k & \cdots & x_{t\,p}^k \end{bmatrix}$$

The second step, consists in normalizing the data of W_t^k by calculating it's standard score S_t^k as explained by Equation 3. The reason of using normalized data resides in the difference of scales in which metrics and data are collected. Furthermore, using normalized data allows a better control on the detection threshold.

$$S_{ij}^k = \frac{W_{ij}^k - \overline{W}_{.j}^k}{\sigma(W_{.j}^k)} \tag{3}$$

Contrarily to the basic PCA presented in Section 3.1, our approach, relies on the computation of the whole eigenvectors $(e_{1t}^k, e_{2t}^k, \ldots, e_{pt}^k)$ related to all the eigenvalues $(\lambda_{1t}^k, \lambda_{2t}^k, \ldots, \lambda_{pt}^k)$ of Equation 1, which constitutes the third step in the detection process. That way, our approach considers all the data set without any information loss. The covariance matrix used in the eigenvectors computation are obtained through Equation 4.

$$C_t^k = \frac{1}{n}(S_t^k)^T \times S_t^k \tag{4}$$

The set of the p eigenvectors constitutes a factorial space, represented by M_t^k the $p \times p$ eigenvector matrix, $M_t^k = [e_{1t}^k, \ldots, e_{pt}^k]$. This factorial space entity represents the heart of our approach. Indeed, in [11], we showed that the factorial space composed by the eigenvectors, defines tenants' activities in general and the botcloud's activity in particular. We also showed that, whatever the attack rate, the factorial space of a botcloud is almost constant. In addition, it appears always as an outlier of legitimate activities. All that has led us to define a generic factorial space that represents a botcloud realizing a DDoS flooding attack. The latter serves as a reference R for our detection algorithm. In other words, unlike most of approaches that use PCA for outlier detection, our approach compares the workload with a defined outlier pattern, which is the factorial space R. Any similarity with this pattern is considered as a potential attack.

Consequently, the fourth step, is the comparison of the calculated M_t^k with R. To that aim, we use the notion of dissimilarity between matrices. The dissimilarity measure between the two matrices which we name D_t^k, is calculated by the Frobenius norm $||M_t^k - R||_F$ [18] as depicted in Equation 5

$$D_t^k = ||M_t^k - R||_F = \sqrt{\sum_{i=1}^{p}\sum_{j=1}^{p} |(M_t^k - R)_{ij}|^2} \tag{5}$$

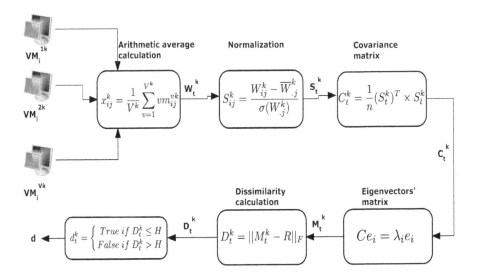

Fig. 1. Detection algorithm steps

Finally, we fix a threshold that we name H to decide whether or not the dissimilarity D_t^k value stands for a DDoS attack. The decision rule d_t^k is given by

$$d_t^k = \begin{cases} True \; if \; D_t^k \leq H \\ False \; if \; D_t^k > H \end{cases} \quad (6)$$

The Figure 1 summarizes the described detection steps in detail.

4   Evaluation and Discussion

4.1   Evaluation Framework

In this section we present the results we obtained for the evaluation of our detection algorithm. We note that our algorithm treats simultaneously all monitored tenants.

For the evaluation, we have used the real traces (logs) we obtained every minute in [10] by injecting them into a simulator built on the R tool[4]. Table 2 summarizes the different elements we monitored and that characterize these experimentations. We have realized five experimentations. For each experiment, we have a botcloud realizing an UDP flood attack at different rates, from 8 MB/s up to 80 MB/s per source, reaching aggregated attack rates of 328 MB/s to 3.125 GB/s. For each experiment, we present the results we obtained through facing the botcloud's activity to 25 other legitimate tenants picked randomly, which represents a large workload of hundreds of VMs.

---

[4] http://www.r-project.org

In order to evaluate our detection algorithm, we have varied the decision threshold H from 1.29 to 1.42. 1.29 constitutes the lower bound of H because it represents the highest dissimilarity value between the reference factorial space R and the botcloud while realizing the different attacks. Regarding the upper bound, we have varied H by steps of 0.03 till having 5% of error rate, which corresponds to the 1.42 value. For the current study, we initialized our algorithm with $w = 7$. Thus, the detector relies on a sliding window W of 7 minutes. The choice of w represents the subject of a study that is left for future work.

Table 2. Summary of the scenarios' numerical parameters

UDP flood attack rate	#Physical servers	#Tenants (incl. attack.)	#VMs (incl. attackers)	#Attacking VMs
8 MB/s	41	123	1,288	41
16 MB/s	41	118	1,261	41
40 MB/s	43	123	1,310	43
56 MB/s	41	114	1,241	41
80 MB/s	40	103	1,198	40

4.2 Evaluation Results

We have computed the confusion matrix of all the simulations we conducted. A confusion matrix contains information about actual and predicted classifications done by a classification system. From the latter, we have calculated different statistical indicators such as Receiver Operating Characteristic (ROC) curves, Accuracy, Error rate, Matthews Correlation Coefficient, Positive and Negative Predictive Values.

Accuracy and Error Rate. The accuracy[5] of a measurement system is the degree of closeness of measurements of a quantity to that quantity's true value. It has a value between 0 and 1. Figure 2.a describes the accuracy values obtained over the five experimentations. We note that the highest ACC we obtained corresponds to $H = 1.32$, which are 0.9955, 0.9944, 0.9957, 0.9955 and 0.9939. These Accuracy values reflect the efficiency of our algorithm. In similar way, the error rate measurement which represents the opposite of the accuracy and defined by the remoteness of measurements of a quantity to that quantity's true value. So, lower is the error rate, more reliable is the detection. Figure 2.b describes the error rates obtained over the five experimentations. We note that the lowest ERR rates we obtained are 0.0045, 0.0056, 0.0043, 0.0045 and 0.006, which corresponds to $H = 1.32$.

---

[5] http://www.bipm.org/en/publications/guides/

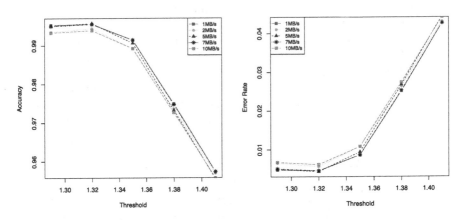

Fig. 2. Accuracy and Error rate graphs ; (a) Accuracy (b) Error rate

Positive and Negative Predictive Values. The positive and negative predictive values (PPV and NPV respectively) are the proportions of positive and negative results in statistics and detection tests that are true positive and true negative results. The PPV and NPV describe the performance of the detection. Closer are PPV and NPV values from 1, better is the detection. Figure 3 describes the obtained values of PPV and NPV over the five experimentations. For both measures the highest values we obtained over the experimentation belongs to $H = 1.32$. The PPV obtained values are: 0.9474, 0.9500, 0.9545, 0.9535 and 0,9444. Concerning the NPV measure we always got values over than 0.99. These values are very close from 1, which again reflects the efficiency and good prediction of our algorithm.

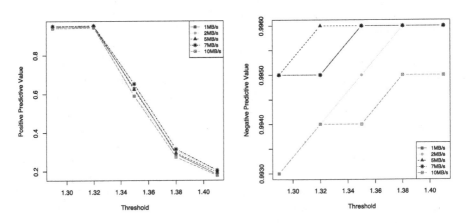

Fig. 3. Predictive values graphs; (a) Positive Predictive Values; (b) Negative Predictive Values

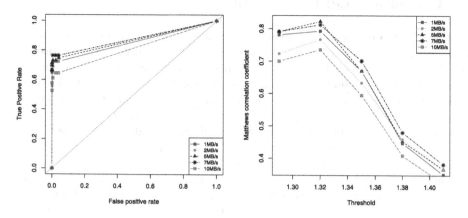

Fig. 4. ROC and Matthews correlation coefficient; (a) ROC curves; (b) Matthews correlation coefficient

ROC Curves and Matthews Correlation Coefficient. Figure 4.a represents the different ROC curves we obtained. In the five cases, the drawn curve is always widely on top of the bisector, which prove the efficiency of our algorithm.

The Matthews correlation coefficient (MCC) [19] is used as a measure of the quality of binary (two-class) classifications. It represents a correlation coefficient between the observed and predicted binary classifications; it returns a value between -1 and +1. A coefficient of +1 represents a perfect prediction, 0 no better than random prediction and -1 indicates total disagreement between prediction and observation. Figure 4.b describes MCC values we obtained over the experimentation. The highest MCC values we obtained belongs also to $H = 1.32$, which are 0.7927, 0.7669, 0.8224, 0.8120 and 0.7352. These results reflect the good prediction of our algorithm.

The consistency of the results over the threshold variation confirms the efficiency of our algorithm. We also note that the best threshold we got is 1.32. Over this threshold, we have got a very good performance: an Accuracy rate always over 99%, an Error rate always less than 0.6%, a PPV value rate always over than 94% and a NPV value always higher than 99%. These results are obtained through the comparison with a generic factorial space obtained through a botcloud realizing attacks at defined rates (between 8MB/s and 80MB/s per source). The best detection results are obtained through the experimentation at 40MB/s (median value of attack rates). Indeed, we got better performances through 40MB/s experiment because the respective botcloud's factorial space is the closest from R.

The obtention of such very good results is due to the use of the arithmetic average in a centralized approach. However, due to the complexity of the detection algorithm, a distributed approach is mandatory. Consequently, we plan to study such an implementation to see whether the detection performances undergo degradations.

5   Conclusion and Future Work

In this paper, we have addressed the problem of the conversion of the cloud computing into an attack vector. To remediate the problem, we have presented a novel approach based on PCA and system metrics, which enables a source-based detection of DDoS flooding attacks in a cloud computing environment. We have validated our approach by a simulation approach that relies on a real traces that we obtained through *in situ* experimentations. We have proved the efficiency and resiliency of our detection algorithm over the different statistics that took into account dozens of tenants that involve hundreds of virtual machines activities which represents a large workload amount.

These results only represent a step of our work. A short-term future work will focus on proposing a fully distributed approach of our detection algorithm, able to deal with scalability issues. Mid-term future work consists in extending this study in order to characterize other attacks such as application level attacks and even to detect infected legitimate VMs exhibiting an almost an almost normal behavior. Finally, our long-term research direction will look at the development of an autonomous self-protection system for CSPs against DDoS attacks leveraged by a cloud infrastructure.

Acknowledgment. This work is supported by the (Contrôle Autonome et Sécurité dans le Cloud Computing (CASCC)) research project, which is founded by the Champagne-Ardenne region.

References

1. Pedram, H., Jia, J., Daria, R.: Botcloud an emerging platform for cyber-attacks (October 2012), http://baesystemsdetica.blogspot.fr
2. Clark, K.P., Warnier, M., Brazier, F.M.T.: Botclouds - the future of cloud-based botnets? In: Leymann, F., Ivanov, I., van Sinderen, M.J., Shishkov, B.B. (eds.) Proceedings of the 1st International Conference on Cloud Computing and Services Science (CLOSER 2011), pp. 597–603. Science and Technology Publications (2011)
3. Peng, T., Leckie, C., Ramamohanarao, K.: Survey of network-based defense mechanisms countering the DOS and DDOS problems. ACM Computing Surveys (CSUR) 39(1) (2007)
4. Dean, D.J., Nguyen, H., Gu, X.: Ubl: unsupervised behavior learning for predicting performance anomalies in virtualized cloud systems. In: Proceedings of the 9th International Conference on Autonomic Computing, ICAC 2012, pp. 191–200. ACM (2012)
5. François, J., Aib, I., Boutaba, R.: Firecol: a collaborative protection network for the detection of flooding DDoS attacks. IEEE/ACM Trans. Netw. 20(6), 1828–1841 (2012)
6. Dash, D., Kveton, B., Agosta, J.M., Schooler, E., Chandrashekar, J., Bachrach, A., Newman, A.: When gossip is good: Distributed probabilistic inference for detection of slow network intrusions. In: Proceedings of the 21st National Conference on Artificial Intelligence, AAAI 2006, vol. 2, pp. 1115–1122. AAAI Press (2006)

7. Zhou, C.V., Karunasekera, S., Leckie, C.: A peer-to-peer collaborative intrusion detection system. In: 2005 13th IEEE International Conference on Networks, Jointly Held with the 2005 IEEE 7th Malaysia International Conference on Communication, vol. 1, p. 6 (2005)

8. Li, J., Lim, D.-Y., Sollins, K.: Dependency-based distributed intrusion detection. In: Proceedings of the DETER Community Workshop on Cyber Security Experimentation and Test 2007, DETER, p. 8. USENIX Association (2007)

9. Mirkovic, J., Reiher, P.: D-ward: a source-end defense against flooding denial-of-service attacks. IEEE Transactions on Dependable and Secure Computing 2(3), 216–232 (2005)

10. Badis, H., Doyen, G., Khatoun, R.: Understanding botclouds from a system perspective: a principal component analysis. In: Network Operations and Management Symposium (NOMS 2014). IFIP/IEEE (May 2014) (accepted paper)

11. Badis, H., Khatoun, R., Doyen, G.: A factorial space for a system-based detection of botcloud activity. In: Sixth IFIP International Conference on New Technologies, Mobility and Security (NTMS 2014). IFIP/IEEE (March 2014) (accepted paper)

12. Chun, B., Culler, D., Roscoe, T., Bavier, A., Peterson, L., Wawrzoniak, M., Bowman, M.: Planetlab: an overlay testbed for broad-coverage services. SIGCOMM Comput. Commun. Rev. 33(3), 3–12 (2003)

13. Ruiter, J., Warnier, M.: Privacy regulations for cloud computing: Compliance and implementation in theory and practice. In: Gutwirth, S., Poullet, Y., De Hert, P., Leenes, R. (eds.) Computers, Privacy and Data Protection: an Element of Choice, pp. 361–376. Springer, Netherlands (2011)

14. Wold, S., Esbensen, K., Geladi, P.: Principal component analysis. Chemometrics and Intelligent Laboratory Systems 2, 37–52 (1987), Proceedings of the Multivariate Statistical Workshop for Geologists and Geochemists

15. Shyu, M.-L, Chen, S.-C, Sarinnapakorn, K., Chang, L.W.: A novel anomaly detection scheme based on principal component classifier. Technical report, DTIC Document (2003)

16. Brauckhoff, D., Salamatian, K., May, M.: Applying pca for traffic anomaly detection: Problems and solutions. In: IEEE INFOCOM 2009, pp. 2866–2870 (April 2009)

17. Lee, Y.-J., Yeh, Y.-R., Wang, Y.-C.F.: Anomaly detection via online oversampling principal component analysis. IEEE Transactions on Knowledge and Data Engineering 25(7), 1460–1470 (2013)

18. Meyer, C.D.: Matrix analysis and applied linear algebra, vol. 2. SIAM (2000)

19. Baldi, P., Brunak, S., Chauvin, Y., Andersen, C.A.F., Nielsen, H.: Assessing the accuracy of prediction algorithms for classification: an overview. Bioinformatics 16(5), 412–424 (2000)

Software Defined Networking to Improve Mobility Management Performance

Morteza Karimzadeh, Anna Sperotto, and Aiko Pras

Design and Analysis of Communication Systems (DACS), University of Twente,
The Netherlands
{m.karimzadeh,a.sperotto,a.pras}@utwente.nl

Abstract. In mobile networks, efficient IP mobility management is a crucial issue for the mobile users changing their mobility anchor points during handover. In this regard several mobility management methods have been proposed. However, those are insufficient for the future mobile Internet in terms of scalability and resource utilization as they mostly follow the centralized management approach owning several inherent restrictions. In this research a novel mobility management approach relying on the OpenFlow-based SDN architecture is proposed. Such an approach manages mobility in a scalable fashion while optimally utilizing the available resources. This approach is also appropriate for the cloud-based Long Term Evolution *(LTE)* system, in order to (i) keeping sessions active during handover, and (ii) providing traffic redirection when a virtual machine (*e.g.,* a mobility anchor point), migrates from one virtualization platform to another, while keeping the on-going sessions running, as well. This research is currently in its initial phase and is planned to eventuate as a Ph.D. thesis at the end of a four year period.

1 Introduction

Recently, Telecommunication networks (*e.g,* 3G and 4G cellular networks) and Mobile networks (*e.g,* WiMAX and WiFi) have increasingly become the major access method to the Internet and data services. Accordingly, many networks currently experience a rapid growth in the number of mobile subscribers and wireless data traffic. Over the last few years, wireless operators' networks have rapidly turned into full IP-based networks for both voice and data, thus stimulating an underlying IP mobility support. Mobility management refers to a set of mechanisms to keep ongoing-sessions continuity while a mobile user changes his/her physical channel, access network or communication protocol. Real-time IP multimedia applications such as Video Conferencing, Voice over IP (*VoIP*), Game net, download/upload of large size files (*particularly in cloud computing environment*) are examples of such notably demanded applications in mobile network environments, in which supporting IP mobility and seamless session continuity is a necessity for the users changing their mobility anchor points during inter-operator and intra-operator/technology handovers.

A. Sperotto et al. (Eds.): AIMS 2014, LNCS 8508, pp. 118–122, 2014.

Various mobility management mechanisms may employ different layers of the OSI protocol stack to handle their functionalities [1]. In the physical layer, mobility management carries out the detach and attach operations to different access points during handover. In the network layer, mobility support means to deal with the change in the sub-network. Mobility support in this layer may be based on routing (used *e.g.*, in Cellular IP [2]) or mapping (used *e.g.*, in Mobile IP (*MIP*) [3] and Proxy Mobile IP (*PMIP*) [4]). In the transport layer, mobility management focuses on keeping the on-going TCP connection, though IP address is changing (used *e.g.*, in Mobile Stream Control Transmission Protocol (*M-SCTP*) [5]). In the application layer, a particular design is considered to tackle mobility issues for each application type (used *e.g.*, in the Session Initiation Protocol (*SIP*) [6]), or a middle ware may be implemented between applications of two nodes to manage mobility, such as WiSwitch [7]. The network layer based scheme is the most popular one offering transparent mobility support to all kinds of applications. MIP [3], PMIP [4], and 3GPP mobility management [8], are examples of such scheme.

Most of these solutions rely on a centralized mobility management entity which is in charge of both control and data planes [9],[4],[8]. Centralized mobility management inclines to several restrictions such as centralized management of one/several hierarchical tunnels for each Mobile Node *(MN)*, data processing overhead to perform encapsulations/de-capsulation functions during tunneling updates, network bottleneck, single point of failure and non optimal routing (*particularly when MN and correspondent node are close to each other but are both far from the mobility anchor point*) [10],[11],[12]. Centrally managed IP mobility in the current mobile Internet is not scalable enough to efficiently deal with demands raised by ever-growing number of mobile users of new generation of applications seeking for IP mobility.

Over the last few years, researches aiming to tackle limitations in centralized mobility management have been emerged. Double NAT (*D-NAT*) [13], Distributed Mobility Anchoring (*DMA*) [14], Inter-domain DMM, Local IP Access (*LIPA*)/Selected IP Traffic Offload (*SIPTO*) [15] are examples of such approaches. In this regard as discussed in [16] Software Defined Networking (*SDN*)/OpenFlow approach outperforms existing solutions.

SDN [17] has emerged as a new paradigm offering a logically centralized control model which detaches control and data planes, thus enabling direct programming of the control plane and abstracting the underlying infrastructure for applications and services. SDN makes networks programmable, manageable and adaptable to a wider extent, that is ideally suited for highly scalable mobile wireless networks.

OpenFlow [18], as the most common communication protocol used in SDN approach, can significantly facilitate traffic management by accessing the control plane and the data plane of switches and routers over the network (*e.g.*, Internet architecture). Capabilities offered by OpenFlow would be as an enabler to improve IP mobility management, such that each traffic path could be traced from an Internet Ingress node (*e.g.*, Internet PoPs) to an Egress node (*e.g.*, router at the edge of access network) as a separate flow, and traffic could be redirected to a new mobility anchor point without any IP address translation or modification. Consequently, it eliminates the need for IP and GPRS Tunneling Protocol (GTP) tunneling respectively in wireless and cellular networks demanded for mobility management and diminishes data processing and traffic overhead in a large scale as a result of optimum encapsulations/de-capsulation, handover and location signaling. Hereby it brings in more scalability with the increasing number of MNs.

Given that the OpenFlow-enabled switches and routers comprise a set of actions that give the possibility to modify the transiting packet headers belonging to a specific flow, as well as the ability of dynamic configuration of flow tables in switches and routers via OpenFlow Controller (OC), we believe the OpenFlow-based SDN architecture could be as a promising approach notably enhancing mobility management in terms of scalability and network resource utilization in the future mobile Internet.

The rest of the paper is organized as follows: in Section 2, we introduce our objective, detail the research questions, and describe the proposed approaches. Following Section 2, Section 3 outlines the sketched procedures to evaluate and validate the proposal. Finally in Section 4, we wrap up the paper.

2   The Objective, Research Questions and Approaches

The objective of this research is to answer the question *"Could OpenFlow-based SDN architecture be used to improve mobility management and support session continuity accordingly?"*. In particular, our research addresses the following research questions:

1. *Is the current mobility management approach well-suited for the future mobile Internet?*
2. *How OpenFlow-based SDN architecture could be used to support session continuity?*
3. *Which OpenFlow-based SDN approach is better-fitted to support mobility management?*

The first question discovers the main constraints of utilizing the centralized mobility management approach in the future mobile Internet, and investigates the superseded mobility management scheme (*i.e.*, distributed mobility management) and compares it with the centralized one. Comprehensive literature review is the first step of the plan. Further, quantitative measurements and analysis of some relevant performance metrics (*e.g.*, resource utilization and delay), using NS3-LENA [19] simulation environment will be carried out, complementing the comparison. As network and traffic data utilized in the simulation environment always have deviations from real ones, real-world measurements are thought of as further evaluation, if possible.

By question 2, we figure out how capabilities of OpenFlow-based SDN architecture [17],[18] could be utilized to enable and further enhance mobility management. OpenFlow-enabled switches are augmented with a set of actions that could be applied to flow-specific packets providing further capabilities [18]. *Set-Field*, as the most relevant one for our purpose, provides the possibility to OpenFlow switches to modify packets' and frames' headers. A combination of *Set-Field* and *Output* (*identifying the output interface*) actions, could be used to provide dynamic per-flow forwarding and redirection. Flow tables and action lists in OpenFlow-enabled switches are added and modified by the OC utilizing dedicated secure connections.

Further, in order to find out which mobility management network structure could be better-fitted to the next generation mobile networks, we will benefit from [20],[21], which extend current IP mobility solutions for flat architectures and describe the requirements for distributed management based on IPv6 networks. In the distributed framework, the data plane *(partially distributed)* or both the data plane and control plane *(fully distributed)* are distributed among the mobility anchors located at different network segments *(usually at the edge of the access network)*, and MNs are served by a closer anchor entity accordingly.

Answering question 3, we investigate which of the full or partial OpenFlow approaches is better-suited to be integrated to the operator's transport network to fulfill session continuity requirements and support mobility management functionality. In the first approach, all routers in the transport network are OpenFlow-enabled and no modification of the packets is needed for traffic redirection. Whereas, in the partial approach, only the routers placed at the edges of the transport network are OpenFlow-enabled and traffic redirection on the transport network is based on layer 3 routing instead of flow forwarding. In this approach packets' headers must be modified at the edge of the transport network (at the Ingress and Egress switches).

3   Evaluation and Validation

In line with question 3, the proposed solutions, will be evaluated based on different sets of experiments implemented within the NS3-LENA simulation environment and various predefined metrics (*e.g,* scalability, signaling overhead, etc.) will be measured and analyzed. Further, within the context of the Mobile Cloud Networking (*MCN*) project [22], we intend to implement a prototype of the proposed OpenFlow-based SDN architecture in OpenStack [23] virtualization test bed as a supplementary validation.

4   Final Considerations

The main objective of this research, will be achieved within a period of four year, as part of a Ph.D thesis. This research has been funded by the EU FP7 MCN project (#318109) and EU FP7 Flamingo Network of Excellence (ICT-318488).

References

1. Akyildiz, I.F., Xie, J., Mohanty, S.: A Survey of Mobility Management in Next-Generation All-IP-Based Wireless Systems. IEEE Wireless Communications, 16–28 (2004)

2. Valko, A.G.: Cellular IP: A New Approach to Internet Host Mobility. ACM SIG-COMM Computer Communication Review (1999)
3. Johnson, D., Perkins, C., Arkko, J.: Mobility Support for IPv6. IETF RFC 3775 (2004)
4. Gundavelli, S., Chowdhury, K., Devarapalli, V., Patil, B., Leung, K., et al.: Proxy Mobile IPv6. IETF RFC 5213 (June 2008)
5. Riegel, M., Tuexen, M.: Mobile SCTP. IETF draftriegeltuexen-mobile-sctp-09.txt) (2007 expired)
6. Rosemberg, J., Schulzrinne, H., Camarillo, G., Johnston, A., Sparks, R., Handley, A., Schooler, E.: SIP: Session Initiation Protocol. IETF RFC 3261 (2002)
7. Giordano, S., Lenzarini, D., Puiatti, A., Vanini, S.: WiSwitch: Seamless Handover between Multi-provider Networks. In: Proceedings of Second Annual Conference on Wireless On-demand Network Systems and Services (WONS 2005), pp. 224–235 (2005)
8. 3GPP Technical Specification 29.060, General Packet Radio Service (GPRS); GPRS Tunnelling Protocol (GTP) across the Gn and Gp interface (Release 8), http://www.3gpp.org
9. Johnson, D., Perkins, C., Arkko, J., et al.: Mobility support in IPv6. IETF RFC 3775 (June 2004)
10. Bertin, P., Bonjour, S., Bonnin, J.-M.: Distributed or centralized mobility? In: IEEE Global Telecommunications Conference, GLOBECOM 2009, p. 16. IEEE (2009)
11. Chan, H.A., Yokota, H., Xie, J., Seite, P., Liu, D.: Distributed and Dynamic Mobility Management in Mobile Internet: Current Approaches and Issues. Journal of Communications 6(1), 415 (2011)
12. Bokor, L., Faigl, Z., Imre, S.: Flat architectures: Towards scalable future internet mobility. In: Domingue, J., et al. (eds.) Future Internet Assembly. LNCS, vol. 6656, pp. 35–50. Springer, Heidelberg (2011)
13. Liebsch, M.: Per-Host Locators for Distributed Mobility Management. IETF Internet draft (work in progress) (2013)
14. Seite, P., Bertin, P., Lee, J.H.: Distributed Mobility Anchoring. IETF Internet draft (work in progress) (2013)
15. 3GPP Technical Specification 23.829, Local IP Access and Selected IP Traffic Offload (LIPA-SIPTO) (Release 10), http://www.3gpp.org/DynaReport/23829.htm
16. Karimzadeh, M., Valtulina, L., Karagiannis, G.: Applying SDN/OpenFlow in Virtualized LTE to Support Distributed Mobility Management(DMM). In: 4th International Conference on Cloud Computing and Services Science (2014)
17. ONF official website, https://www.opennetworking.org/ (visited in December 2013)
18. The OpenFlow Switch Specification. Version 1.3.0, http://archive.openflow.org (visited in December 2013)
19. The LTE/EPC Network Simulator, http://networks.cttc.es/mobile-networks/software-tools/lena/ (visited in November 2013)
20. Liu, D., Yokota, H., Seite, P., Korhonen, J., Chan, H.A. (ed.): Requirements for Distributed Mobility Management. IETF Internet draft, work in progress (2013)
21. Liebsch, M., Karagiannis, G., Seite, P.: Distributed Mobility Management-Framework and Analysis. IETF Internet draft (work in progress) (2013)
22. EU FP7 Mobile Cloud Networking project, http://www.mobile-cloud-networking.eu/site/ (visited in September 2013)
23. The OpenStack Cloud Software, https://www.openstack.org/ (visited in December 2013)

Future of DDoS Attacks Mitigation in Software Defined Networks

Martin Vizváry and Jan Vykopal

Institute of Computer Science, Masaryk University, Brno, Czech Republic
{vizvary,vykopal}@ics.muni.cz

Abstract. Traditional networking is being progressively replaced by Software Defined Networking (SDN). It is a new promising approach to designing, building and managing networks. In comparison with traditional routed networks, SDN enables programmable and dynamic networks. Although it promises more flexible network management, one should be aware of current and upcoming security threats accompanied with its deployment. Our goal is to analyze SDN accompanied with OpenFlow protocol from the perspective of Distributed Denial of Service attacks (DDoS). In this paper, we outline our research questions related to an analysis of current and new possibilities of realization, detection and mitigation of DDoS attacks in this environment.

Keywords: Software Defined Networking, SDN, Distributed Denial of Service Attack, DDoS, OpenFlow, security, detection, mitigation.

1 Introduction

Even though computing has advanced over the past decades, the networking principles have remained mostly unchanged. Traditional networks are built using switches and routers. Every vendor uses a proprietary operating system and configuration in these network devices. Emerging clouds and Internet of Things demand scalable and dynamic networks. However, building a suitable network with centralized management in such a heterogeneous environment is very expensive. One new architecture that replaces traditional networking is Software Defined Networking (SDN). SDN abstracts network control from the underlying infrastructure of the network. This abstraction enables applications and network services to treat the network as one logical entity. This could increase the potential for the better mitigation of security threats.

A DDoS attack is an attempt to make a network or server resource unavailable to its intended users. The attack is relatively easy to perform, hard to defend against, and the attacker is rarely traced back. The target of a DDoS attack could be any online business, government or critical infrastructure. Increasing numbers of DDoS attacks in current networks also increases the awareness of them and makes them a major threat to today's networks. The deployment of SDN will not stop attackers, however, it could make mitigation techniques more effective and their deployment more flexible.

A. Sperotto et al. (Eds.): AIMS 2014, LNCS 8508, pp. 123–127, 2014.

Our research will be dedicated to an analysis of security challenges in SDN from the point of view of DDoS attacks. Although SDN promises more flexible network management, one should be aware of current and upcoming security threats accompanied with the deployment of SDN. The abstraction of data and control plane devices introduces new potential threats.

The remainder of this paper is organized into four sections. Section 2 briefly describes the state of the art in SDN. Section 3 states our hypothesis and research questions. Section 4 outlines the scientific approach. Section 5 summarizes this paper.

2   Software Defined Networking

SDN is an emerging network architecture. It is supported by many large companies listed on Open Networking Foundation[1] list [3], e. g., Google [4] or Cisco Systems [2]. SDN is based on the abstraction of a data plane from a control plane. This abstraction makes networks more programmable and flexible. Figure 1 describes the basic SDN architecture.

The control plane consists of one or more SDN controllers. The controller maintains a global view of the network. It defines the forwarding rules of the devices in the data plane and performs all complex functions. All devices in the data plane are remotely configured by the controller via well-known and vendor-neutral API. It allows the controller to manage different types of devices from different vendors. The data plane contains simple forwarding devices, e. g., switches. From the point of view of the controller, devices in the data plane could act as a single logical entity. These devices forward all traffic according to rules in flow tables. If there is not a matching forward rule for a packet, the packet is forwarded to the controller. The communication between the controller and data plane devices needs a suitable standard. Such standard seems to be the widely supported OpenFlow protocol [6]. It provides an open and standard way for a controller to direct communication with a network device in the data plane.

Many SDN and OpenFlow security challenges have been proposed in the literature [8]. We will focus on DDoS attacks since they have become a major threat in modern-day networks. Due to the centralization of controller and flow table limitations in data plane devices, there is an increased potential for new DDoS attacks in SDN networks as well.

3   Hypothesis and Research Questions

Our hypothesis is that *SDN provides an ideal platform for distributed detection and mitigation of DDoS attacks.* SDN emerges as a promising network paradigm. The new concept of networking guarantees programmable and dynamic networks. They could react faster and with better efficiency to necessary changes in

---

[1] The organization dedicated to the promotion of SDN through open standards development.

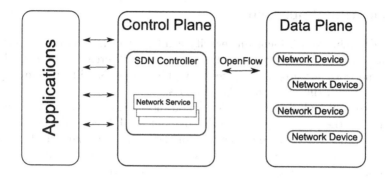

Fig. 1. Software Defined Networking architecture schema

networking. This could help to mitigate the DDoS attack. However, the attacks could also take advantage of the overhead of the SDN controller. We split our research into the following three research questions:

1. *What differences does SDN bring compared to traditional networks and its monitoring?*

   This research question aims to gain an understanding of SDN that separates the networking into the data and control plane. We will analyze and compare the differences between SDN and current networks. The research will also cover the analysis of monitoring possibilities in SDN.

2. *What are SDN specific security vulnerabilities both on the data and control planes? In particular, what known or new vulnerabilities of SDN can be abused by attackers in DDoS attacks?*

   The goal of this question is to analyze possible abusive attributes of the data and control plane. At first, we will focus on open-source solutions, e. g., Open vSwitch [1]. We will analyze possibilities of DDoS attacks abusing data and control plane devices as a bottleneck, reflector or amplifier. Abstraction of the control plane from the data plane might cause serious overhead when there are too many requests from the data plane. Also the misconfiguration or direct abuse of the central controller or one of the data plane devices could cause denial of network access for users.

3. *How to optimally mitigate DDoS attacks in Software Defined Networks?*

   The main goal of this question is to find a method to optimally mitigate spoofed and non-spoofed DDoS attacks in a SDN environment. We will analyze different DDoS attack methods and propose the optimal way for mitigating attacks. We will also pay attention to the trace-back of the source of an attack using the advantages of the SDN architecture.

4   Scientific Approach

In our research, we will focus on security challenges in DDoS attacks detection and mitigation in SDN environment. At first, we will create a state of the art in SDN network monitoring and security. This analysis will provide required understanding of the SDN and related issues.

Next, we will analyze attack, defense and monitoring mechanisms in current networks and the possibility of their deployment in SDN environment. Monitoring is nowadays mostly done at the host or network level in attacked networks. There are many variants of DDoS attacks as well as defense mechanisms against them proposed for current networks [10]. We believe that those methods could be adopted in SDN. Flow-based techniques are mostly used for the detection of DDoS attacks. Due to the flow-based nature of SDN, it is possible to make detections in both planes. However, detection mechanisms deployed in the controller without proper aggregation of network traffic could overload the communication among control and data plane. Also, the flow table in a network device has limitations. Shin et al. [9] proposed that some of these issues could be resolved by adding some minimal intelligence to the data plane devices.

The main goal of our research is to mitigate the attack using SDN architecture. For the sake of simplicity, we consider two groups of DDoS attacks. The first group targets the computing power. The second group exceeds available bandwidth. The first group could be mitigated using a SDN infrastructure of the attacked organization. We could use all network devices as one logical switch to load balance the network traffic through the network. This load balancing of attack traffic gives us the possibility to configure as many filtering rules as possible to maximize the amount of dropped malicious traffic. However, for the second group, this option is not effective. We have to stop the attack closer to the source of traffic, e. g., country of origin, or ISP of the attack source. Even though this mitigation technique requires a cooperation of involved providers in the route of the attack and complex reconfiguration of ISP routing tables, the flexible SDN environment could make this reconfiguration easier. The first SDN application that programs networks for DoS security against network flood attacks is Radware DefenseFlow [7]. However, it is not a "pure" SDN solution and it still has to cooperate with dedicated mitigation hardware.

At last, to prove our hypotheses, we will prepare a pure SDN infrastructure. We will use an environment prepared in Cybernetic Proving Ground (CPG) project [5]. In this environment, we will create set of synthetic and real traffic based data sets and experimentally verify the hypothesis.

5   Summary

Research questions 1 and 2 aim to obtain a thorough understanding of SDN in the context of DDoS attacks. It is crucial to understand SDN for answering the third research question. Our goal in research question 3 is to find the optimal way to mitigate DDoS attack using the SDN infrastructure. The main goal should be achieved within a period of three years as a part of a PhD thesis.

Acknowledgments. This material is based upon work supported by Cybernetic Proving Ground project (VG20132015103) funded by the Ministry of the Interior of the Czech Republic.

References

1. Open vSwitch – An Open Virtual Switch. Project website, http://openvswitch.org/ (accessed January 27, 2014)
2. Cisco. Software-Defined Networking: Why We Like It and How We Are Building On It. White paper, Cisco Systems, San Jose, CA, USA (2013)
3. Open Networking Foundation. Member Listing – Open Networking Foundation. Website, https://www.opennetworking.org/membership/member-listing (accessed January 21, 2014)
4. Jain, S., Kumar, A., Mandal, S., Ong, J., Poutievski, L., Singh, A., Venkata, S., Wanderer, J., Zhou, J., Zhu, M., Zolla, J., Hölzle, U., Stuart, S., Vahdat, A.: B4: Experience with a Globally-Deployed Software Defined Wan. In: Proceedings of the ACM SIGCOMM 2013 Conference on SIGCOMM, SIGCOMM 2013, pp. 3–14. ACM, New York (2013)
5. Kouřil, D., Rebok, T., Jirsík, T., Čegan, J., Drašar, M., Vizváry, M., Vykopal, J.: Cloud-based Testbed for Simulation of Cyber Attacks. In: Proceedings of the 2014 IEEE Network Operations and Management Symposium, NOMS 2014 (to appear, 2014)
6. Open Networking Foundation. Software-Defined Networking: The New Norm for Networks. White paper, Open Networking Foundation, Palo Alto, CA, USA (2012)
7. Radware. DefenseFlow – Software Defined Networking Application. Product website, http://www.radware.com/Products/DefenseFlow/ (accessed January 21, 2014)
8. Scott-Hayward, S., O'Callaghan, G., Sezer, S.: SDN Security: A Survey. In: Proceedings of the Software Defined Nnetworks for Future Networks and Services (SDN4FNS 2013), pp. 1–7 (2013)
9. Shin, S., Yegneswaran, V., Porras, P., Gu, G.: AVANT-GUARD: Scalable and Vigilant Switch Flow Management in Software-defined Networks. In: Proceedings of the 2013 ACM SIGSAC Conference on Computer Communications Security, CCS 2013, pp. 413–424. ACM, New York (2013)
10. Zargar, S.T., Joshi, J., Tipper, D.: A Survey of Defense Mechanisms Against Distributed Denial of Service (DDoS) Flooding Attacks. IEEE Communications Surveys Tutorials 15(4), 2046–2069 (2013)

Towards Decentralized, Energy- and Privacy-Aware Device-to-Device Content Delivery

Leonhard Nobach and David Hausheer[*]

Peer-to-Peer Systems Engineering Lab, TU Darmstadt, Germany
{lnobach,hausheer}@ps.tu-darmstadt.de

Abstract. Device-to-Device (D2D) content delivery is a new approach to directly exchange content between mobile devices, which allows to offload traffic from infrastructure-based networks and thus reduces the risk of congestion. While centralized D2D approaches rely on the mobile operator to discover nearby devices and initiate a content transfer, in decentralized D2D the devices autonomously and opportunistically organize themselves to deliver content to each other. The latter approach is more flexible as it does not depend on a single operator, however, it typically requires more energy for scanning other devices. Another issue is privacy, since the decentralized approach reveals a user's interest for content to all devices in proximity. Therefore, this paper sketches an new approach towards decentralized energy- and privacy-aware D2D content delivery. The proposed approach addresses the energy loss that occurs when constantly and spontaneously scanning multiple unknown devices for content. Furthermore, the paper identifies privacy requirements and proposes first steps towards a privacy-aware D2D solution.

Keywords: Device-to-Device, Content Delivery, Privacy, Energy, Decentralization, Delay-Tolerance, Opportunistic Networking.

1 Introduction

As people are sharing more higher-resolution multimedia content, traffic demand in the Internet is constantly increasing. Today, content is transferred mostly from a content provider's server to a consumer's device. Different types of content delivery can be distinguished: *Live* content is immediately consumed after creation, including a short transmission delay. *On-Demand* delivery refers to content that is commonly consumed an arbitrary but significant amount of time after creation, whenever a particular consumer requests it. For example, most of the web content is delivered this way. *Video-on-Demand (VoD)* services deliver movies and video clips on request, which are typically very bandwidth-intensive. Although less bandwidth-consuming, music, applications and software updates are also content types appropriate for on-demand delivery.

---

[*] This work has been supported in parts by the European Union (FP7/#317846, SmartenIT and FP7/#318398, eCousin) and the German DFG (CRC 1053, MAKI).

A. Sperotto et al. (Eds.): AIMS 2014, LNCS 8508, pp. 128–132, 2014.

Delivering copies of content to a large number of receivers is challenging in terms of network load. Many carriers use IP Multicast to deliver live content to their own customers. However, in the current public Internet, multicast is not widely implemented between carriers. For on-demand content delivery, multicasting is not applicable, as content has to be delivered to every consumer by the time of request. Content Delivery Networks (CDNs) place replica servers in proximity of the access network, which offloads the content provider's uplink and inter-carrier transits. However, the consumer's access network itself is typically not affected by the traffic reduction.

Device-to-Device (D2D) content delivery transmits content from a consumer's mobile device directly to another one in range. This way, infrastructure utilization is reduced especially for the transfer of popular content in crowded areas. Also, the quality of experience (QoE) can be increased in case of bandwidth-limited infrastructures. D2D content delivery only is effective if a certain device density and content popularity is given. If there are few devices in range or the content is unpopular, chances are high that there is no device in range serving the content. D2D content delivery mechanisms can be distinguished by the type of content *discovery* mechanism used.

Centralized D2D content discovery [1] [2] [6] relies on the cellular operator locating content in range and triggering the transfer between devices. For that, an operator requires data like the position as well as information about available and requested content. In contrast, a *decentralized* [10] mechanism lets the devices organize the discovery and transfer of relevant content themselves. Such an operator-independent service, when standardized, is available to and communicates with every device, not only the devices under contract with the operator. Furthermore, it can even work in the absence of a mobile infrastructure.

However, current link-layer protocols widely implemented in consumer electronics (e.g., IEEE 802.11 [7]) are focused on low-delay and reliable communication between devices previously known to each other. Using the default 802.11 MAC layer, discovering content on any device currently in range involves an exchange of multiple management frames and unnecessarily frequent medium listening (ATIM window), leading to an increased energy consumption. Additionally, requesting content by broadcasting leads to an unintended disclosure of user interest to all devices in communication range. Attackers may also flood requests for privacy-sensitive content and track devices answering it. Previous approaches did not investigate how these issues can be mitigated, except that they switched to a centralized, operator-dependent solution [1] [2] [6].

Based on this finding, the goal of this work is to propose a new operator-independent approach towards D2D content delivery between mobile devices, while addressing energy-efficiency and privacy, starting at the link layer. The remainder of this paper is structured as follows. In Section 2, a modification of the 802.11 data link layer for energy-efficient, opportunistic content discovery is sketched. Also, the aforementioned privacy concerns are addressed and first countermeasures are proposed. Moreover, Section 3 discusses related work, while Section 4 concludes this paper.

2   Energy- and Privacy-Aware Content Discovery

The proposed discovery mechanism follows a single hop D2D approach. While content delivery can also be done over multiple hops, for the purpose of stability, medium availability, energy conservation, and the lack of incentives for intermediate nodes, this approach is not considered here. The discovery mechanism involves two roles, a content requester (CR) and a content provider (CP), where a device can take both roles at the same time. The CR maintains a predicted table of content identifiers likely to be consumed in the future, while the CP maintains a cache of provided content. Prediction and caching strategies are not part of this paper.

As the devices are previously unknown to each other, they communicate by broadcasting link-layer frames in their proximity, either content requests (active) or content advertisements (passive). The frames contain a list of content identifiers. To be able to receive each other's frames, devices must agree on certain physical parameters like the 802.11 channel and rate, which may be done at roll-out time. In order not to drain the battery, the opportunistic broadcast mechanism works without any previous device scanning, participating in distributed beaconing, or handshake. Instead, a broadcast is only answered by CPs providing (active) or CRs requesting (passive) the particular content, other devices remain silent upon reception. This certainly involves changes in IEEE 802.11's MAC Sublayer Management Entity (MLME) [7]. The changes must not interfere with standard 802.11 operation.

Conserving energy also incorporates the decision when to power on and off the transmitters, referred to as *sleep scheduling*. Increased wake-up intervals and smaller wake-up periods may conserve energy, but also increase the delay as messages have to stay longer in the buffer to wait for the next wake-up. Fortunately, such a wait-to-send delay in the area of seconds is not a concern for decentralized content discovery. Instead, finding a good way to synchronize these wake-up periods between devices that are spontaneously in contact to each other is a major challenge. An approach suitable to this problem would lead to synchronized listen-sleep periods as depicted in Figure 1.

To increase privacy of the discovery mechanism, two approaches are proposed. First, a clear-text identifier is replaced with a hash-salt combination, where the salt changes in every request. This way, only devices in possession of the content identifier understand the request. Secondly, the usage of anonymous addresses in wireless media hardens the tracking of devices. Therefore, MAC addresses used for opportunistic requests can be randomly chosen and frequently changed.

3   Related Work

Golrezaei et al. [6] investigate an approach for distributed caching. Although they first propose to establish femtocells controlled by small base-station-like nodes called *helpers*, they later consider a pure D2D communication system where the mobile devices play the helper role themselves. In the latter, the D2D exchange

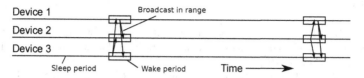

Fig. 1. Expected result of sleep scheduling for broadcast messaging. Devices power on at the same time, broadcast content requests in this time window and power off again.

is completely controlled by the operator, which knows the device's position, as well as the content that is currently cached by every device.

Bao et al. [1] [2] propose a centralized mechanism, where the network operator tracks the location of mobile devices. The operator then identifies areas with a high device density (data spots). Whenever a certain density is given, content requests are mediated by the operator, which initiates a WiFi connection between the requester and a device in proximity having the desired content.

An approach for decentralized content discovery was proposed by Ma and Jamalipour [10]. Evaluated costs are focused on bandwidth consumption and disk space. Nevertheless, optimizing energy consumption was not addressed, although this has been done for Bluetooth [12] [5].

Boldrini et al. [3] exploit a user's social relationship to decide where to place content. Cost evaluations concern limited bandwidth and cache. Distributed sleep synchronization for energy conservation in MANETs has been addressed by Jiang et al. [8], as well as Choi et al. [4], but these approaches are not focused on broadcast discovery between devices previously unknown to each other.

In the area of privacy, much research has been done and is underway in the area of opportunistic networks (ONs) [9], but regarding *content delivery* in ONs, very few exist. Privacy was addressed by Shikfa et al. [11], given prior key distribution and using intermediate nodes.

4   Summary and Future Work

In this paper, a new approach towards decentralized D2D content delivery has been proposed. The operator-independent approach shows clear advantages as it even works in the absence of an infrastructure. Moreover, the paper sketched a solution how energy and privacy issues can be mitigated.

To identify the situations in which D2D content delivery is effective, likely urban environments with a high device density and providers of popular content, request and position traces of a large cellular operator will be evaluated. In addition, user incentives for *providing* content via D2D communication have to be provided. Mechanisms to measure D2D contribution and possible rewards have to be designed. Furthermore, the approach sketched in Section 2 will be further developed to a complete protocol. The last steps towards a solution include an energy- and mobility-aware simulation and a prototype implementation. In parallel, social-content interdependencies and their exploitation will be investigated.

References

1. Bao, X., Lee, U., Rimac, I., Choudhury, R.R.: DataSpotting: Offloading Cellular Traffic via Managed Device-to-Device Data Transfer at Data Spots. SIGMOBILE 14(3), 37–39 (2010)
2. Bao, X., Lin, Y., Lee, U., Rimac, I., Choudhury, R.R.: DataSpotting: Exploiting Naturally Clustered Mobile Devices to Offload Cellular Traffic. In: IEEE INFOCOM, pp. 420–424 (2013)
3. Boldrini, C., Conti, M., Passarella, A.: ContentPlace: Social-Aware Data Dissemination in Opportunistic Networks. In: MSWiM, pp. 203–210 (2008)
4. Choi, B.J., Shen, X.: Adaptive Asynchronous Sleep Scheduling Protocols for Delay Tolerant Networks. IEEE Transactions on Mobile Computing 10(9), 1283–1296 (2011)
5. Drula, C., Amza, C., Rousseau, F., Duda, A.: Adaptive Energy Conserving Algorithms for Neighbor Discovery in Opportunistic Bluetooth Networks. IEEE Journal on Selected Areas in Communications 25(1), 96–107 (2007)
6. Golrezaei, N., Dimakis, A., Molisch, A., Caire, G.: Wireless Video Content Delivery through Distributed Caching and Peer-to-Peer Gossiping. In: ASILOMAR, pp. 1177–1180 (2011)
7. IEEE Computer Society: IEEE Standard for Information Technology – Telecommunications and Information Exchange between Systems – Local and Metropolitan Area Networks – Specific Requirements – Part 11: Wireless LAN Medium Access Control (MAC) and Physical Layer (PHY) Specifications. IEEE Std 802.11-2012 (2012)
8. Jiang, J.R., Tseng, Y.C., Hsu, C.S., Lai, T.H.: Quorum-based Asynchronous Power-Saving Protocols for IEEE 802.11 Ad Hoc Networks. Mobile Networks and Applications 10(1-2), 169–181 (2005)
9. Lilien, L., Kamal, Z.H., Bhuse, V., Gupta, A.: Opportunistic Networks: The Concept and Research Challenges in Privacy and Security. In: WSPWN, pp. 134–147 (2006)
10. Ma, Y., Jamalipour, A.: A Cooperative Cache-based Content Delivery Framework for Intermittently Connected Mobile Ad Hoc Networks. IEEE Transactions on Wireless Communications 9(1), 366–373 (2010)
11. Shikfa, A., Onen, M., Molva, R.: Privacy in Content-based Opportunistic Networks. In: WAINA, pp. 832–837 (2009)
12. Wang, W., Motani, M., Srinivasan, V.: Opportunistic Energy-efficient Contact Probing in Delay-Tolerant Applications. IEEE/ACM Transactions on Networking 17(5), 1592–1605 (2009)

Goal-Oriented Monitoring Adaptation: Methodology and Patterns

Antoine Toueir, Julien Broisin, and Michelle Sibilla

IRIT, University Toulouse III - Paul Sabatier
118 rue de Narbone, 31062 Toulouse, France
{toueir,broisin,sibilla}@irit.fr

Abstract. This paper argues that autonomic systems need to make their distributed monitoring adaptive in order to improve their "comprehensive" resulting quality; that means both the Quality of Service (QoS), and the Quality of Information (QoI). Thus, we propose a methodology to design monitoring adaptation based on high level objectives (*goals*) related to the management of quality requirements. One of the advantages of adopting a methodological approach, is that monitoring reconfiguration will be conducted through a consistent adaptation logic. Starting from a model-guided monitoring framework, we introduce our methodology to assist human administrators in eliciting the appropriate quality goals piloting the monitoring. Moreover, some monitoring adaptation patterns falling into reconfiguration *dimensions* are suggested and exploited in a cloud provider case-study illustrating the adaptation of Quality-Oriented monitoring.

Keywords: Quality requirements, adaptive monitoring, autonomic systems, goal-oriented adaptation.

1 Introduction

Autonomic systems that are implemented by virtue of their four characteristics self-configuration, self-optimization, self-healing and self-protection, are serving the main principle of making them self-managed to achieve high level objectives [1]. In practice, the four self-* characteristics are realized by implementing the MAPE-K (*Monitoring, Analyzing, Planning, Executing - Knowledge*) loop modules. This implementation is either embedded within a resource, or distributed over several resources. However, the monitoring module of MAPE-K loop plays a crucial role, since wrong decisions might be taken by the analyzing & planning modules, if they were provided with interrupted or wrong information. Therefore, autonomic systems need to ensure the quality of information (*e.g.*, correctness, freshness, timeliness, accuracy, etc.) exposed by the distributed monitoring modules.

Within autonomic systems, monitoring is usually quality-oriented. In other words, the underlying monitoring instruments metrics and evaluates them against quality specifications expressed via *Service Level Agreements* (SLAs) or management high level objectives. Since the management system could provide the

A. Sperotto et al. (Eds.): AIMS 2014, LNCS 8508, pp. 133–146, 2014.

possibility to renegotiate or modify the QoS specification afterward, and also, various management needs could be distinguished during the management system lifetime, the monitoring system has to adapt its behavior according to these new requirements. To resume, the monitoring of autonomic systems has to be capable of configuring the underlying gathering mechanisms (*i.e.*, polling & notification) carrying the monitoring functions (*e.g.*, measuring, gathering, evaluating, filtering, etc.) starting from quality specification, as well as reconfiguring those mechanisms based on quality requirements.

Most of the time, reconfiguration is held through ad-hoc logic. But this approach isn't suitable for reuse in other scenarios, and also doesn't satisfy high level objectives; which are extended at the autonomic system whole scale. To overcome these issues, first, we adopted the *Requirements Engineering* methodology to design monitoring adaptation; it starts from high level goals, and ends up with the (re)configuration of monitoring mechanisms. However, reconfiguration questions such as: why to delay launching some monitoring mechanisms? Why to substitute remote agents? What determine the instrumentation of particular set of metrics but not another one? need to be answered. In other words, identifying goals representing the "starting point" for deriving monitoring (re)configuration is a big challenge. Thus, besides adaptation methodology, this paper answers these questions by proposing monitoring adaptation patterns to assist human administrators in designing meaningful adaptations, that increase the overall quality of autonomic systems.

The paper is organized as follows: Section 2 points out the weaknesses of other monitoring adaptation approaches; Section 3 gives an overview of the monitoring framework at the basis of our contributions; the methodology of designing goal-oriented adaptive monitoring is presented in Section 4; the reconfiguration dimensions as well as monitoring adaptation patterns are discussed in Section 5 and then applied on a case-study in Section 6; finally, we conclude by listing our perspectives in Section 7.

2   Related Work

This section enumerates some existing trends focusing on (i) adapting the QoS monitoring in autonomic systems [2,3,4,5,6], and (ii) designing patterns regarding the distributed deployment as well as the adaptation of MAPE loop modules [7,8,9].

Collecting additional metrics or joining managed resources is addressed in [2,3,5] either to adapt monitoring to meet SLA modifications, or to deal with the managed scope changes, or even to operate a "minimal" monitoring that is able to be extended in case of SLA violations. Indeed, the capability of scaling up/down the monitored metrics and resources is important as an adaptation action. But, it isn't clear whether this capability could be applied in other scenarios for distinct objectives, if so, how that could be feasible.

Runtime deployment of monitoring resources (*i.e.*, managers, probes) is discussed in [3,4,6] either to integrate monitoring into the SLA management lifecycle of large scale systems, or to replace failed managers, or even to monitor metrics concerning particular paths or segments. But here also, besides the undeniable gains of deploying monitoring resources during runtime, we don't see how the system administrators can orchestrate the monitoring adaptation of the distributed modules among several collaborating managers. The orchestration isn't a trivial task, because a given quality objective may need to be extended on several managers and treated differently on each of them. Thus, a "simple deployment" of new monitoring resources isn't enough to realize orchestration.

Inspired from the autonomic computing reference architecture proposed in [7], patterns regarding the distribution of the MAPE loop modules were proposed in [8,9]. Those patterns are useful in term of design reuse as well as clarifying the application contexts and benefits, but they target mainly the deployment of the monitoring modules rather than the monitoring behavior itself. That is, once the autonomic system is designed and deployed based on the proposed patterns, the monitoring conserves its behavior. Consequently, the management system knowledge won't exceed a "maximum ceiling" and the management will be limited regarding treating new situations; as it has specific vision reflecting the same aspects all the time.

To resume, most of the studied work focuses either on the auto-configuration of monitoring, or on the reconfiguration of the functional system based on the knowledge produced from the QoS monitoring, or even the reconfiguration of the monitoring itself based on static purposes. Contrary to the studied work, we argue that increasing the QoS of the whole system begins from designing adaptive monitoring, that is derived from and satisfies high level quality requirements, and interpreted by several managers.

3   The Enriched Adaptive Monitoring Framework

Our approach is based on a 3-layered framework [10,11,12] illustrated in Figure 1, and defines three capabilities required to control monitoring: being configurable, adaptable and governable. This framework operates monitoring mechanisms without any consideration regarding agents or management protocols.

The **configurability layer** stands on the Distributed Management Task Force (DMTF) Common Information Model (CIM) standard. This low level layer aims at representing, in addition to the managed resources, the metrics [13] and their gathering mechanisms as well [10]. Moreover, those models have been enriched with the concept of *Monitoring Mode*. The latter encapsulates: metrics (*Aspects of Interest* to be instrumented), constraints (thresholds to be checked once associated metrics are instrumented), indications (notifications to be raised once metrics are violated), as well as two types of subscriptions to deliver both metrics values and raised indications to the appropriate destinations (see Figure 1). The **adaptability layer** provides an interface encapsulating operations to be applied on the lower layer models. Those operations constitute a "control interface" to update the attributes of both monitoring modes and metrics, thus the underlying gathering mechanisms will be reconfigured, and consequently the monitoring adapts its behavior. Finally, the **governability layer** is the top level layer representing the "intelligence" of the monitoring adaptation. To express the quality requirements, it uses Event/Condition/Action (ECA) policies to describe *when* and *how* adaptation should take place, that is, they determine the situations during which the adaptability layer operations should be invoked.

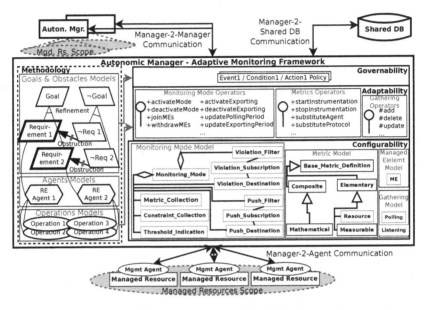

Fig. 1. Adaptation Methodology & Enriched Monitoring Framework

4   A Goal-Oriented Methodology for Adaptive Quality-Oriented Monitoring

Thinking that one of the existing software engineering approaches should answer our needs, we looked forward a suitable method for designing monitoring adaptation. The origin of Requirements Engineering (RE) goes back to the need to avoid crucial mistakes committed at the project design phase, and aims at building systems solving real-world problems. This methodology applies iterative activities about *"eliciting, evaluating, documenting, consolidating and changing the objectives, functionalities, assumptions qualities and constraints that the system-to-be should meet based on the opportunities and capabilities provided by new technologies"* [14]. Among multiple RE approaches, **K**eep **A**ll **O**bjectives **S**atisfied (KAOS) is adopted as RE goal-oriented method, due to its formal assertion layer that proves correctness and completeness of goals [15].

In KAOS the system-to-be is divided into various models. The **goal models** elicit goals representing high level behavioral prescriptions of the system-to-be (the monitoring system in this study). Each goal may serve one or more objectives, and a given goal is realized through the cooperation of several components or actors, the so-called *Agents*[1]. Goals are decomposed into sub-goals via a refinement process (see Section 6), where the most refined goals are called *Requirements*, or *Leaf Goals*; in KAOS, each of those leaf goals is assigned to a specific agent in order to be realized. Others goals, depicted within the **obstacle models**, are deduced from the goal models and prevent the satisfaction of the latter. In our study, since goals converge on the quality of monitoring, their obstacles will be related to the monitoring failures. The **operation models** are composed of the sets of internal operations carried by agents in order to realize the *Leaf Goals*. Finally, the **object models** identify the system-to-be objects.

By iterating refinement process on goals and obstacles, leaf goals will be identified. Once leaf goals are determined, both of ECA policies (to be inserted into the governability layer) and agents (invoking operations of the adaptability layer) will be reconnoitered. Thus, monitoring adaptation is automatically handled, and high level goals remain satisfied. However, human administrators have to refine manually the high level objectives they want to reach, in order to identify the leaf goals. To facilitate this task, we investigated the monitoring aspects that are subject to adaptation. As a result, we have identified various leaf goals belonging to four *dimensions* (*i.e.,* Spatial, Metric, Temporal, Exchange) [16]. In Section 5, we pursuit in proposing monitoring adaptation patterns falling into those dimensions, in order to assist human administrators in refining goals.

5   Dimensions and Patterns

With regard to refinement process, besides the basic AND/OR-decompositions, we rely on some predetermined correct and complete refinement patterns proved mathematically [17]. Those patterns refine *Achieve* goals of the form $P \Rightarrow \Diamond Q$ (see Table 1), and written in *Linear Temporal Logic* (LTL) classical operators where $\Diamond$, $\Box$ and $\mathcal{W}$ mean respectively *some time in the future, always in the future*, and *always in the future unless*. Starting from a given goal (P), *milestone pattern* identifies one or many intermediate goals ($R, [...]$) that must be reached orderly before reaching the ultimate one (Q). Rather, *case pattern* identifies the set of different and complete cases ($P1, P2$) for reaching final goals ($Q1, Q2$) that OR-decompose the ultimate goal (Q). Finally, the *guard pattern* requires the recognition of a condition (R) before achieving the ultimate goal (Q).

In order to clarify the exploitation contexts, pattern goals and requirements, as well as the various situations in which they may apply to, our pattern structure encompasses: context, pattern refinement, and examples. Notice that we are focusing on adaptation actions taken at the autonomic manager side only. Thus, investigating adaptations at the agent side is out of scope. In addition, the patterns are refined using KAOS graphical language [14].

---

[1] Notice that *Agents* in networks and systems management are entities responding to management requests coming from other management entities called *Managers*; therefore the term "*Agent*" in RE has a different meaning.

Table 1. Patterns Refining *Achieve* Goals $(P \Rightarrow \Diamond Q)$ [17]

Pattern	Subgoal 1	Subgoal 2	Subgoal 3
Milestone Pattern	$P \Rightarrow \Diamond R$	$R \Rightarrow \Diamond Q$	
Case Pattern	$P \wedge P1 \Rightarrow \Diamond Q1$	$P \wedge P2 \Rightarrow \Diamond Q2$	$\Box(P1 \vee P2)$ $Q1 \vee Q2 \Rightarrow Q$
Guard Pattern	$P \wedge \neg R \Rightarrow \Diamond R$	$P \wedge R \Rightarrow \Diamond Q$	$P \Rightarrow P \mathcal{W} Q$

5.1 Exchange Dimension Pattern

Context. Relying on IBM blueprint reference architecture [7], autonomic systems could distribute the MAPE loop over multiple collaborating autonomic managers. Each of which is responsible for managing particular scope of managed resources. Patterns belonging to this dimension are useful to overcome metrics gathering and delivering problems. Those problems could affect either metrics values, communication reliability between the information sources and destinations, or even on trustworthiness of those sources and destinations.

Pattern Refinement. Communications inside autonomic system could be classified according to the entities involved in information exchange (*i.e.*, managers, agents, shared databases). Therefore, we identify three communication classes: Manager-2-Agent, Manager-2-Manager, and Manager-2-Shared Database (see Figure 1). By taking into consideration push and pull modes[2], along with previous communications classes, we use *case pattern* for the first two refinement levels to cover all possible cases. Based on the triplet ⟨ *Information Source, Communication Protocol, Information Destination* ⟩, the Manager-2-Agent pull mode will be OR-decomposed into *Substitute Agent* and *Substitute Protocol* leaf goals. Rather, *Substitute Protocol* and *Substitute Destination* OR-decompose both Manager-2-(Manager/Shared DB) push mode. Besides, *Activate/Deactivate Polling & Exporting* leaf goals are elicited to launch and stop polling & exporting (see Figure 2a).

Since a manager responds to pull requests in both Manager-2-(Manager/Shared DB) pull mode communications, it is considered as agent (because it is the source of information); therefore, this case becomes identical to Manager-2-Agent pull mode. Moreover, adaptation actions related to Manager-2-Agent push mode are not treated because they need to be held at the agent side.

Examples. This pattern is suitable for the following cases: (1) Increasing accuracy or precision of pulled/pushed metrics values, by replacing information source. (2) Querying more available agents, or blocking fake agents trying to integrate the distributed management system. (3) Securing the communication between information sources and destinations. (4) Modifying information destination when changing the topology of collaborating autonomic managers.

---

[2] In *pull*, entity needing information solicits the one possessing it, that responds with queried information; while in *push*, entity possessing information reports it to others.

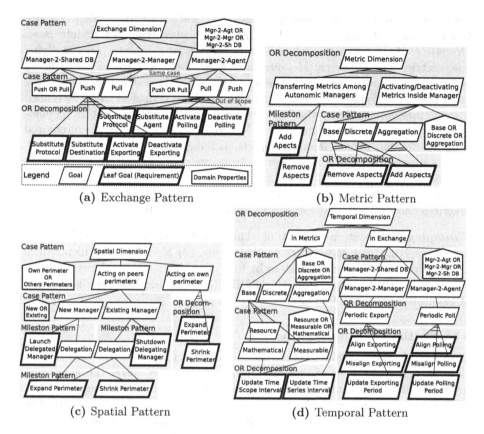

(a) Exchange Pattern

(b) Metric Pattern

(c) Spatial Pattern

(d) Temporal Pattern

Fig. 2. Dimensional Patterns

5.2 Metric Dimension Pattern

Context. The main idea behind building autonomic systems is to delegate decisions, that human administrators are used to make, to the autonomic systems themselves. Thus, to be able to make "wise" decisions, monitoring system needs to instrument specific metrics that could be activated/deactivated according to the management needs during runtime. Patterns belonging to this dimension are useful to control the trade-off between constructing richer knowledge and monitoring the information that is necessary for management.

Pattern Refinement. Metric instrumentation must be thought at the whole management system level. In other words, a given autonomic manager could activate/deactivate instrumentation of particular metrics, but when deactivating metrics on that manager, it doesn't mean necessarily that those metrics are "abandoned", because they could be transferred to other collaborating autonomic manager on which they are activated. These two cases are OR-decomposing the first refinement level. Regarding metrics manipulation inside autonomic manager, the second refinement level uses *case pattern* to cover metric classes. Our research exploits both CIM Metric Model [18] classifying metrics into *Base, Discrete & Aggregation*, as well as our mathematical extension [13] classifying base metrics into *Resource, Measurable & Mathematical*. Each of these classes is OR-decomposed using *Add Aspects* and *Remove Aspects* leaf goals. On the other hand, the transfer of metrics among autonomic managers could be refined through *milestone pattern*, when metrics are activated on the collaborating manager first (*Add Aspects* in Figure 2b, as Subgoal 1 in Table 1), and then removed from the delegating one (*Remove Aspects*, as Subgoal 2).

It is worthy to precise that previously mentioned *Aspects* are representing "metric definitions", rather than "metric values". The former encompasses attributes related to the nature of metric (*e.g.*, data type, unit), while the latter describes the instrumented values and their relevant contexts.

Examples. This pattern can be applied in the following cases: (1) Troubleshooting, or applying root cause analysis algorithms. (2) Modifying the hierarchical topology of the management system by instrumenting aggregated metrics to be exported to other managers or shared DBs. (3) "Engineering" the distribution of monitored metrics among autonomic managers.

5.3   Spatial Dimension Pattern

Context. As mentioned earlier, in autonomic system, each manager is responsible for managing a set of managed resources. In many cases, the number of users consuming the autonomic system services may oscillate rapidly, or even become quite important in term of size. Thus, managed resources are subject to be joined/withdrawn during runtime. Patterns belonging to this dimension are useful to react to the important changes of the managed resources scope.

Pattern Refinement. As management of autonomic systems is orchestrated by the collaboration of multiple autonomic managers, each of which can act on its own perimeter, as well as the perimeters of its collaborating peers. Thus, the first refinement level uses *case pattern* to cover these two cases. In fact, acting on its own perimeter is OR-decomposed using *Expand* and *Shrink Monitoring Perimeter* leaf goals to join/withdraw resources respectively into its managed scope. Rather, acting on others perimeters is refined using *case pattern* into deploying a new manager, or soliciting an existing one. First, the case of deploying a new manager is refined using *milestone pattern* into launching manager (*Launch Delegated Manager* in Figure 2c, as Subgoal 1 in Table 1), and then, delegating perimeter (*Delegation*, as Subgoal 2). In its turn, delegation goal is also refined through *milestone pattern* into joining delegated perimeter on the delegated manager (*Expand Perimeter*, as Subgoal 1), and then, deleting this perimeter from the delegating manager (*Shrink Perimeter*, as Subgoal 2). About the second case, where acting is held on existing manager, it is refined twice, using *milestone pattern*, into delegating the whole perimeter to the delegated manager (*Delegation*, as Subgoal 1), and then shutting down the delegating one (*Shutdown Delegating Manager*, as Subgoal 2).

Examples. This pattern is suitable for the following cases: (1) Load balancing of monitoring among autonomic managers. (2) Supporting scalability of the autonomic systems. (3) Decreasing the number of monitoring resources.

5.4   Temporal Dimension Pattern

Context. Temporal aspects are decisive factors in adapting monitoring behavior. Notice that the previous patterns are explained without considering time notions, but in fact, they imply some temporal aspects. Patterns belonging to this dimension are useful to overcome, among others, both temporal violations and scheduling problems, as well as to tune the analysis over the instrumented metrics. However, these two cases are far from being exhaustive, and time intervenes in a lot of other cases.

Pattern Refinement. Regarding information exchange, once again, we use *case pattern* to represent the same cases identified in *exchange* dimension. Obviously, dealing with information exchange temporal aspects, means that exchange is done iteratively and not once. Thus, Manager-2-Agent case is OR-decomposed into periodic poll, and both Manager-2-(Manager/Shared DB) cases are OR-decomposed into periodic export. We distinguish two levels of temporal granularity: the fine-grained level deals with an individual polling (exporting), whereas the coarse-grained level addresses a collective polling (exporting). Based on this distinction, we identify various leaf goals OR-decomposing periodic poll (export), where: *Update Polling (Exporting) Period* to update the frequency of a given polling (exporting), *Align Polling (Exporting)* to launch a set of synchronized parallel pollings (exported metrics) at the same time, and *Misalign Polling (Exporting)* to launch pollings (exported metrics) according to a "relative offset" delaying their launching moments one another (see Figure 2d).

Regarding metrics calculation, we identify the case of modifying the temporal interval covered by the metric value[3]. Therefore, *case pattern* is used twice to cover all possible metric classes previously mentioned. But, we refine only measurable, mathematical & aggregation metrics, because time has a sense in their calculation, but not the others. Thus, we OR-decompose measurable & mathematical metrics using *Update Time Scope Interval*, while *Update Time Series Interval* OR-decomposes aggregation metrics (see Figure 2d).

Examples. This pattern is suitable for the following cases: (1) Controlling (*e.g.*, relaxing, stressing) the monitoring load on autonomic managers, network paths among autonomic managers and shared DBs, as well as remote agents. (2) Tuning temporal parameters of metrics analysis.

6   Case-Study

Context. Our scenario rolls in a cloud data center providing to the virtual machines (VMs) owners a continuous monitoring of their enforced SLAs metrics.

---

[3] For instance, the *throughput* is not an instantaneous metric, and the validity of its value equals to the temporal interval through which that value was measured.

Each VM integrates two agents (primary: *MIB-II SNMP* & secondary: *SBLIM ProviderCmpiBase*) providing metrics reflecting the performance level of that VM. In most large scale systems, distributed agents push metrics periodically; in our case, agents push metrics each 10 seconds to specific pre-configured autonomic managers. We assume that our studied SLA template distinguishes two time-slots: metrics must be refreshed at the client side with a freshness falling into the range of [3-6] seconds during the first time-slot, and a range of [30-40] seconds for the second one. The SLAs metrics values are instrumented and delivered automatically through polling and exporting respectively in a manner that, once new SLA is enforced, the autonomic managers pull metrics with the lowest freshness value (3 seconds).

Objectives. Based on the data center management strategies, human administrators identify three high level monitoring goals: *Respect Metrics Freshness* makes sure that SLAs are monitored appropriately regarding freshness, *Minimize Monitoring Cost* aims at limiting the resources dedicated to monitoring as much as possible, and *React to Gathering Problems* operates resilient gathering mechanisms after analyzing the potential reasons of gathering problems.

Patterns. Several patterns could be exploited to refine the first objective. During the first time-slot, we use the *temporal pattern* to relax polling & exporting by updating their periods (*Update Polling & Exporting Period* in Figure 3) with respect to the highest freshness range (6 seconds). If delivering freshness violates the highest freshness, that would be a result of overloading manager [16], thus we apply the *spatial pattern* as a second alternative, and consequently, a new autonomic manager will be deployed to assist the overloaded one (*Launch Delegated Manager, Expand Perimeter & Shrink Perimeter*). As a third alternative, and in case that the overloaded autonomic manager monitors non-SLAs metrics (*i.e.,* physical servers healthiness), the *metric pattern* could be applied to transfer them to other manager, in order to relax the first one (*Add & Remove Aspects*). Since the second time-slot freshness ([30-40] seconds) is greater than agents push period (10 seconds), there is no need to poll metrics, nor to export all received metrics. Rather, we apply the *temporal pattern* to update the exporting period from [3-4] to [30-40] seconds (*Update Exporting Period*), and consequently, the first time-slot pollings will be stopped (*Deactivate Polling*).

The second objective is refined using *spatial pattern* in order to shutdown recently deployed managers, during the first time-slot. Thus, an underloaded manager delegates its whole perimeter to another one, and shutdowns itself (*Expand Perimeter, Shrink Perimeter & Shutdown Delegating Manager*). During the second time-slot, autonomic managers already deliver to clients around one-third of the metrics pushed by agents, thus no adaption actions are to be taken in regard with minimizing monitoring resources.

As the third objective deals with gathering problems (*e.g.,* lack of collected information), autonomic managers would act on the *exchange pattern*. Notably, they substitute either remote agent or communication protocol (*Substitute Agent & Protocol* in Figure 3). But, if "failures" at the agent side cause information lack, in such case substituting protocol won't solve the problem. Therefore, we act on the *metric pattern* by launching troubleshooting to acquire more knowledge (*Add Aspects*) required to determine the appropriate substitution.

For all previous objectives, autonomic managers adapt their monitoring if they recognize adaptation stimuli. Therefore, we exploit *guard pattern* to apply adaptation actions (*Adaptation* in Figure 3, as Subgoal 2 in Table 1) as response to specific stimulus (*Guard*, as Subgoal 1), while maintaining the current monitoring behavior unless adaptation takes place (*Unless*, as Subgoal 3).

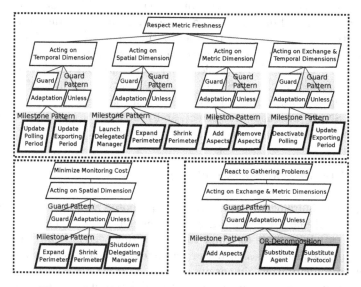

Fig. 3. Case-Study High Level Objectives Refinement

Applying Leaf Goals. In our case-study, autonomic managers are CIM servers operating model-guided monitoring. Moreover, the healthiness indicators of the physical servers, as well as each SLA template, are converted into a monitoring mode each, whereby metrics and constraints are encapsulated.

The *Update Polling/Exporting Period* leaf goals are realized through applying the corresponding methods on all SLA monitoring mode instances to stretch the time interval of collecting/delivering metrics.

The *Expand Perimeter* leaf goal is realized in two manners: first, in case of delegating managed resources to another autonomic manager, whereby the same SLA templates are already enforced (*i.e.,* SLAs monitoring modes are already instantiated), the delegated manager will **join** the yet transfered managed resources in their SLA monitoring mode instances. Otherwise the delegated manager will **activate** the appropriate monitoring mode instances over the transfered resources. However, the *Shrink Perimeter* leaf goal is realized through withdrawing the determined managed resources from their SLA monitoring modes.

Each metric definition instance belonging to a SLA monitoring mode is systematically associated with a *listening* instance to update that metric with the pushed values. But, the same metric definition is also associated with a polling instance to pull its values according to the SLA period. However, *Deactivate Polling* leaf goal is applied on all SLA monitoring mode instances to stop polling and consequently *listening* continues to instrument associated metrics with the agents push period.

Both *Add/Remove Aspects* leaf goals are realized respectively through monitoring mode activation/deactivation. Therefore, to transfer the servers healthiness indicators, the corresponding monitoring mode will be activated on the delegated manager and deactivated from the delegating one. Rather, autonomic manager activates the "gathering troubleshooting" mode to determine whether it must substitute agent or protocol. This mode encapsulates metrics collected from remote agents SNMPv2-MIB variables, such as: *snmpInBadVersions & snmpInBadCommunityNames*[4]. If the SNMP messages querying agent don't increment the "gathering troubleshooting" mode metrics of that agent, it means that the synthesized SNMP messages are correct, and probably the problem comes from the agent itself; in that case, *Substitute Agent* is applied.

7   Conclusion and Perspectives

Based on the Requirements Engineering, we proposed a goal-oriented approach for designing self-managed monitoring in autonomic systems. This approach assists human administrators to adapt the monitoring system behavior regarding quality requirements. We designed four reusable monitoring adaptation patterns falling into reconfiguration dimensions.

About the perspectives, and in order to validate our approach, we need to consider two validation levels. First, the completeness and correctness of the patterns refinement must be validated. Using proof theory, we can avoid missing some necessary requirements, and also, we can discover the available alternatives to refine a given goal [17]. On the other hand, once the monitoring system adaptation is modeled as a *transition system* (*i.e.,* set of states and transitions) through the *Temporal Logic*, we need to determine the critical properties to be checked (*i.e.,* invariance, safety, eventuality, fairness, and precedence) [19]. Using model checking, the properties satisfaction is checked, either on particular state, or path, or even the whole system model. Apart from validation, and besides enriching patterns, adaptation actions at the agent side need to be investigated, and orchestrated with those applied at the autonomic manager side.

---

[4] These variables describe the number of SNMP messages delivered to a SNMP agent with unsupported version and unknown "community string", respectively .

References

1. Kephart, J.O., Chess, D.M.: The vision of autonomic computing. Computer 36(1), 41–50 (2003)
2. Grefen, P., Aberer, K., Ludwig, H., Hoffner, Y.: Crossflow: Cross-organizational workflow management in dynamic virtual enterprises. International Journal of Computer Systems Science & Engineering 15, 277–290 (2000)
3. Roxburgh, D., Spaven, D., Gallen, C.: Monitoring as an sla-oriented consumable service for saas assurance: A prototype. In: 2011 IFIP/IEEE International Symposium on Integrated Network Management (IM), pp. 925–939 (2011)
4. Thongtra, P., Aagesen, F.: An adaptable capability monitoring system. In: 2010 Sixth International Conference on Networking and Services (ICNS), pp. 73–80 (2010)
5. Munawar, M.A., Reidemeister, T., Jiang, M., George, A., Ward, P.A.S.: Adaptive monitoring with dynamic differential tracing-based diagnosis. In: De Turck, F., Kellerer, W., Kormentzas, G. (eds.) DSOM 2008. LNCS, vol. 5273, pp. 162–175. Springer, Heidelberg (2008)
6. Nobre, J.C., Granville, L.Z., Clemm, A., Prieto, A.G.: Decentralized detection of sla violations using p2p technology. In: Proceedings of the 8th International Conference on Network and Service Management, pp. 100–107. International Federation for Information Processing (2012)
7. IBM Corp.: An architectural blueprint for autonomic computing. IBM White Paper (June 2005)
8. Weyns, D., et al.: On patterns for decentralized control in self-adaptive systems. In: de Lemos, R., Giese, H., Müller, H.A., Shaw, M. (eds.) Self-Adaptive Systems. LNCS, vol. 7475, pp. 76–107. Springer, Heidelberg (2013)
9. Ramirez, A.J., Cheng, B.H.C.: Design patterns for developing dynamically adaptive systems. In: Proceedings of the 2010 ICSE Workshop on Software Engineering for Adaptive and Self-Managing Systems, SEAMS 2010, pp. 49–58 (2010)
10. Moui, A., Desprats, T., Lavinal, E., Sibilla, M.: A cim-based framework to manage monitoring adaptability. In: 2012 8th International Conference on Network and Service Management (CNSM) and 2012 Workshop on Systems Virtualiztion Management (SVM), pp. 261–265 (2012)
11. Moui, A., Desprats, T., Lavinal, E., Sibilla, M.: Information models for managing monitoring adaptation enforcement. In: International Conference on Adaptive and Self-adaptive Systems and Applications (ADAPTIVE), Nice, July 22-27, pp. 44–50 (2012)
12. Moui, A., Desprats, T., Lavinal, E., Sibilla, M.: Managing polling adaptability in a cim/wbem infrastructure. In: 2010 4th International DMTF Academic Alliance Workshop on Systems and Virtualization Management (SVM), pp. 1–6 (2010)
13. Toueir, A., Broisin, J., Sibilla, M.: Toward configurable performance monitoring: Introduction to mathematical support for metric representation and instrumentation of the cim metric model. In: 2011 5th International DMTF Academic Alliance Workshop on Systems and Virtualization Management (SVM), pp. 1–6 (2011)
14. Van Lamsweerde, A.: Requirements Engineering: From System Goals to UML Models to Software Specifications. Wiley (2009)
15. Van Lamsweerde, A.: Requirements engineering in the year 00: a research perspective. In: Proceedings of the 2000 International Conference on Software Engineering, pp. 5–19 (2000)

16. Toueir, A., Broisin, J., Sibilla, M.: A goal-oriented approach for adaptive sla monitoring: a cloud provider case study. In: LATINCLOUD 2013, Maceió, Brazil (December 2013)
17. Darimont, R., Van Lamsweerde, A.: Formal refinement patterns for goal-driven requirements elaboration. In: Proceedings of the 4th ACM SIGSOFT Symposium on Foundations of Software Engineering - SIGSOFT 1996, pp. 179–190 (1996)
18. DMTF Applications Working Group: Base metrics profile (December 2009)
19. Goranko, V.: Temporal logics for specification and verification. In: Proceedings of the European Summer School in Logic, Language and Information, ESSLI 2009 (2009)

Detection of Network Flow Timestamp Reliability

Martin Žádník, Erik Šabík, and Václav Bartoš

CESNET, a. l. e.,
Zikova 4, 160 00 Prague, Czech Republic
{zadnik,sabik,bartos}@cesnet.cz

Abstract. Network flow measurement and analysis are important parts of network management and security. Flow data analysis is a challenging task which is often rendered harder by pitfalls in a monitoring pipeline. In this paper we focus on timestamps since many analysis procedures utilize timestamps to reveal various characteristics of network traffic. Unfortunately, the timestamps are not always that reliable as it may seem. We propose an algorithm to estimate the percentage of correctly assigned timestamps to flow records with respect to the sequence of a request and a response flow. We simulate various timestamp failures and we evaluate the failures using the proposed algorithm. We demonstrate the usage of the algorithm in the use case of bidirectional flow orientation.

1 Introduction

Network administrators as well as service providers need to measure and analyse network traffic for maintenance, security and planning [7]. One popular approach is based on network flows. The flows are measured at observation points (e.g. routers, probes) and the flow records are exported to collectors for storage and analysis. Flow monitoring enables various security and management applications to reveal information about the state of network and its network traffic as well as the state of services and the behavior of connected machines (e.g. to detect infected machines).

Flow records contain timestamps besides other statistics. The timestamps usually express start and end of a flow. The flow start timestamp captures a significant event from the analysis perspective. For example, the start timestamps offer a possibility to identify initiators of communications (i.e. to establish bidirectional flow orientation [12]), distinguish and profile hosts [11], measure TCP response time [8] and order flows according to their arrival at the observation point.

The utilization of start timestamps may improve the data analysis but only if the start timestamps are reliable. This is often not the case based on our experience from practical deployments as well as based on the cases studied in the literature. For example, in [2] the authors state: "Furthermore, the flow timestamps have proved to be sometimes unreliable and more often, the request and reply flows have identical timestamps due to the granularity of the timestamps."

A. Sperotto et al. (Eds.): AIMS 2014, LNCS 8508, pp. 147–159, 2014.

On the other hand, if the monitoring pipeline provides reliable timestamps the subsequent analysis methods may utilize this knowledge to improve on their results. To this end, we propose an algorithm to estimate reliability of start timestamps in the flow records belonging to a particular observation point. The algorithm assumes that a flow generated in reaction (response flow) cannot precede the initiating flow (request flow). The algorithm selects a certain subset of flow records and compares their start timestamps with another heuristic utilizing port numbers. The correlation provides an estimate on the reliability of the timestamps. The algorithm consumes only little amount of resources not to slow down any subsequent analysis.

We evaluate the algorithm on real packet and flow traces. To assess a baseline we utilize traces with reliable timestamps. Subsequently the algorithm is evaluated on traces containing originally as well as artificially generated timestamp failures.

In order to show the contribution of utilizing timestamps (if reliable) we propose a biflow orientation algorithm utilizing timestamp reliability estimate to modify its function when the timestamps are not reliable.

The rest of the paper is organized as follows. Related work on timestamp failures and timestamp utilization is discussed in Section 2. Section 3 and 4 describe the proposed timestamp reliability estimate algorithm and biflow orientation algorithm respectively. Section 5.2 analyzes several data sets and evaluates the algorithm on a problem of biflow orientation. The paper is concluded with summary and future work in Section 6.

2   Related Work

2.1   Timestamp Failures

Failures and errors in the monitoring pipeline are not an exception as documented in several works. In [4], [6] the authors investigate various flow measurement tools and look for artifacts caused by design decisions or implementation constraints. Besides other artifacts the authors found out that a certain flow exporter reports incorrect start times in a case a flow is exported due to an active timeout. Moreover, they analyze the effects of *flow learn failures* on flow data. The authors state in [6]: "Our experiments have shown that the first packets of flows are more likely to be subject to flow learn failures, because subsequent packets of accounted flows are matched until the records are expired". As a result some start timestamps need not necessarily correspond to the first packets in the flows. The timing artifacts may also be caused by the poor resolution of timestamps and this issue is analyzed closer in [9]. Also an underlying platform/system hosting the measurement process may introduce some timing issues, e.g. so called interrupt coalescence [10].

The timing error may appear also due to a design option. The work [13] characterizes timing errors in flow data caused by collection and export via NetFlow v9 [3]. The work identifies three sources of errors in the measurement methodology. These errors may lead to the timing bias in the order of a second.

Other causes of timing errors are not that well documented. The following list of potential timestamp issues is definitely not complete but summarizes our experience from real deployment.

Buffers. A timestamp must be assigned to each packet upon its arrival at the physical interface. Otherwise a packet may be subject to buffering resulting in an arbitrary delay in hardware (network card) and software (host memory) buffers. Since the buffers are usually dedicated per each interface some packets may or may not be buffered. As a result the order of packets at physical interfaces need not necessarily conform to the order of timestamps assigned by software. High-speed packet capture solutions usually utilize large buffers to increase transfer efficiency and to sustain short overloads. This results in an even larger unpredictability of the correct timestamp assignment in software.

Packet drop/sampling. A metering process may drop packets if overloaded or may sample packets deliberately. In both cases some first packets are lost resulting in a mismatch between the true start of a flow and the start timestamp stored in a flow record.

Timestamp representation. An inconsistent interpretation of timestamp format may result in a timestamp error as well. For example, a 64-bit timestamp may represent seconds (upper 32 bits) and a remainder (lower 32 bits). In the first case the remainder is represented as a number of 233 picosends intervals to fully utilize all 32 bits whereas in the second case the remainder is represented as a number of nanoseconds, i.e. utilizing only 30-bits. An error of up to 750 ms may appear if a timestamp stored in the first representation (e.g. by hardware) is interpreted as the second (e.g. by a flow measurement tool).

Deduplication. In certain metering infrastructures a flow may be measured multiple times since it traverses multiple observation points. Deduplication process merges corresponding flows into a single record. Based on the configured rules the order of flows (their start timestamps) may change during the deduplication process.

The low reliability of timestamps is also demonstrated on a popular collector NfDump [5] since the collector implements biflow orientation based on port numbers only.

2.2   Timestamp Analysis

The time characteristics of flow exporters are analyzed in [9] from the perspective of one way delay (OWD) measurement. An offline algorithm is proposed to derive an exporter profile based on flow data. The profile captures clock skew, clock offset, resolution, bias and accuracy of timestamps. The profiles are inferred by correlation of records belonging to traversing flows (flows seen on at least two exporters). Therefore the algorithm needs at least two exporters (a reasonable assumption for OWD measurement) but the algorithm does not account for timestamp errors described in Section 2.1. The algorithm infers ordering of flows (request-response) based on timestamps and it is therefore susceptible to errors described in Section 2.1. The profiling algorithm would benefit from the knowledge of timestamp reliability derived by our algorithm. Therefore we consider our algorithm to be orthogonal since their algorithm focuses on different error types, utilize different heuristics and report different results.

NfSight tool [2] utilizes Bayesian classifier to identify clients and servers. The classifier combines timestamp, port and IP address heuristics. The classifier is trained and evaluated using an annotated data set, i.e. server and clients are known a priori. The evaluation shows that the start timestamps in their data set are heavily biased. The ability of start timestamps to correctly identify biflow orientation is very low (25%) if the difference of the timestamp is lower than 1 second (see [2] page 4, Fig. 2). According to the evaluation 95% accuracy is reached only in cases where the difference is more than 5 seconds.

Clearly, each data set (exporter) may produce flow records of various reliability and therefore on a different data set the training phase would construct a different classifier. However, it is problematic in a real deployment to train the classifier due to various limitations, e.g. it is not always possible to capture reliable raw packet dump to apply annotation mechanisms. Therefore, we consider our work to be complementary to [2] since our algorithm does not require any training though it may reach lower precision when utilized in the use case of the biflow orientation. Also the output of our biflow orientation algorithm may serve as an input of the classifier if the training phase is feasible.

Minarik et al. [11] proposed an extension of host profiling with bidirectional flows. A request flow is identified by its start timestamp, i.e. the flow with an earlier start timestamp is a request. If the timestamps are not reliable the port number heuristic is utilized (a higher source port and a lower destination port is considered to appear in request). Our work extends the idea further by an algorithm to detect timestamp failure automatically. Moreover, we propose a decision tree to improve biflow orientation by combining timestamp and port heuristics.

3   Timestamp Reliability Algorithm

The goal of the algorithm is to estimate the percentage of flow records with a valid start timestamp. For the purpose of our work we consider start timestamps to be valid if the timestamps of a request flow precedes the timestamp of a flow generated in response. In our work, we utilize term flow to denote a set of packets with the same 5-tuple (IP addresses, port numbers and protocol number). The algorithm sets out its estimate according to the correlation of start timestamps with a request/response heuristic based on port numbers. Please note that our algorithm is able to estimate bad ordering of the timestamps but not their accuracy.

The algorithm starts by selecting flow records that are relevant from the perspective of start timestamps or port numbers. Let A denotes a set of all flow records, $T \subset A$ denotes a subset of flow records that is possible to evaluate based on start timestamps, $P \subset A$ denotes a subset of flow records that is possible to evaluate based on port number heuristic. $T_{req,resp} \subset T$ is a subset of flow records denoted by timestamps as requests and responses respectively. $P_{req,resp} \subset P$ is

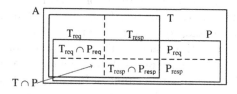

Fig. 1. Network flows split into sets according to timestamp and port number heuristic

a subset of flow records denoted by port numbers as requests and responses respectively. The sets are depicted in Fig. 1.

The subset T contains only flow records meeting following conditions.

1. The flow record corresponds to a flow in reverse direction, i.e. there are two flows forming a bidirectional flow in the set A. If a flow is only unidirectional it is not possible to distinguish request or response flow based on its start timestamp. A flow may be unidirectional due to various reasons such as its reverse flow is not observed (e.g. asymmetric routing), reverse flow is discarded (e.g. flow sampling), server is not responding and many others.
2. The bidirectional flow record accounts for a TCP connection.
3. The record contains TCP SYN flags for both directions. In that case the record is considered to account for the first packets of each flow since a flow may be reported as a sequence of flow records by the observation point due to, e.g., inactive and active timeouts, full flow cache or replacement policy.
4. The start timestamps in the record must differ otherwise it is not possible to decide the flow ordering.

The subset P contains flow records that is possible to validate by the port number heuristic. The utilization of port numbers rules out flow records with protocols other than TCP or UDP. The heuristic compares destination port number (destinationTransportPort) with source port number (sourceTransport-Port). The heuristic classifies only flow records when one of the port numbers is lower than 1024 and the other is higher than or equal to 1024. If destinationTransportPort is lower than 1024 then the flow record is considered to be a request. The utilized classification condition is rather strict to achieve high confidence in the classified samples (a more vague rule would be, for example one of the port numbers is lower and the other is higher).

The algorithm selects an intersection $T \cap P$ and classifies these flow records by timestamps and ports. The estimate e on the timestamp reliability is expressed as the ratio of the number of flow records classified as requests/responses by the timestamps and the ports in mutual agreement and the number of flow records in the intersection plus $|T_equal|$:

$$e = \frac{|T_{req} \cap P_{req}| + |T_{resp} \cap P_{resp}|}{|T \cap P| + |T_{equal}|}, \tag{1}$$

where T_{equal} is a subset of TCP bidirectional records with TCP SYN flags but containing equal start timestamps thus filtered out of T by the fourth condition. If the start timestamp and port heuristic agree on flow ordering then e reaches 100% provided the start timestamps differ. If there are bidirectional flows with equal timestamps or the timestamps do not conform to port heuristic than e drops to 50% under normal circumstances. If e drops below 50% then it means that start timestamps and port numbers are in negative correlation. We also suggest to consider e value only if size of $|T|$ is at least five percent of all flows and the number of all flows is sufficiently large (e.g. 10 million flows).

4   Biflow Orientation Algorithm

We propose a flow orientation algorithm that decides the orientation based on timestamps and port number heuristic. The decision algorithm is driven by timestamp reliability estimate e. The algorithm orients the flows according to the decision tree depicted in Fig. 2.

Upon a flow or biflow arrival the algorithm follows the tree from root to leaves. If the flow is single then the port numbers must determine the flow orientation. If it is a bidirectional flow then the timestamps decide the orientation first but only if the timestamps can be trusted. The trust is expressed by the condition C_t which includes reliability estimation, flow start heuristic and condition on differing timestamps:

$$C_t : e > R \wedge (TCP \wedge SYN \vee (\neg TCP \wedge duration < D)) \wedge t_1 \neq t_2, \quad (2)$$

where R is a reliability threshold. Values t_1, t_2 are start timestamps which must differ to determine the order of flows. The second expression identifies flows in which the start timestamps belong to the first packet of the flows. We consider these flows either to be TCP flows with SYN flags or non-TCP flows lasting less than D seconds. The flow fragmentation occurs when the flow duration reaches active timeout (e.g. 300 seconds) under normal circumstances. Therefore records describing long flows (duration close to active timeout) are more likely to be fragments of a long lasting flow and do not account for the first packet of a flow in most cases. The algorithm omits the flow reassembly procedure due to its memory cost and selects flows that are significantly shorter than active timeout. Still the algorithm may account for the last fragment of a flow accidentally. According to our traces, we suggest to setup the thresholds $R = 80\%$ and $D = 180s$. This balances the classification gain when utilizing timestamps and possible errors introduced by incorrect timestamps or fragmented flows.

If the condition C_t does not hold the algorithm proceeds with port number classification. This requires the ports to be available and to differ from each other. The classification results in request/response biflow orientation, single request/response flow and unknown orientation.

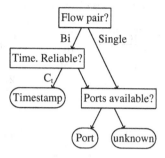

Fig. 2. Bidirectional flow orientation decision tree (C_t is condition described in expression (2))

5   Evaluation

We analyze our data sets to determine the dependency between timestamps and port number heuristic from the perspective of timestamp reliability estimation algorithm. Subsequently we evaluate our biflow orientation algorithm under various timestamp failures.

5.1   Data Sets

The experiments are carried out on three data sets. As a baseline we utilize a data set with verified timestamps. The timestamps are assigned by hardware prior to any buffering and offers nanosecond resolution. Manual analysis of the data set confirmed that the start timestamps are in line with the expected flow ordering. The baseline data set consists of raw packets observed during one day interval on a 10 Gbps backbone network link (link between CESNET and ACONET NRENs (National Research and Educational Network). The packets are aggregated into flow records offline thus no packet drop appears. The packet aggregation was performed by a program written specifically for this task (setup: inactive timeout 30 s, active timeout 300 s, do not interpret TCP flags, no memory limit). The second data set consists of flow records observed during one day interval on an Internet connection of a campus network. This data set consists of flow records which were aggregated online by a metering probe. These two data sets were thinned by accounting only first fifteen minutes of each hour (data set A - backbone (baseline), data set B - campus). In addition to our data sets, we also include data set that is publicly available. This data set was captured on WIDE backbone samplepoint-F on a 155 Mbps line [1]. Again the flow records were aggregated offline hence the only timestamp errors may come from the utilized capture solution (no details are available). Tab. 1 shows basic characteristics of the utilized data sets.

Fig. 3 displays cumulative distribution function of time differences (de facto a round trip time (RTT)) between start timestamps of the bidirectional flows. The

Table 1. Volumes of utilized data sets

	Flows [mil.]	Packets [mil.]	Bytes [bil.]	Interval
data set A - Aconet	266	10379	8887	2014/01/10 0:00 - 23:15
data set B - VUT	190	7595	6668	2013/12/02 0:00 - 23:15
data set C - Mawi	8	58	27	2014/02/10 14:00 - 14:15

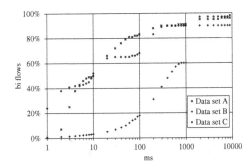

Fig. 3. Time differences between start timestamps of bidirectional flows (please note the logarithmic scale of the x-axis)

data set A and B exhibit similar properties – 90% of start timestamp differences fit into 1000 ms interval. Whereas data set C exhibit longer RTTs – 90% of start timestamp differences fit into 2000 ms interval.

We apply various modifications to data set A to observe dependency between certain timestamp failures and our estimation algorithm as well as our orientation algorithm. Three types of the artificial modifications are proposed:

1. To swap the start timestamps in bidirectional flows with probability $p_w = \{0.01, 0.02, 0.05, 0.1, 0.2, 0.5\}$. The modified data set is denoted as, for example, $A_{p_w=0.1}$. Such a modification may simulate buffering issues.
2. To set up start timestamps to the same value in case the difference between timestamps is less than d ms, $d = \{1, 2, 5, 10, 20, 50\}$. The modified data set is denoted as, for example, $A_{d=1}$. This modification may simulate poor timestamp resolution.
3. To apply random packet sampling prior to flow aggregation with probability $p_s = \{0.01, 0.02, 0.05, 0.1, 0.2, 0.5\}$ (the higher the sampling probability p_s the more packets is accounted for measurement). The modified data set is denoted as, for example, $A_{p_s=0.1}$. This modification may simulate packet drops and sampling.

5.2   Experimental Results

First, we conduct experiments to determine the correlation between start timestamps and port heuristics. If the correlation between port and timestamps is

Table 2. Breakdown of data sets into subsets

Data set	$|A|$ [mil. flows]	$|T|$	$|P|$	$|T \cap P|$	$|T_{req} \cap P_{req}|+$ $|T_{resp} \cap P_{resp}|$	$|T_{equal}|$	e
A	266	19%	43%	18%	18%	0.02%	100%
B	190	27%	61%	22%	12%	0.04%	54%
C	8	6%	30%	5%	5%	0.7%	89%

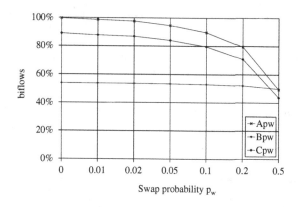

Fig. 4. Impact of the timestamp swap modification on the timestamp reliability estimate e

high in case of the non-modified data set and if it differs in case of a modified data set then the reliability estimate algorithm can estimate cases of timestamp failures successfully. Tab. 2 breaks down the flow records in the data sets A, B and C into the subsets utilized in Eq. (1).

The baseline set A exhibit nearly perfect correlation between timestamps and port numbers as $|T_{req} \cap P_{req}| + |T_{resp} \cap P_{resp}|$ and $|T \cap P|$ are of equal size. Therefore the reliability may be worsened by $|T_{equal}|$ only. On the other hand the timestamps and ports correlation is low in the data set B. This conforms already suspicious results presented in Fig. 3 where the cumulative distribution of start timestamp differences is significantly lower to other data sets. Therefore we infer that these start timestamps already bear significant artifacts introduced by the monitoring pipeline. Tab. 2 also shows that in the case of the data set C the size of T is quite low but still above our threshold of 5% out of all flows. On the other hand the correlation of timestamps and ports is high (89%).

The impact of the first modification (start timestamp swap) on e is depicted in Fig. 4. The higher the number of swapped start timestamps the lower e. In case of the data set B the decrease of e is slow since the correlation between timestamps and port numbers is already bad in the first place. The second modification (equalizing timestamps) is applied on the data sets and the result is depicted in Fig. 5. Again Fig. 5 shows that with larger number of equal timestamps the estimation decreases.

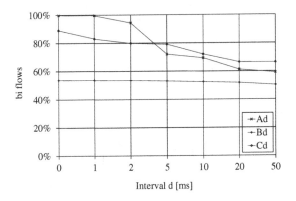

Fig. 5. Impact of the timestamp resolution modification on the timestamp reliability estimate e

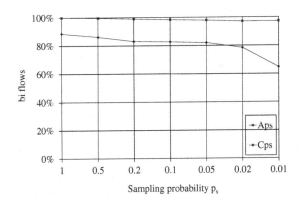

Fig. 6. Impact of the sampling modification on the timestamp reliability estimate e

In case of data set modification by packet sampling we are not able to modify data set B since this data set consists of the flow records only and it is not considered for evaluation. Fig 6 depicts the behavior of e when the sampling rate decreases. Since the data set B consists of already aggregated flow records it is omitted from the evaluation. In case of data set C the estimate decreases with the decreasing sampling rate. In case of the data set A the e remains high despite higher sampling rate but the size of T quickly decreases below 5% for $A_{p_s \leq 0.2}$. Therefore the e should be considered low and timestamps should not be utilized. The experiments with the modified data sets show that the estimate e reacts on start timestamps errors as expected. We proceed with the experiments on the bidirectional flow orientation to demonstrate the ability of e to control

Table 3. Comparison of TREE and PORT algorithms in bidirectional orientation problem (nd - not defined)

Flow type	Data set Classified by	A Flows [mil]	A PORT	A TREE	B Flows [mil]	B PORT	B TREE	C Flows [mil]	C PORT	C TREE
Single flow	port	134	60%	60%	27	43%	43%	1.6	71%	71%
	unknown		40%	40%		57%	57%		29%	29%
Bi. flow	port		88%	39%		71%	20%		74%	7%
	timestamp	132	0%	57%	164	0%	70%	1	0%	75%
	unknown		12%	4%		29%	10%		26%	18%
Bi. flow	errors		8%	0%		nd	nd		8%	0%

the decision algorithm as well as the advantage of bidirectional flow orientation utilizing start timestamps in parallel to port numbers.

First we evaluate our orientation algorithm (TREE) against port number heuristic (PORT) on all non-modified data sets. The port heuristic classifies only such flow records in which one of the port numbers is lower than 1024 and the other is higher than or equal to 1024. The Tab. 3 depicts the capability of each algorithm to classify single flows and bidirectional flows. The single flows are always classified by port numbers since timestamps may only be utilized in case of bidirectional flows. Naturally, some single flows do not match the condition of PORT heuristic and are classified unknown. The bidirectional flows may be classified either by port or timestamps in case of TREE and only by ports in case of PORT. Naturally, some bidirectional flows cannot be oriented neither by timestamps nor by ports and these flows are marked unknown.

On the data set A the PORT heuristic is able to determine 88% of flows belonging to 66 mil. bidirectional flow (132 mil. flows). Since we know that the data set A contains verified timestamps than we can utilize classification results of TREE as a ground truth to estimate errors of PORT. As a result, if PORT is utilized 88% of bidirectional flows is classified but with 8% of errors. On the other hand TREE is able to classify 96% of bidirectional flows without an error. In case of data set B the timestamps cannot be trusted but if utilized the number of classified flows would reach 90% in comparison with only 71% in case of PORT. The classification results for data set C are similar to data set A since the timestamps are deemed correct.

Tab. 4 captures the behavior of TREE algorithm on modified data set A_{p_w}. As the number of swapped timestamps decreases the bidirectional flow algorithm starts to utilize timestamps for orientation. If the timestamps have been used when $p_w = 0.5, p_w = 0.2$ then the classification error would be quite large, 29% and 12% respectively. At the same time when TREE starts to utilize timestamps the error decreases further as well as the percentage of non-oriented biflows.

Tab. 5 captures the behavior of TREE algorithm on modified data set A_d. The algorithm stops utilizing timestamps upon $d = 20, d = 50$ although if the timestamps were used then the percentage of non-oriented flows and the

Table 4. Modified data sets A_w and the impact on bidirectional flow orientation algorithm (bidirectional flows only, [t] and [p] mark values belonging to TREE and PORT respectively)

	A	A_{p_w}					
		0.5	0.2	0.1	0.05	0.02	0.01
port	39%[t]	88%[p]	88%[p]	39%[t]	39%[t]	39%[t]	39%[t]
timestamp	57%[t]	0%[p]	0%[p]	57%[t]	57%[t]	57%[t]	57%[t]
unknown	4%[t]	12%[p]	12%[p]	4%[t]	4%[t]	4%[t]	4%[t]
errors	0%[t]	8%[p] 29%[t]	8%[p] 12%[t]	6%[t]	3%[t]	1%[t]	1%[t]

Table 5. Modified data sets A_d and the impact on bidirectional flow orientation algorithm (bidirectional flows only)

	A	A_d [ms]					
		1	2	5	10	20	50
port	39%[t]	39%[t]	41%[t]	51%[t]	53%[t]	88%[p]	88%[p]
timestamp	57%[t]	57%[t]	55%[t]	44%[t]	42%[t]	0%[p]	0%[p]
unknown	4%[t]	4%[t]	4%[t]	5%[t]	5%[t]	12%[p] 6%[t]	12%[p] 7%[t]
errors	0%[t]	0%[t]	0%[t]	1%[t]	1%[t]	8%[p] 2%[t]	8%[p] 3%[t]

number of errors would be lower. This is a prize given by the fact that we cannot anticipate which timestamp error appears on a given network.

6   Conclusion

The paper proposed two algorithms – first one to estimate the timestamp reliability and the second to orient bidirectional flows according to start timestamps and port numbers. Our future work will test the algorithms further to fully evaluate the performance of the classifiers on empirical data sets containing timestamp failures.

Acknowledgment. This research has been partially supported by the CES-NET Large Infrastructure project no. LM2010005 funded by the Ministry of Education, Youth and Sports of the Czech Republic.

References

1. The mawi archive (2014), `http://mawi.wide.ad.jp/mawi/`
2. Berthier, R., Cukier, M., Hiltunen, M., Kormann, D., Vesonder, G., Sheleheda, D.: Nfsight: netflow-based network awareness tool. In: Proceedings of the 24th International Conference on Large Installation System Administration, LISA 2010, pp. 1–8. USENIX Association, Berkeley (2010),
`http://dl.acm.org/citation.cfm?id=1924976.1924988`

3. Claise, B.: Cisco Systems NetFlow Services Export Version 9. RFC 3954 (Informational) (October 2004), http://www.ietf.org/rfc/rfc3954.txt
4. Cunha, Í., Silveira, F., Oliveira, R., Teixeira, R., Diot, C.: Uncovering artifacts of flow measurement tools. In: Moon, S.B., Teixeira, R., Uhlig, S. (eds.) PAM 2009. LNCS, vol. 5448, pp. 187–196. Springer, Heidelberg (2009)
5. Haag, P.: Nfdump - netflow processing tools (2013), http://sourceforge.net/projects/nfdump/
6. Hofstede, R., Drago, I., Sperotto, A., Sadre, R., Pras, A.: Measurement artifacts in netFlow data. In: Roughan, M., Chang, R. (eds.) PAM 2013. LNCS, vol. 7799, pp. 1–10. Springer, Heidelberg (2013)
7. Hughes, E., Somayaji, A.: Towards network awareness. In: LISA, pp. 113–124. USENIX (2005), http://dblp.uni-trier.de/db/conf/lisa/lisa2005.html
8. Jiang, H., Dovrolis, C.: Passive estimation of tcp round-trip times. SIGCOMM Comput. Commun. Rev. 32(3), 75–88 (2002), http://doi.acm.org/10.1145/571697.571725
9. Kogel, J.: One-way delay measurement based on flow data: Quantification and compensation of errors by exporter profiling. In: 2011 International Conference on Information Networking (ICOIN), pp. 25–30 (January 2011)
10. McPherson, S., Ortega, A.: Analysis of internet measurement systems for optimized anomaly detection system design. CoRR abs/0907.5233 (2009), http://dblp.uni-trier.de/db/journals/corr/corr0907.html
11. Minarik, P., Vykopal, J., Krmicek, V.: Improving host profiling with bidirectional flows. In: Proceedings of the 2009 International Conference on Computational Science and Engineering, CSE 2009, vol. 3, pp. 231–237. IEEE Computer Society, Washington, DC (2009), http://dx.doi.org/10.1109/CSE.2009.23
12. Trammell, B., Boschi, E.: Bidirectional Flow Export Using IP Flow Information Export (IPFIX). RFC 5103 (Proposed Standard) (January 2008), http://www.ietf.org/rfc/rfc5103.txt
13. Trammell, B., Tellenbach, B., Schatzmann, D., Burkhart, M.: Peeling away timing error in netFlow data. In: Spring, N., Riley, G.F. (eds.) PAM 2011. LNCS, vol. 6579, pp. 194–203. Springer, Heidelberg (2011)

Enhancing Network Intrusion Detection by Correlation of Modularly Hashed Sketches

Martin Drašar, Tomáš Jirsík, and Martin Vizváry

Institute of Computer Science, Masaryk University,
Botanická 68a, 61200 Brno, Czech Republic
{drasar,jirsik,vizvary}@ics.muni.cz

Abstract. The rapid development of network technologies entails an increase in traffic volume and attack count. The associated increase in computational complexity for methods of deep packet inspection has driven the development of behavioral detection methods. These methods distinguish attackers from valid users by measuring how closely their behavior resembles known anomalous behavior. In real-life deployment, an attacker is flagged only on very close resemblance to avoid false positives. However, many attacks can then go undetected. We believe that this problem can be solved by using more detection methods and then correlating their results. These methods can be set to higher sensitivity, and false positives are then reduced by accepting only attacks reported from more sources. To this end we propose a novel sketch-based method that can detect attackers using a correlation of particular anomaly detections. This is in contrast with the current use of sketch-based methods that focuses on the detection of heavy hitters and heavy changes. We illustrate the potential of our method by detecting attacks on RDP and SSH authentication by correlating four methods detecting the following anomalies: source network scan, destination network scan, abnormal connection count, and low traffic variance. We evaluate our method in terms of detection capabilities compared to other deployed detection methods, hardware requirements, and the attacker's ability to evade detection.

1 Introduction

With the dramatic development of network technology over last few years, the number of Internet users and traffic volume has increased. Globally, the number of Internet users is forecast to increase from 1.9 billion users in 2010 to 3 billion in 2015. The amount of the traffic per average Internet user is estimated to grow from 7.3 gigabytes per month to 61.8 gigabyte per month. Furthermore, global consumer internet traffic is about to reach nearly 60 exabytes per month in two years.[15] Along with the growth of the traffic volume, we monitor an increase in the attack count. There was a 42 % increase in the targeted attacks in 2012 and more than 5 thousands of new vulnerabilities were discovered.[16]

Given the immense volume of traffic and arising computational complexity, deep packet inspection becomes inefficient as a method for attack detection

A. Sperotto et al. (Eds.): AIMS 2014, LNCS 8508, pp. 160–172, 2014.

and prevention in large-scale networks. Therefore, behavioral detection methods based on flow analysis have been deployed to detect attackers. Behavioral detection methods distinguish the attackers from valid users by comparing either how their behavior resembles known anomalous behavior or how their behavior deviates from valid behavior. Since there are many types of attacks, various methods have been invented to detect them. Simple methods monitor basic network characteristics and are based on naïve thresholds, while more sophisticated methods employ statistics or behavioral profiling based on more complex characteristics.

Real-life deployment of behavior detection methods has its problems, though. Most methods described in current papers exhibit an excessive false positive ratio and their deployment is subject to base-rate fallacy [1]. Because security administrators need to identify attackers with nearly absolute certainty, the parameters of methods are set to minimize the false positive ratio. However, this minimization results in higher false negative ratios and consequently higher number of undetected attacks. There is also an issue with limited detection capabilities. Currently available methods are usually able to detect a set of attacks that are synergistic in their nature, e.g., port scanning and malware propagation. Methods that employ some form of event correlation to reduce false positives usually focus on events with identical dimensions and are unable to take into account the inherent uncertainty of some events.

Based on the previous discussion, we identify following research questions:

1. How can we correlate diverse anomaly reports from different sources with different dimensions?
2. Can the correlation be done efficiently enough to permit deployment on high speed networks?
3. What is the impact of correlation on the false positive and negative ratio?

To answer the stated questions we apply the following approach. First we propose a correlation mechanism based on modularly hashed reversible sketches and discuss its advantages and drawbacks. Then we use our preliminary implementation and deploy it in a network with more than 15.000 machines to assess its efficiency by comparison with already deployed detection methods.

This paper is organized into five section. In Section 2 we give a brief background on base-rate fallacy, current state of statistic anomaly correlation, and the concept of sketches. In Section 3 we explain in detail the concept of modular key hashing scheme and our correlation method. In Section 4 we evaluate the method both from theoretical standpoint and by experiments on a set of attacks. In Section 5 we conclude our paper and present focus of our future research.

2   Background

In this section we present background for our work. First, we introduce a phenomenon of base-rate fallacy of detection methods in real-life networks. Then we briefly describe the approaches to lower false positives of detected events using statistic correlation, and conclude with description of sketches.

2.1   Base-rate Fallacy

A base-rate fallacy is a phenomenon of Bayesian statistics. The base-rate fallacy is committed when available statistical data are ignored in favor of specific data to make a probability judgment. Base-rate fallacy in network intrusion detection is well described by Axelsson [1]. Briefly, it states that false positive ratios (FP) in units of percent are treated as a remarkable success in papers. However, in real-life and large-scaled networks, due to the large amount of examined anomalies, this FP ratio would result in an excessive number of false alarms.

A closer examination of various detection methods shows that even though authors often claim very high detection efficiency, their results are still not suitable for deployment in real networks. For example, Casas et al. [2] in their clustering method for detection of DoS attacks present a FP ratio 1-3.5 %. Francois et al. [6] who detect bots using link analysis and clustering, give a FP ratio of 2 %. This is equivalent to several thousand false alarms in real-life deployment. Even if they lowered the FP to 0,1 % by slightly reducing the true positive ratio, it still represents several hundred FPs.

2.2   Statistic Correlation of Events with the Same Dimensions

Statistical correlation of events from more sources is a natural approach for lowering false positives. This approach is typically used in networks where data is gathered from multitude of sources, such as sensor networks. One approach for correlating the results of methods used in sensor networks is proposed by Idé et al. [9]. However, this approach requires homogeneity of gathered data that typical networks cannot provide.

For IP networks, a number of approaches was suggested that correlate events with the same dimensions to confirm an attack. They can process flows in separate time windows [6,7], detect unexpected changes in time series [10,21], or measure co-occurrence of events of the same dimensions across multiple data sources. [14]

There are, however, no correlation mechanisms that we know of that can correlate temporally dependent events of different dimensions, e. g., a small increase in the communication of multiple sources and a large increase in the communication to one destination.

2.3   Sketches

Next approach to network management and anomaly detection are sketches. In the area of anomaly detection, sketches are mostly used for detection of heavy changes and heavy hitters, usually in the form of top percentile of traffic [3,13,22].

A sketch is a probabilistic data-stream aggregation technique that projects a high dimensional network events into a smaller set of dimensions, by hashing the event descriptors. In our case an event is a network flow and descriptors are fields of a flow, e. g. source and destination addresses and ports. A sketch is then defined by one or more hash functions and a hash table with bucket count equal to the output size of a hash function. Upon each new event a hashing function is applied to event descriptors and the result is used as a key to identify a bucket in the hash table that gets its value updated. Thus information about the entire traffic can be stored in a limited and arbitrarily set space that is dictated by the output size of a hashing function. This is an immense advantage for processing of large data streams, because the hashing can be done very fast and the memory footprint is constant, regardless of the traffic volume. Sketches also have linear structure that enables easy arithmetic operations between different sketches.

Sketches have some disadvantages, though. Most notably collisions and necessity to maintain a structure for sketch reversing due to irreversibility of hashes. Collisions of hash functions could be solved using a k-ary sketch proposed by Krishnamurthy et al. [11]. The k-ary sketch consists of H hash tables of size K. Each incoming event is then hashed by H hashing functions into H tables. This duplication enables to lower collisions to desired levels by modifying H and K. An approach to hashing reversal is proposed by Schweller et al. [17,18], who achieved reasonable reversibility while keeping low memory footprint, high throughput and detection accuracy.

Given their properties, sketches can be used beyond the detection of heavy hitters and heavy changes. Thanks to their linearity, they can be also used for correlation of anomalies and events with different dimensions.

3 Correlation of Modularly Hashed Sketches

In the following section we will discuss the concept of modular hashing and explain how it can be used for the correlation of detected anomalies.

3.1 Modular Hashing

Generally, sketching algorithms work with k-universal hashing functions that take the entire input and produce a sketch key in one step. This approach, however, has two drawbacks. The first one is inherent to the nature of hashing functions. Keys are not easily reversible to their original value and reconstructing the original value in naïve implementation may require checking all possible inputs. The second is related to the essence of hashing functions that aim to mangle as much bits of input as possible, thus destroying dependencies between input descriptors. In case of multidimensional events with more descriptors (e.g., source and destination IP addresses, and source and destination ports, where various anomalies can manifest), it is very problematic to reconstruct the nature of an anomaly given only a key and a value.

The reversibility problem was already addressed using numerous approaches, but we have chosen to adapt the method of modular hashing proposed by Schweller et al. [18]. They have demonstrated that by relaxing requirements on hash k-universality and then hashing input by separate parts (octets of IP address in their case), it is possible to efficiently reverse keys of a sketch to their original value. We propose to extend this idea even further and hash each input descriptor separately and then concatenating the result. In this paper we use this notion of a key hashing an input event: $K(I) = K(i_1, \ldots, i_n \mid i \in I) = h(i_1)\| \ldots \|h(i_n)$. Input descriptors that are hashed to a key are referred to in this paper as key parts.

Our proposed modular hashing scheme enables easy reversibility as well as preserving dependencies between descriptors, which are two key properties for our correlation method. These will be described next.

3.2   Correlation

Our proposed correlation method is built to work with the uncertainty that is inherent in all anomaly detection methods. This uncertainty is usually dealt with by setting high enough detection thresholds, but this entails the increase in false negatives that we are trying to overcome. Instead of setting one threshold for each detection method that is to be correlated, we are working with uncertainty expressed as an anomaly score. This score represents the possibility that any given network traffic is in fact an anomaly. To this end we operate with two different types of sketches. The first one is the *source sketch*. This sketch accumulates input data and is subject to periodic analysis. The second one is the *analyzed sketch*. This sketch is a result of application of analytic function on a *source sketch*. The function prototype is: $f : S \to S$.

The high-level algorithm for our correlation method is presented in pseudo-code in Algorithm 1. On the input it takes analyzed sketches and returns sources of identified anomalies. The algorithm works in four distinct phases: accumulation, analysis, combination, and aggregation.

Algorithm 1. High-level overview of the correlation algorithm

---

Input: Set of analyzed sketches

1 **begin**
2 | accumulate sketches with the same key structure;
3 | **while** *there are sketches left to analyze* **do**
4 | | scan sketches for anomaly scores going over threshold;
5 | | combine sketches that have non-empty intersection;
6 | | aggregate combined sketches with the same key structure;
7 | | discard already analyzed sketches;
8 | **end**
9 **end**

Accumulation Phase. In the first phase of the algorithm, anomaly scores of sketches with identical key parts are summed. This phase is ran only once at the beginning. A simple sum of values was selected as an appropriate mechanism, because on the input, there are analyzed sketches whose values are weighted to be in the same value range. After this phase, the algorithm is left with a set of analyzed sketches that have different key parts, e.g., K(source IP address, destination port), K(destination port, destination IP address), and K(source IP address, destination IP address).

Analysis Phase. In the second phase of the algorithm, analyzed sketches are checked for values crossing an anomaly threshold, and anomalies are eventually reported. Sketches are linearly scanned for values greater or equal than the anomaly threshold. Such values are marked in each of the arrays for each hash function in a sketch. If for a given source IP address the value is greater or equal to the anomaly threshold in each array, then the source IP address is reported as anomalous. The reversing processes of our algorithm is identical to the one proposed by Schweller et al. [18], which is available as an open-source solution [12], and not explained here for the sake of brevity.

Combination phase. In the third phase, sketches with different key parts are combined to create new sketches that capture the influences of original sketches. Each two sketches that share at least one key part are combined together. The result of such combination is a new sketch whose key is a union of key parts of the original sketches, e.g., for two sketches with keys K(source IP address, destination port) and K(destination IP address, destination port), the resulting sketch will have a key K(source IP address, destination IP address, destination port). The principle of this combination is illustrated in the Algorithm 2. For each non-null value v_1 in the sketch s_1, all non-null values v_i of the sketch s_2 which have the same value of shared key parts are added together. The result of this addition is stored in the new sketch s with the key which is the union of keys for v_1 and all v_i.

Example of such combination is given in Table 1.

Aggregation Phase. In the fourth phase, sketches resulting from the combination phase with identical key parts are aggregated together. Sketches that were input to the combination phase do not enter the aggregation phase and are discarded, because their influence is already present in the combined sketches. The purpose of this phase is to eliminate the growing number of sketches that can result from the previous phase. This phase is almost the same as the accumulation phase, but values in buckets sharing the same key are not added together. Only the higher value is kept to prevent the superfluous rapid growth of values that would result from the repeated addition of anomaly scores from each input sketch.

Table 1. Example of sketch combination

SIP	DPORT	Value		DPORT	DIP	Value		SIP	DIP	DPORT	Value
A_1	B_1	X_1	$\oplus$	B_1	C_1	Y_1	=	A_1	C_1	B_1	$X_1 + Y_1$
A_1	B_2	X_2		B_1	C_2	Y_2		A_1	C_2	B_1	$X_1 + Y_2$

Algorithm 2. Combination of sketches with different key parts

---

Legend: s_c, s_1, s_2: Sketches

$\qquad P_x$: Set of key parts of sketch x

$\qquad s(P_y)$: New sketch with key having key parts P_y

$\qquad h(p)$: Hash of a value of a key part p

$\qquad H(p)$: All possible hash values of a key part p

$\qquad V(s, K)$: Values of sketch s at key K in all sketch tables

Input : Two sketches s_1 and s_2

Output: Combined sketch s_c

1 **begin**

2 $\quad$ $s_c \leftarrow$ *new sketch* $s(P_{s_1} \cup P_{s_2})$;

3 $\quad$ **for** $\{p_1, \ldots, p_m \in (P_{s_1} \cap P_{s_2})\}$ **do**

4 $\quad\quad$ $V(s_c, K_1 \cup K_2) \leftarrow V(s_1, K_1) + V(s_2, K_2) \mid$

$\qquad\qquad K_1 = (h(p_1) \parallel \ldots \parallel h(p_m) \parallel H(p_m) + 1 \parallel \ldots \parallel H(p_{|P_{s_c}|})) \wedge$

$\qquad\qquad K_2 = (h(p_1) \parallel \ldots \parallel h(p_m) \parallel H(p_m) + 1 \parallel \ldots \parallel H(p_{|P_{s_c}|})) \wedge$

$\qquad\qquad V(s_1, K_1) \neq 0 \wedge V(s_2, K_2) \neq 0$;

5 $\quad$ **end**

6 **end**

---

4   Method Evaluation

To evaluate the efficiency of the proposed method, we have decided to measure its properties on a real-life network traces containing attacks against Secure Shell (SSH) and Remote Desktop Protocol (RDP) services. We have chosen dictionary attacks because they inherently manifest themselves in several aspects. This was noted by Hellemons et al. [8] and Vykopal [19]. They discovered that port scanning often precedes dictionary attacks. They have also found flow counts typical for such attacks. Also Drašar [4] has revealed that for automated dictionary attacks low variance in flow count is symptomatical. Based on their observations we have decided to implement four sketch-based methods covering four different aspects of dictionary attacks.

4.1   Particular Detection Methods

The first sketch method is *source network scan detection*, which measures the number of unsuccessful connections from one IP address to a given port. This method is implemented on top of a sketch with a key K(source IP address and destination port). The second sketch method is *destination network scan detection*, which measures the number of unsuccessful connections to one IP address on a given port. The point of this method is to keep the link between attacking and attacked computers if, for example, one computer is used for scanning and the other for attacking. This method is implemented on top of a sketch with a key K(destination IP address and destination port). The third sketch method is detection of *abnormal number of connections*, which measures the number of successful flows from one source IP address. The point of this method is to reveal computers that initiate an abnormally large number of connections which is always suspicious in case of dictionary attacks. This method is implemented on top of a sketch with a key K(source IP address and destination port). The fourth method is *low traffic variance detection*, which measures whether connections from one IP address to one port exhibit a near-constant pattern. It is implemented on top of a sketch with key K(source IP address and destination port).

In the traditional settings, methods such as the proposed ones have thresholds separating anomalies from normal traffic based on heuristic or statistical properties. However, this approach forces a binary view on an inherently multivalued one. For example, given a threshold of 30 scanning attempts per five-minute time window, is it reasonable to expect that an IP address with 29 is not anomalous? Rather, it could be argued that the IP address is not anomalous with very low probability. To quantify these probabilities in the aforementioned detection methods, we have analyzed traffic going over the perimeter of Masaryk University's network.

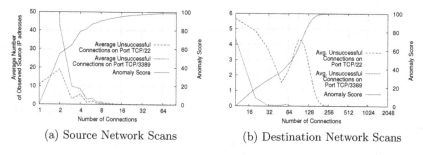

(a) Source Network Scans   (b) Destination Network Scans

Fig. 1. Anomaly scores of detection methods

An analysis of traffic in the past year has given us an important insight into the nature of certain traffic aspects and also outlined an approach for measuring anomaly scores in our four detection methods. For *source network scan detection*, we have counted all unsuccessful connections to a given port in five-minute window frame by each communicating IP address. We have then made a histogram of the average number of IP addresses initiating such connections. The result is depicted in Figure 1a. Even a cursory look at the graph reveals that more than 90 % of IP addresses made less then five unsuccessful connections in five-minute time window. Based on this observation, we have decided to set a threshold for maximal anomaly score to a value that represented ~1 % of most active traffic sources. That is, in case of *source network scan detection* more than 100 scan attempts were evaluated to maximal anomaly score. Anomaly score for a lower number of scan attempts is set to be proportional to how common these attempts are in a network, i. e.: a ratio of a percentile of given number of connections to difference between minimal and maximal percentile: $\frac{percentile\_of\_measured\_connections - minimal\_percentile}{1 - minimal\_percentile}$. The same approach was used for the *destination network scan detection*, whose result can be seen in Figure 1b, and for *abnormal number of connections*, whose results can be seen in Figure 2a. Anomaly scores for *low traffic variance detection* were based on a paper by Drašar [4] and set as an inverse of relative difference in flow count.

4.2   Experiment

To test the efficiency of our method, we have analyzed one week of traffic over the perimeter of Masaryk University. This networks connects about 15.000 active computers every day and the data throughput ranges from about 1 Gbit/s at night to 8 Gbit/s at peak hours. Because this data is not annotated, we have used two already deployed methods for the detection of bruteforce attacks against SSH and RDP services to verify our results. These are pattern matching methods based on a research done by Vykopal [19]. Both methods work by identifying machines that were scanning the network in the previous week and then attempted to log into one or more targets. The SSH detection method uses the following pattern: more than 10 scanning attempts on port TCP/22, connects with more than 10 target machines, performs more than 3 login attempts on each connected host. The RDP detection method uses this one: more than 5 scanning attempts on port TCP/3389, connects with at least one target machine, performs more than 14 login attempts in case of one target or more than 4 in case of multiple targets. Detected attackers are blocked from accessing the network for at least a day.

Data from our experiments can be found in Table 2. The table summarizes the number of anomalies as well as unique IP addresses (in parentheses) that were marked as anomalous by *abnormal number of connection detection*, by accumulation of method with the same key parts and by combination of all methods. The remaining three particular methods are not included, because no anomaly crossed the anomaly threshold. Numbers for the two reference methods are included as well.

4.3   Discussion

Given the high thresholds of our reference methods, we regard all their results as true positives. This view is also reinforced by deployment experience – in three years of the SSH attack detection and two years of the RDP attack detection no identified attack was challenged as a false positive. To estimate false positive ratio of our proposed method we have then analyzed sample of identified attacking IP addresses not detected by our reference methods. In this sample, all addresses were confirmed to be attackers. Although not everything was checked, we have a very high confidence that the rest was true positive too. Estimation of false negative ratio is even more complicated. As the reference methods are in a way subset of a detection of our proposed method, there are no measured false negatives. However, we believe that there still may be attacks evading our detection, because our thresholds are still relatively high. Complete and rigorous

Table 2. Detected anomalies on ports TCP/22 and TCP/3389 in one week traffic

Anomalies	Connection	Accumulation	Combination	Reference methods
TCP/22	2679 (116)	10045 (264)	26408 (551)	(47)
TCP/3389	53 (20)	2175 (1079)	0	(878)

SNS	*Source Network Scan Detection*
DNS	*Destination Network Scan Detection*
Connection	*Abnormal Number of Connections Detection*
Variance	*Low Traffic Variance Detection*
Accumulation	*Accumulation of* SNS, Connection, Variance
Combination	*Combination of* SNS, DNS, Connection, Variance

evaluation of positive and negative ratios would require annotated datasets that to our knowledge do not yet exist.

Despite certain gaps in the evaluation, we were able to make some key observations:

- The correlation of data leads to an increase in detection accuracy and number of detected anomalies that surpasses capabilities of particular detection methods. This observation is in accord with observation of other researchers [5,14,21].
- Even an unoptimized algorithm for correlation was able to process five minute long windows of traffic over the perimeter of Masaryk University in units of seconds. This observation is very promising for deployment in large networks.
- It was confirmed by overall anomaly scores for dictionary attacks on the SSH service (see Figure 2b), symptoms of network scanning, connection count, and low variance are strongly correlated.
- No results in combination of sketches for the RDP service verified our observation from production use that malware targeting this service does not precede attacks with large-scale scanning, but rather attacks the first computer available.

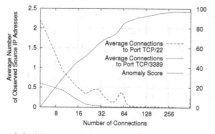   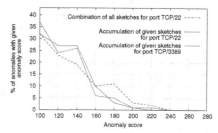

(a) Abnormal Number of Connections   (b) Accumulation and Combination

Fig. 2. Anomaly scores of a detection method and overall anomaly scores of accumulation and combination

Our proposed correlation method can be a powerful tool for the detection of attacks that are intentionally hidden, as was described in [20], because it adds together small anomalies that would be otherwise unseen or ignored. It also enables the sharing of workloads for different detection methods. For example, our two reference methods both check for scanning IP addresses and the same computation is done twice. With correlation, this computation can be seamlessly shared, thus saving computational resources.

Sketch-based methods have proven to be usable and fast enough even on high-speed networks [18]. Our proposed method builds on this foundation and is expected to work in a two tier model. In the first tier, *source sketches* accumulate data from switches, routers, probes, etc. with fixed memory and computational constraints. In the second tier, analyses of these sketches and their correlation are done on more powerful hardware with much relaxed requirements. The correlation phase requires much more memory, because linear growth in key size requires exponential growth in sketch size. There are, however, some optimization techniques that can lower the memory requirements. One can lower key sizes by intentionally limiting the range of possible values. For example, the network space of Masaryk University is only 2^{16} addresses, so we could shrink the destination IP key size from 12 bits to only 6. One can also discard values over anomaly threshold from combination phase and switch in later iterations from sketches to hash tables. By omitting already reported anomalies, the number of events to process falls significantly and hash tables can be much more memory and CPU efficient, even for very large keys.

5   Conclusion

In this paper we presented an approach to correlation based on modularly hashed reversible sketches. We proposed an algorithm that correlates anomaly reports from different sources.

The detection algorithm, based on k-ary sketches, has proved to be a suitable tool for correlation of events with different dimensions. We conducted an experiment in which we deployed the proposed method into a university's network. Even though the method's algorithm was unoptimized, it performed well enough to analyze the five-minute time windows in units of seconds. Compared to other deployed methods, the algorithm was able to detect more anomalies without an increase in the number of false positives.

Our future work will concentrate on addition of new detection methods for correlation. We will also explore possibilities for optimization.

Acknowledgments. This paper is supported by the Czech Ministry of Interior under Identification code VF2013201531.

References

1. Axelsson, S.: The Base-rate Fallacy and the Difficulty of Intrusion Detection. ACM Trans. Inf. Syst. Secur. 3(3), 186–205 (2000)
2. Casas, P., Mazel, J., Owezarski, P.: Unsupervised Network Intrusion Detection Systems: Detecting the Unknown without Knowledge. Computer Communications 35(7), 772–783 (2012)
3. Cormode, G., Muthukrishnan, S.: What's new: finding significant differences in network data streams. In: Proceedings of the IEEE INFOCOM, vol. 3, pp. 1534–1545 (2004)
4. Drašar, M.: Protocol-Independent Detection of Dictionary Attacks. In: Bauschert, T. (ed.) EUNICE 2013. LNCS, vol. 8115, pp. 304–309. Springer, Heidelberg (2013)
5. Fontugne, R., Borgnat, P., Abry, P., Fukuda, K.: MAWILab: Combining Diverse Anomaly Detectors for Automated Anomaly Labeling and Performance Benchmarking. In: Proceedings of the 6th International Conference, Co-NEXT 2010, pp. 8:1–8:12. ACM, New York (2010)
6. François, J., Wang, S., State, R., Engel, T.: BotTrack: Tracking Botnets Using NetFlow and PageRank. In: Domingo-Pascual, J., Manzoni, P., Palazzo, S., Pont, A., Scoglio, C. (eds.) NETWORKING 2011, Part I. LNCS, vol. 6640, pp. 1–14. Springer, Heidelberg (2011)
7. Goldfarb, J.: Identifying Anomalous Network Traffic Through the Use of Client Port Distribution. In: CERT FloCon Workshop, Vancouver, Washington, USA (2006),http://www.cert.org/flocon/2006/presentations/clientport_dist1205.pdf (January 11, 2014)
8. Hellemons, L., Hendriks, L., Hofstede, R., Sperotto, A., Sadre, R., Pras, A.: SSHCure: A Flow-Based SSH Intrusion Detection System. In: Sadre, R., Novotný, J., Čeleda, P., Waldburger, M., Stiller, B. (eds.) AIMS 2012. LNCS, vol. 7279, pp. 86–97. Springer, Heidelberg (2012)
9. Idé, T., Papadimitriou, S., Vlachos, M.: Computing Correlation Anomaly Scores Using Stochastic Nearest Neighbors. In: Proceedings of the IEEE International Conference on Data Mining, pp. 523–528 (2007)
10. Ishibashi, K., Kondoh, T., Harada, S., Mori, T., Kawahara, R., Asano, S.: Detecting Anomalies in Interhosts Communication Graph. In: CERT FloCon Workshop, Scottsdale, Arizona, USA (2009), http://www.cert.org/flocon/2009/presentations/Ishibashi_GraphAnomalies.pdf (accessed January 11, 2014)
11. Krishnamurthy, B., Sen, S., Zhang, Y., Chen, Y.: Sketch-based Change Detection: Methods, Evaluation, and Applications. In: Proceedings of the 3rd ACM SIGCOMM, IMC 2003, pp. 234–247. ACM, New York (2003)
12. Network Systems Lab. Opensketch (2013), https://github.com/USC-NSL/opensketch
13. Li, A., Han, Y., Zhou, B., Han, W., Jia, Y.: Detecting Hidden Anomalies Using Sketch for High-speed Network Data Stream Monitoring. Applied Mathematics and Information Sciences 6(3), 759–765 (2012)
14. Mahimkar, A., Lall, A., Wang, J., Xu, J., Yates, J., Zhao, Q.: SYNERGY: Detecting and Diagnosing Correlated Network Anomalies, http://www.research.att.com/export/sites/att_labs/techdocs/TD-7KEJWS.pdf (accessed January 11, 2014)
15. IEEE 802.3 Ethernet Working Group. IEEE 802.3TM Industry Connections Ethernet Bandwidth Assessment (July 2012), http://www.ieee802.org/3/ad_hoc/bwa/BWA_Report.pdf

16. Synmatec Corporation. Internet Security Threat Report 2013 (April 2013), http://www.symantec.com/security_response/publications/ threatreport.jsp

17. Schweller, R., Chen, Y., Parsons, E., Gupta, A., Memik, G., Zhang, Y.: Reverse Hashing for Sketch-based Change Detection on High-speed Networks. Technical report, Proceedings of the INFOCOM (2004)

18. Schweller, R., Gupta, A., Parsons, E., Chen, Y.: Reversible Sketches for Efficient and Accurate Change Detection over Network Data Streams. In: Proceedings of the 4th ACM SIGCOMM, IMC 2004, pp. 207–212. ACM, New York (2004)

19. Vykopal, J.: A Flow-Level Taxonomy and Prevalence of Brute Force Attacks. In: Abraham, A., Lloret Mauri, J., Buford, J.F., Suzuki, J., Thampi, S.M. (eds.) ACC 2011, Part II. CCIS, vol. 191, pp. 666–675. Springer, Heidelberg (2011)

20. Vykopal, J., Drašar, M., Winter, P.: Flow-based Brute-force Attack Detection, pp. 41–51. Fraunhofer Research Institution AISEC, Garching near Muenchen (2013)

21. Yan, R., Shao, C.: Hierarchical Method for Anomaly Detection and Attack Identification in High-speed Network. Information Technology Journal 11(9), 1243–1250 (2012)

22. Zhang, Y., Singh, S., Sen, S., Duffield, N., Lund, C.: Online Identification of Hierarchical Heavy Hitters: Algorithms, Evaluation, and Applications. In: Proceedings of the 4th ACM SIGCOMM, IMC 2004, pp. 101–114. ACM, New York (2004)

Next Generation Application-Aware Flow Monitoring

Petr Velan and Pavel Čeleda

Institute of Computer Science, Masaryk University
Botanická 68a, Brno, Czech Republic
{velan,celeda}@ics.muni.cz

Abstract. Deep packet inspection (DPI) and IP flow monitoring are frequently used network monitoring approaches. Although the DPI provides application visibility, detailed examination of every packet is computationally intensive. The IP flow monitoring achieves high performance by processing only packet headers, but provides less details about the traffic itself. Application-aware flow monitoring is proposed as an attempt to combine DPI accuracy and IP flow monitoring performance. However, the impacts, benefits and disadvantages of application flow monitoring have not been studied in detail yet. The work proposed in this paper attempts to rectify this lack of research. We also propose a next generation flow measurement for application monitoring. The flows will represent events within the application protocol, e.g., web page download, instead of packet stream. Finally, we will investigate the performance of different approaches to application classification and application parsing with a computational complexity in mind.

Keywords: flow, network measurement, application monitoring, IPFIX.

1 Introduction

The number of different applications communicating over the Internet is ever increasing and so is the need for application-aware network monitoring. However, building network monitoring systems is always a compromise between accuracy and performance. The more information processed, the more accurate the monitoring system is. However, thorough examination of the traffic is computationally expensive [14,18].

Application flow monitoring is a network monitoring approach created to exploit the benefits of deep packet inspection (DPI). Integration of the DPI into flow monitoring allows for information aggregation, which provides better performance than the DPI alone. However, the impacts, benefits and disadvantages of application flow monitoring have not been studied in detail yet. Therefore, we will research the impact of application flow monitoring on flow exporters. Then we will propose improvements to the application flow monitoring that will help to cope with any challenges discovered during the research. We also believe that it is possible to utilize a newly acquired application information to improve the

A. Sperotto et al. (Eds.): AIMS 2014, LNCS 8508, pp. 173–178, 2014.
© IFIP International Federation for Information Processing 2014

quality of the flows. Based on experiences gained during the research, we will propose a next generation flow measurement for application monitoring. The flows will match events within the application protocol, e.g. web page download, instead of packet stream. This approach will provide more context to monitored traffic, which will improve network security, the quality of service and the quality of experience. Finally, to address the monitoring of high-speed networks, we will investigate the performance of different approaches to application classification and application parsing with a computational complexity in mind.

The rest of the paper describes the motivation for our research and introduces the proposed research in more detail.

2   Motivation

This section describes problems of the current generation of application flow monitoring and identifies areas of research that should be addressed.

The NetFlow protocol originally designed by Cisco has been used for almost 20 years now [1]. The first version widely deployed was NetFlow version 5 [5]. The protocol was designed to provide information about network traffic up to the transport layer. The fixed message format was found to be inadequate and NetFlow version 9 [7] was introduced. However, even this protocol limits the data that can be transferred to several simple fixed-length types. Modern measurements often require a definition of new elements, possibly of variable length. Based on NetFlow v9, the IETF defined IP Flow Information Export protocol [9] (IPFIX). This protocol allows us to define private organization-specific elements with complex types and of variable length. The IPFIX protocol is essential for application flow monitoring since it allows us to transfer application information in a standardized manner. Cisco is also using the IPFIX protocol and proposed a specification of application information export [8]. Based on their work, new IPFIX information elements have been added to [16].

The current generation of application flow monitoring uses the same principles as the first generation of NetFlow. Each flow is created as an aggregation of packets with the same key elements [23]. These elements are taken from link, network and transport layers. The information about application protocols are added as new elements to existing flow records, as shown by [6]. Little research has explored the possibilities of using the application information to improve the measurement itself. In [10] we have shown that the information from IPv6 tunnels can be used to create flows with finer granularity. We expect that the information from application protocols can be utilized in a similar manner to create more detailed flow records. There are other unexplored possibilities for improvements in application flow monitoring. The measurement process can be optimized based on observed application, which might lead to performance and quality improvements.

The application-aware flow monitoring inspects the network traffic in more detail than IP flow monitoring. Providing more detailed information about the traffic has a negative impact on the monitoring process performance. Standard flow cache [19] was not designed for application data. Therefore, methods to cope with the extensive amount of data gained from application monitoring need to be researched. The amount of data from measurements might cause an overload of the service network. We believe that possibilities of IPFIX data stream compression should be examined to find solution similar to [3].

The IP flow monitoring is designed to focus on communication consisting of packet streams. This approach is certainly useful for network management [4,11]. However, users are more focused on applications than the network itself. To comply with this trend, content providers need to ensure so called Quality of Experience, which reflects the user's subjective experience with a service. Individual flows might be generated as a result of single *event*. An event might be user opening a website or a server performing a planned synchronization. Information about several flows being part of one event is lost in the current application flow monitoring paradigm. This is a shortcoming that should be addressed.

One of the benefits of application flow monitoring over DPI is its processing speed. However, adding protocol analyzers for new applications degrades the performance. We have described this problem using HTTP protocol as an example in [25]. The authors of [21] propose an automated way to construct application parsers and also analyze their performance. However, the absence of a ground truth and methodology for comparing performance of application protocol analyzers makes comparison of different approaches difficult. Traffic traces used to evaluate anomaly detection methods are freely available and widely used [15]. Similar traces must be provided to create comparable conditions for the evaluation of application protocol analyzers, together with a suitable methodology.

3   Proposed Research and Approach

The aim of our work is to research a next generation flow monitoring system. The new system will be based mainly on the application layer instead of the network layer. To aid this research, we will investigate new approaches in application flow monitoring to make the measurement process more accurate and scalable. We have found that various services such as intrusion detection systems, quality of service and quality of experience measurements are significantly limited by the data provided by flow exporters. Providing high quality data will lead to improvements in all of these areas. The next generation flow monitoring will also enable the development of new methods for network security and management. The main research questions are as follows:

1. *How can information from multiple packet streams be aggregated to single application event and how can we utilize application events to design the next generation flow monitoring?*

Instead of working with flows based on packet streams, the next generation flow monitoring system will be based on events. One event may encompass more than one packet stream. We believe, that this architecture will allow the processing of more complex events than the collection of individual packet streams.

2. *What are the impacts of application protocol measurement on flow exporters?*

To research the next generation flow monitoring system, we need to understand how the addition of application layer information affects the flow exporters. We have already encountered several issues when adding application information to basic flow records. The extracted application data need to be stored for each flow record, which causes the flow records to grow significantly. The result is a large memory consumption of the flow cache, which in turn causes ineffective caching and performance degradation. We will measure the effects of large flow records and propose an alternative approach to solve this problem.

3. *How can application protocol information be used to improve flow measurement quality?*

Using information from the application layer can improve the flow measurement quality and efficiency. We believe that we can utilize application specific information to tailor the flow exporter for distinct protocols. For example, a DNS request is usually sent using only one packet, so the resulting flow record can be exported almost immediately. However, some applications, e.g., video streaming, generate large number of packets over a period of time [13], therefore the inactive timeout should be longer. By analyzing the behavior of major application protocols we can make the flow cache management more effective. If the short flows are exported sooner, the memory requirements of the flow cache might be decreased, which would improve overall performance. Research on flow cache timeouts without considering application protocol information was done in [22].

4. *What are the limits of application protocol measurement on high-speed networks?*

To evaluate the proposed next generation flow monitoring system, we need to build a prototype of a next generation flow exporter. We will use this exporter to compare the results of the new system with existing flow monitoring solutions [2,20]. Since the flow monitoring is frequently used for high-speed network monitoring [12,17,24], we need to design our flow exporter to handle such speeds. The processing of application protocols makes this task even more challenging, since each packet needs to be analyzed more thoroughly to gain the necessary information.

4   Conclusions

In this paper, we presented our goals for future research on application flow monitoring. We aim to analyze the impact of application protocol measurement on flow monitoring. Our contribution includes a study of the quality of generated flow data and of flow monitoring performance. We also propose the next generation application flow monitoring where the flows are merged into network events.

Acknowledgments. This material is based upon work supported by Cybernetic Proving Ground project (VG20132015103) funded by the Ministry of the Interior of the Czech Republic.

References

1. Brownlee, N.: Flow-Based Measurement: IPFIX Development and Deployment. IEICE Transactions on Communications 94(8), 2190–2198 (2011)
2. Network Situational Awareness group at CERT, Carnegie Mellon University.: Yet Another Flowmeter, http://tools.netsa.cert.org/yaf/ (cited January 18, 2014)
3. Chen, S., Ranjan, S., Nucci, A.: IPzip: A Stream-Aware IP Compression Algorithm. In: Data Compression Conference, DCC 2008, pp. 182–191 (March 2008)
4. Chen, T.M., Hu, L.: Internet Performance Monitoring. Proceedings of the IEEE 90(9), 1592–1603 (2002)
5. Cisco: NetFlow Export Datagram Format (2014), http://www.cisco.com/en/US/docs/net_mgmt/netflow_collection_engine/3.6/user/guide/format.html (cited January 18, 2014)
6. Cisco: Network Based Application Recognition, NBAR (2014), http://www.cisco.com/en/US/products/ps6616/products_ios_protocol_group_home.html (cited January 18, 2014)
7. Claise, B.: Cisco Systems NetFlow Services Export Version 9. RFC 3954 (Informational) (October 2004), http://www.ietf.org/rfc/rfc3954.txt
8. Claise, B., Aitken, P., Ben-Dvora, N.: Cisco Systems Export of Application Information in IP Flow Information Export (IPFIX). RFC 6759 (Informational) (November 2012), http://www.ietf.org/rfc/rfc6759.txt
9. Claise, B., Trammell, B., Aitken, P.: Specification of the IP Flow Information Export (IPFIX) Protocol for the Exchange of Flow Information. RFC 7011 (INTERNET STANDARD) (September 2013), http://www.ietf.org/rfc/rfc7011.txt
10. Elich, M., Velan, P., Jirsík, T., Čeleda, P.: An Investigation Into Teredo and 6to4 Transition Mechanisms: Traffic Analysis. In: Turgut, D., Aschenbruck, N., Tölle, J. (eds.) 38th Annual IEEE Conference on Local Computer Networks (LCN 2013), Sydney, Australia, pp. 1046–1052 (2013)
11. Estan, C., Keys, K., Moore, D., Varghese, G.: Building a Better NetFlow. In: Proceedings of the 2004 Conference on Applications, Technologies, Architectures, and Protocols for Computer Communications, SIGCOMM 2004, pp. 245–256. ACM, New York (2004), http://doi.acm.org/10.1145/1015467.1015495
12. Estan, C., Varghese, G., Fisk, M.: Bitmap Algorithms for Counting Active Flows on High-speed Links. IEEE/ACM Trans. Netw. 14(5), 925–937 (2006), http://dx.doi.org/10.1109/TNET.2006.882836
13. Fioreze, T., Oude Wolbers, M., van de Meent, R., Pras, A.: Finding Elephant flows for optical networks. In: 10th IFIP/IEEE International Symposium on Integrated Network Management, IM 2007, pp. 627–640 (2007)
14. Gao, M., Zhang, K., Lu, J.: Efficient packet matching for gigabit network intrusion detection using TCAMs. In: 20th International Conference on Advanced Information Networking and Applications, AINA 2006, vol. 1, 6 p. (2006)

15. Gogoi, P., Bhuyan, M.H., Bhattacharyya, D.K., Kalita, J.K.: Packet and Flow Based Network Intrusion Dataset. In: Parashar, M., Kaushik, D., Rana, O.F., Samtaney, R., Yang, Y., Zomaya, A. (eds.) IC3 2012. CCIS, vol. 306, pp. 322–334. Springer, Heidelberg (2012), http://dx.doi.org/10.1007/978-3-642-32129-0_34

16. IANA: IP Flow Information Export (IPFIX) Entities (2014), http://www.iana.org/assignments/ipfix (cited April 07, 2014)

17. Iannaccone, G., Diot, C., Graham, I., McKeown, N.: Monitoring Very High Speed Links. In: Proceedings of the 1st ACM SIGCOMM Workshop on Internet Measurement, IMW 2001, pp. 267–271. ACM, New York (2001), http://doi.acm.org/10.1145/505202.505235

18. Lai, H., Cai, S., Huang, H., Xie, J., Li, H.: A Parallel Intrusion Detection System for High-Speed Networks. In: Jakobsson, M., Yung, M., Zhou, J. (eds.) ACNS 2004. LNCS, vol. 3089, pp. 439–451. Springer, Heidelberg (2004), http://dx.doi.org/10.1007/978-3-540-24852-1_32

19. Muenz, G., Claise, B., Aitken, P.: Configuration Data Model for the IP Flow Information Export (IPFIX) and Packet Sampling (PSAMP) Protocols. RFC 6728 (Proposed Standard) (October 2012), http://www.ietf.org/rfc/rfc6728.txt

20. ntop: nProbe (2014), http://www.ntop.org/products/nprobe/ (cited January 18, 2014)

21. Pang, R., Paxson, V., Sommer, R., Peterson, L.: Binpac: A Yacc for Writing Application Protocol Parsers. In: Proceedings of the 6th ACM SIGCOMM Conference on Internet Measurement, IMC 2006, pp. 289–300. ACM, New York (2006), http://doi.acm.org/10.1145/1177080.1177119

22. Quan, L., Heidemann, J.: On the Characteristics and Reasons of Long-lived Internet Flows. In: Proceedings of the 10th ACM SIGCOMM Conference on Internet Measurement, IMC 2010, pp. 444–450. ACM, New York (2010), http://doi.acm.org/10.1145/1879141.1879198

23. Sadasivan, G., Brownlee, N., Claise, B., Quittek, J.: Architecture for IP Flow Information Export. RFC 5470 (Informational), updated by RFC 6183 (March 2009), http://www.ietf.org/rfc/rfc5470.txt

24. Schuehler, D.V., Lockwood, J.W.: A Modular System for FPGA-Based TCP Flow Processing in High-Speed Networks. In: Becker, J., Platzner, M., Vernalde, S. (eds.) FPL 2004. LNCS, vol. 3203, pp. 301–310. Springer, Heidelberg (2004), http://dx.doi.org/10.1007/978-3-540-30117-2_32

25. Velan, P., Jirsík, T., Čeleda, P.: Design and Evaluation of HTTP Protocol Parsers for IPFIX Measurement. In: Bauschert, T. (ed.) EUNICE 2013. LNCS, vol. 8115, pp. 136–147. Springer, Heidelberg (2013)

A Modular Architecture for Deploying Self-adaptive Traffic Sampling

João Marco C. Silva, Paulo Carvalho, and Solange Rito Lima

Centro Algoritmi, Universidade do Minho, Portugal
{joaomarco,pmc,solange}@di.uminho.pt

Abstract. Traffic sampling is seen as a mandatory solution to cope with the huge amount of traffic traversing network devices. Despite the substantial research work in the area, improving the versatility of adjusting sampling to the wide variety of foreseeable measurement scenarios has not been targeted so far. This motivates the development of an encompassing measurement model based on traffic sampling able to support a large range of network management activities, in a scalable way. The design of this model involves identifying sampling techniques through its components rather than a closed unit, allowing to address issues such as flexibility, estimation accuracy, data overhead and computational weight within a narrower and simpler scope. This paper concretises these ideas presenting a modular and self-configurable measurement architecture based on sampling, a framework implementing sampling inherent pieces, and provides first results when deploying the proposed concepts in real traffic scenarios.

1 Introduction

Performing network measurement tasks in today's networks is a continuous challenge attending to the massive traffic volumes involved, to the wide range of possible monitoring objectives to fulfill, sometimes in a near real-time basis and requiring minimal interference with the normal network operation. Aiming at efficient network measurements, traffic sampling techniques are broadly deployed in strategic network nodes, generically called measurement points (MPs). Their main objective is to select a subset of packets which will then be used to estimate network parameters, avoiding processing all network traffic [12], with the potential cost of affecting measurement accuracy [4].

Despite the substantial research work on packet sampling [9] [8] [13], choosing the best sampling technique depends on traffic characteristics or statistics needed by applications [3]. Moreover, most proposals are focused on specific network measurement tasks, aiming at increasing the accuracy estimation of a single network metric or a small set of metrics, which, in turn, may increase the consumption of computational resources (e.g., CPU, memory and storage capacity).

In this way, the lack of an encompassing traffic sampling architecture able to map a large range of network management measurement needs in a scalable and autonomous way, yet attending to existing computational resources constraints, is evident. Knowing that distinct sampling techniques lead to different computational weight and accuracy levels for each metric estimation, this paper proposes a modular and self-adaptive architecture able to accommodate the selection and configuration of sampling techniques according to the requirements of the network task and resources available.

A. Sperotto et al. (Eds.): AIMS 2014, LNCS 8508, pp. 179–183, 2014.

2   Measurement Architecture

A self-adaptive sampling-based measurement architecture is envisioned as comprising three planes, as illustrated in Figure 1. The *management plane* includes tasks deployed directly in MPs or in external management entities (such as in Software-defined Networking approaches). Based on specific requirements of each network task, measurement needs are identified, one or more MPs are selected, and the most suitable sampling technique is chosen and configured. This also involves identifying an information model able to define managed objects in the network, as suggested in [2].

The management plane is also responsible for providing the self-adaptive behavior of the model. Adaptiveness is ruled by a function which, in runtime, balances estimations accuracy and the corresponding computational weight. Taking a set of thresholds for CPU load, memory and data storage consumption, combined with the expected relative error of the metric estimation, the function is able to determine whether to maintain the current sampling technique (and settings) or to introduce a lighter and/or more accurate technique (based on the ongoing requirements and computational constraints).

The *sampling plane* consists mainly of a modular sampling framework able to assist the deployment of current and future sampling approaches, which fragments the sampling techniques into well-defined components according to sampling *granularity*, *selection scheme* and *selection trigger*. Then, each component is further divided into a set of approaches that, once combined, may allow deploying sampling policies in a flexible and scalable way, as illustrated in Figure 1. In brief, these components are: (i) *granularity* - identifies the atomicity of the element under analysis in the sampling

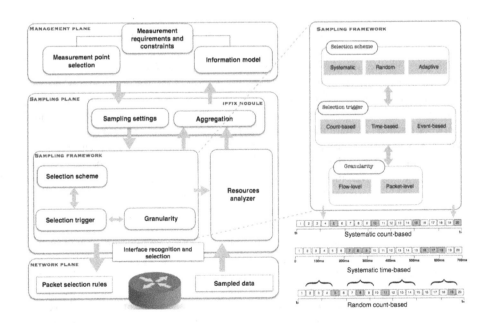

Fig. 1. Architecture description

process: in *flow-level* approach, the sampling process is only applied to packets belonging to a flow or to a set of flows of interest; in a *packet-level* approach, packets are eligible as single independent entities; (ii) *selection scheme* - identifies the function defining which traffic packets will be selected and collected; this scheme may follow a *deterministic*, a *random* or an *adaptive* function; and (iii) *selection trigger* determines the spatial and temporal sample boundaries, may use a *time-based* approach, a *count-based* approach or an *event-based* approach.

To support adaptiveness, a profiler module (*resources analyzer*) monitors the resources consumption in runtime, reporting the current status to the management plane, which will decide on maintaining the sampling policy or setting a new one regarding the measurement needs and resource constraints. A new policy may correspond to a new sampling technique or just a change in the configuration parameters, *e.g.* reducing the sample frequency.

An IPFIX [1] module is responsible for the communication between the management plane and the sampling plane, receiving the sampling settings from the management plane. This module also receives the sampled packets from the network plane, processing them and aggregating relevant fields according to the network task. The aggregation and exporting processes follow IETF guidelines [10] [6] and include results from the resource analyzer, which will then be used for self-adaptation.

At *network plane*, traffic is collected from network interfaces by applying the sample rules defined in the sampling plane. Unprocessed sampled packets are subsequently reported to the sampling plane to be processed, simplifying the network plane.

3   Ongoing Works and Results

According to the measurement architecture, presented in Figure 1, the sampling framework and the resource analyzer were developed in Java using *libpcap*[1], and deployed in a low-cost, open computing device currently used in measurement architectures [11]. The methodology of tests resorts to a quantitative comparison between the computational burden of multiple sampling techniques and policies in presence of similar workloads. The purpose of this comparison is to provide an initial understanding with regards to the relationship between computational requirements and accuracy as afforded by the various sampling techniques. This will facilitate the design of an efficient adaptive module, based on suitable thresholds for specific measurement needs and resource constraints.

Traffic scenarios consist of three workload periods (low, moderate and high) in the network backbone of University of Minho, Portugal along a typical workday, as shown in Table 1. Due to privacy policies only *https* traffic was collected, then submitted to different sampling techniques deployed in the sampling framework, *i.e.*, SystC - Systematic count-based [12], SystT - Systematic time-based [12], RandC - Random count-based [12], LP - Adaptive linear prediction [5] and MuST - Multiadaptive sampling [7].

As shown in Figure 2(a), SystC and MuST require lower CPU consumption, being MuST less demanding during the most critical work scenario. Regarding memory usage, Figure 2(b) demonstrates similar behavior across all techniques and workload scenarios. The volume of data involved in the sampling process (see Figure 2(c)) is higher

---

[1] http://www.tcpdump.org/

for the SystT technique, contrarily to SystC and RandC. Assuming that the computational resource consumption of systematic techniques is proportional to the sampling frequency, Figure 2(d) presents the mean resource consumption for distinct sampling frequencies for SystC technique when applied to the high workload scenario.

Despite the importance of reducing the computational burden of traffic sampling, sampling techniques must still be able to represent the network behavior accurately. Table 1 presents the accuracy results per technique when estimating two metrics useful for traffic characterization, such as mean throughput and number of flows. The results show that the higher storage requirement of SystT delivers a better accuracy in flow identification. Regarding throughput, the relative mean error (RME) is low for all scenarios and techniques (less than 10%). Exceptions are: (i) MuST technique applied to high workload, achieving a significant low error (less than 1%); and (ii) RandC technique applied to moderate workload, with a relative error above 10%.

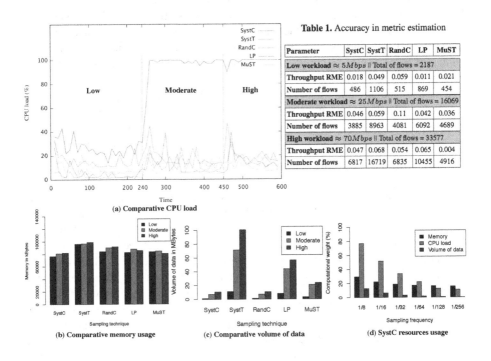

Table 1. Accuracy in metric estimation

Parameter	SystC	SystT	RandC	LP	MuST
Low workload ≈ 5 Mbps ‖ Total of flows = 2187					
Throughput RME	0.018	0.049	0.059	0.011	0.021
Number of flows	486	1106	515	869	454
Moderate workload ≈ 25 Mbps ‖ Total of flows = 16069					
Throughput RME	0.046	0.059	0.11	0.042	0.036
Number of flows	3885	8963	4081	6092	4689
High workload ≈ 70 Mbps ‖ Total of flows = 33577					
Throughput RME	0.047	0.068	0.054	0.065	0.004
Number of flows	6817	16719	6835	10455	4916

(a) Comparative CPU load

(b) Comparative memory usage   (c) Comparative volume of data   (d) SystC resources usage

Fig. 2. Overall results

These preliminary results evince the relevance of tuning traffic sampling (choosing technique, configuration parameters and thresholds), in order to meet distinct measurement requirements and constraints. The present research work proposing a modular and self-adaptive measurement architecture will allow enlarging the scope and efficiency of network measurement tasks through traffic sampling.

Acknowledgements. This work has been supported by FCT - *Fundação para a Ciência e Tecnologia* in the scope of the project: PEst-OE/EEI/UI0319/2014.

References

1. Boschi, E., Mark, L., Quittek, J., Stiemerling, M., Aitken, P.: IP Flow Information Export (IPFIX) Implementation Guidelines - RFC5153. Tech. rep., IETF (2008), https://datatracker.ietf.org/doc/rfc5153/
2. Dietz, T., Claise, B., Quittek, J.: Definitions of Managed Objects for Packet Sampling - RFC6727. Tech. rep., IETF (2013), https://datatracker.ietf.org/doc/rfc6727/
3. Duffield, N.: Sampling for Passive Internet Measurement: A Review. Statistical Science 19(3), 472–498 (2004)
4. Estan, C., Varghese, G.: New directions in traffic measurement and accounting. SIGCOMM Comput. Commun. Rev. 32(4), 323–336 (2002), http://dl.acm.org/citation.cfm?id=964725.633056, http://doi.acm.org/10.1145/964725.633056
5. Hernandez, E.A., Chidester, M.C., George, A.D.: Adaptive Sampling for Network Management. Journal of Network and Systems Management 9(4), 409–434 (2001), http://dx.doi.org/10.1023/A:1012980307500
6. Muenz, G., Claise, B., Aitken, P.: Configuration Data Model for the IP Flow Information Export (IPFIX) and Packet Sampling (PSAMP) Protocols - RFC6728. Tech. rep., IETF RFC 6728 (2012), http://datatracker.ietf.org/doc/rfc6728/?include_text=1
7. Silva, J.M.C., Carvalho, P., Rito Lima, S.: A multiadaptive sampling technique for cost-effective network measurements. Computer Networks (2013), http://www.sciencedirect.com/science/article/pii/S1389128613002491
8. Sommers, J., Barford, P., Duffield, N., Ron, A.: Improving accuracy in end-to-end packet loss measurement. In: Proceedings of the 2005 Conference on Applications, Technologies, Architectures, and Protocols for Computer Communications - SIGCOMM 2005, vol. 35, p. 157. ACM Press, New York (2005), http://dl.acm.org/citation.cfm?id=1080091.1080111
9. Tammaro, D., Valenti, S., Rossi, D., Pescapé, A.: Exploiting packet-sampling measurements for traffic characterization and classification. International Journal of Network Management 22(6), 451–476 (2012), http://doi.wiley.com/10.1002/nem.1802
10. Trammell, B., Wagner, A., Claise, B.: Flow Aggregation for the IP Flow Information Export (IPFIX) Protocol - RFC7015. Tech. rep., IETF (2013)
11. Young, H.: Archipelago measurement infrastructure, http://www.caida.org/projects/ark/
12. Zseby, T., Molina, M., Duffield, N.: Sampling and Filtering Techniques for IP Packet Selection RFC 5475. Tech. rep. (2009), http://datatracker.ietf.org/doc/rfc5475/
13. Zseby, T., Hirsch, T., Claise, B.: Packet Sampling for Flow Accounting: Challenges and Limitations. In: Claypool, M., Uhlig, S. (eds.) PAM 2008. LNCS, vol. 4979, pp. 61–71. Springer, Heidelberg (2008), http://dx.doi.org/10.1007/978-3-540-79232-1_7

Cross-Layer Optimization with Real-Time Adaptive Dynamic Spectrum Management for Fourth Generation Broadband Access Networks

Jeremy Van den Eynde and Chris Blondia

Department of Mathematics and Computer Science
University of Antwerp - iMinds - PATS Research Group
Middelheimlaan 1, 2020 Antwerp, Belgium
{jeremy.vandeneynde,chris.blondia}@uantwerpen.be

Abstract. The upcoming fourth generation of broadband access systems (4GBB) needs to address data rates of up to 1 Gbit/s over twisted-copper pairs. Physical layer techniques like dynamic spectrum management (DSM) aid in increasing the data rate by optimizing the space and frequency domain. However, there is room for improvement in the time dimension that both physical and upper layers can use to their advantage. This paper proposes a bidirectional cross-layer approach to optimize DSM using techniques like scheduling and statistical multiplexing, to mitigate crosstalk, the dominant cause of signal degradation. This in turn should lead to better data rates, more stable networks, and "greener" devices.

1 Introduction

Driven by the emergence of evermore requiring broadband services such as e-business, cloud computing, IPTV and video-conferencing the needs for reliable and fast broadband internet access has become essential to life quality, efficiency and organizations. Quality of service (QoS) requirements for these applications become quite challenging, and thus it is important to improve broadband technologies.

The intermediate step to a global fiber-to-the-home (FTTH) instalment, is the hybrid fiber – copper telephone wires, using the existing telephony DSL infrastructure for the so called *last mile*, identified as the fourth generation broadband (4GBB) access network [12,2].

Increasing VDSL2's datarates (of up to 100 mbit/s) to 1 Gbit/s over these copper wires proves a significant challenge. One of the wireline techniques used to boost data rates is dynamic spectrum management (DSM) [13]. DSM is developed as a means to solve the crosstalk problem. As twisted-copper pairs of different users are merged inside large cable bundles, electromagnetic coupling between neighbouring pairs leads to signal leakage in other users' signals. This is called cross-talk, and is currently the major cause of performance degradation in DSL transmission [4,18].

A. Sperotto et al. (Eds.): AIMS 2014, LNCS 8508, pp. 184–188, 2014.
© IFIP International Federation for Information Processing 2014

Despite the word *dynamic* in DSM, the configuration remains static over time. And thus the time-domain is left unexploited. As the worst-case scenario is envisioned, the settings are very conservative and there is much to gain by taking this dimension into account.

Therefore, we investigate the concept of real-time adaptive DSM, which takes the short time-scale changing environment and requirements into account when calculating the power configuration. This leads to new mechanisms to improve transmission, energy efficiency (e.g. using low-power modes), and stability of the overall network.

However, the physical layer does not have the information that allows for this real-time adaptation and the upper layers could optimize more using physical layer information, hence the need for a cross-layer approach. Cross-layer refers to the exchange of knowledge between layers of the Open Systems Interconnection (OSI) model [1], a layered abstraction of the networking protocol stack (e.g. [14])

In our envisioned model there is a mutual influence between the physical layer and the upper layers (layer two and up). For example, telephony requires a very reliable and constant bit rate (CBR), while web traffic is of highly bursty nature, can cope with loss but needs to be responsive, and background traffic has high bandwidth requirements but does not suffer from delays. This valuable upper layer information can steer the physical layer into assigning three channels with different data and bit-error rates. The physical layer in its turn can report crosstalk, or share common time-frequency slots with other users, to which the upper layers, such as the scheduler, can make decisions.

The goal of this research is the development of a bidirectional cross-layer real-time adaptive DSM optimization framework for mitigating crosstalk by exploiting the time-dimension.

2 Approach

In this research we will investigate the upper layers and work in close collaboration with a researcher that looks at the physical layer optimizations.

The first step in tackling the problem consists of defining a framework with scope, and constructing a multi-layer system model that allows for cross-layer optimization. It includes determining the degrees of freedom and mechanisms, parameters and metrics that can be used for uni- or bidirectional cross-layer optimization.

Metrics of interest include the delay, delay variation, loss, Quality of Experience (QoE), power usage and retransmission probability. Not all metrics will apply for all traffic. E.g. some traffic does not suffer from large delay variation.

Most literature considers a unidirectional information exchange. Linking the several layers with a bidirectional channel results in new possible optimizations. This increase of degrees of freedom might result in unmanageable complexity. Restricting parameters or the degrees of freedom help in handling this. Determining the optimal power configuration, for example, is exponential in complexity [16]. Limiting the update frequency and set of possible bandwidths can alleviate this.

Upstream and downstream have to be treated differently: the latter can be managed centrally as all information is readily available. The upstream traffic, on the other hand, can not be coordinated locally, and thus information exchange with the central office has to be taken into account.

The second phase will focus on the development of a cross-layer optimization approach for the system model.

Main topics of interest here for the upper layer are scheduling and statistical multiplexing. Statistical multiplexing is the merging of several flows such that the required bandwidth is less than the sum of the required bandwidths of the individual flows. Huang [8] shows that this can lead to impressive performance gains in cross-layer settings. Multiplexing has to be considered in a centralized cross-layer setting taking all users into account as there is a positive correlation between crosstalk and data rates in a cable bundle. Furthermore, predicting data and channel behaviour over a short time horizon can enhance the allocation of physical resources and allow for using low power modes, such as stable sleep [10].

The final step comprises a complete and realistic 4GBB simulator with cross-layer optimizations. Using realistic stochastic and worst-case channel models it will be possible to evaluate QoS performance statements, and identify constraints related to the time dimension such as delay, delay variation, retransmission probability and overhead of the upstream communication. The simulation will then be used to compare different scenarios against the G.fast standardization [9].

3   Current State

The current model consists of four building blocks: the application manager, the scheduler, admission control and operational controller. They are depicted in Figure 1 together with possible interactions and an example frequency-time slot mapping, the configuration of bits on the wire.

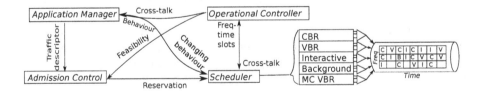

Fig. 1. Model, interactions and frequency-time slot mapping

Upon a new flow requesting access, the application manager translates this request to a long term traffic descriptor, and probes the admission control for a suitable physical layer configuration. If found the scheduler is updated to support the new flow. The scheduler selects packets for transmission for each traffic class (of which there are high reliability CBR, high reliability VBR, interactive traffic, background and multicast VBR). Each of these packets is then mapped to a time-frequency slot, guided by the operational controller. The operational controller uses convex programming to minimize power usage and maximize the frequency-time slot assignment in function of application requirements over all users.

4 Related Work

Previous research is mainly focused on unidirectional cross-layer optimization. For example [3] takes channel state and queue length into account to schedule for optimal throughput. However, the physical layer does not take any of the upper layers' information into account.

Most literature dealing with cross-layer optimization can be found in the wireless network area [3,17,6,11,7,15]. Approaching DSL as a multi-user system, rather than isolated wires, results in similarities between wireless and DSL, and hence allows us to make use of these results. They are different enough (e.g. mobility, MAC, hidden terminal problem ...) that results can not be used directly.

Cross-layer design, such as [11,6], focuses on the principles of decomposition and will be of value for our research.

Relating to the second phase, Çiftçioğlu [3] proposed a predictive block scheduler for a wireless system model. Our aim is to improve this model for a wired setting and provide a more general cross-layer framework.

In contrast to other literature, the FAST copper project [5] focuses on improving DSL. It considers four dimensions: frequency (physical layer allocation), amplitude (shaping at edge), space (network architecture and topology) and time (multiplexing). Whereas FAST focuses on optimizing network performance, we will optimize only the last mile by exploiting the time dimension (scheduling, multiplexing, traffic prediction), and focusing on the QoE.

5 Preliminary Conclusions and Future Work

This paper presented an approach to developing a cross-layer optimization with real-time adaptive DSM for 4GBB. Incorporating the time dimension, mechanisms like scheduling and statistical multiplexing will allow us to mitigate crosstalk, a major source of signal degradation, leading to better data rates, greener devices and more stable networks.

Future work will focus on a more tight collaboration of the physical layer and upper layers, iterative upgrading of the framework and performing simple simulations to evaluate metrics, continuing along the path as in section 2.

Acknowledgement. This work is supported by funds from Research Foundation Flanders (FWO). The authors would like to thank Marijn Scheir for the collaboration.

References

1. Bertsekas, D.P., Gallager, R.G., Humblet, P.: Data networks, vol. 2. Prentice-Hall International (1992)

2. van den Brink, R.F.: Enabling 4gbb via the last copper drop of a hybrid ftth deployment. Broadband, Journal of the SCTE 33(2), 40–46 (2011)
3. Çiftçioğlu, E.N., Gürbüz, Ö.: Scheduling for next generation wlans: filling the gap between offered and observed data rates. Wireless Communications and Mobile Computing 11(5), 654–666 (2011)
4. Cendrillon, R., Moonen, M., Verlinden, J., Bostoen, T., Ginis, G.: Improved linear crosstalk precompensation for dsl. In: Proceedings of the IEEE International Conference on Acoustics, Speech, and Signal Processing, ICASSP 2004, vol. 4, p. iv–1053. IEEE (2004)
5. Chiang, M., Huang, J., Cendrillon, R., Tan, C.W., Xu, D.: Fast copper for broadband access. In: Optics East 2006, p. 639003. International Society for Optics and Photonics (2006)
6. Chiang, M., Low, S.H., Calderbank, A.R., Doyle, J.C.: Layering as optimization decomposition: A mathematical theory of network architectures. Proceedings of the IEEE 95(1), 255–312 (2007)
7. Fu, F., van der Schaar, M.: Decomposition principles and online learning in cross-layer optimization for delay-sensitive applications. IEEE Transactions on Signal Processing 58(3), 1401–1415 (2010)
8. Huang, J., Tan, C.W., Chiang, M., Cendrillon, R.: Statistical multiplexing over dsl networks. In: 26th IEEE International Conference on Computer Communications, INFOCOM 2007, pp. 571–579. IEEE (2007)
9. ITU-T: Recommendation itu-t g.9701 - fast access to subscriber terminals (g.fast) - physical layer specification (2014)
10. Kamitsos, I., Tsiaflakis, P., Ha, S., Chiang, M.: Stable sleeping in dsl broadband access: Feasibility and tradeoffs. In: 2011 IEEE Global Telecommunications Conference (GLOBECOM 2011), pp. 1–6. IEEE (2011)
11. Lin, X., Shroff, N.B., Srikant, R.: A tutorial on cross-layer optimization in wireless networks. IEEE Journal on Selected Areas in Communications 24(8), 1452–1463 (2006)
12. Odling, P., Magesacher, T., Host, S., Borjesson, P.O., Berg, M., Areizaga, E.: The fourth generation broadband concept. IEEE Communications Magazine 47(1), 62–69 (2009)
13. Song, K.B., Chung, S.T., Ginis, G., Cioffi, J.M.: Dynamic spectrum management for next-generation dsl systems. IEEE Communications Magazine 40(10), 101–109 (2002)
14. Srivastava, V., Motani, M.: Cross-layer design: a survey and the road ahead. IEEE Communications Magazine 43(12), 112–119 (2005)
15. Van Der Schaar, M., et al.: Cross-layer wireless multimedia transmission: challenges, principles, and new paradigms. IEEE Wireless Communications 12(4), 50–58 (2005)
16. Vangorp, J., Tsiaflakis, P., Moonen, M., Verlinden, J., Van Acker, K.: Optimal spectrum balancing in multi-user xdsl systems with on/off power loading. In: 2006 IEEE International Conference on Acoustics, Speech and Signal Processing, ICASSP 2006 Proceedings, vol. 4, p. IV. IEEE (2006)
17. Yu, W., Kwon, T., Shin, C.: Multicell coordination via joint scheduling, beamforming and power spectrum adaptation. In: 2011 Proceedings IEEE INFOCOM, pp. 2570–2578. IEEE (2011)
18. Zeng, C., Aldana, C., Salvekar, A.A., Cioffi, J.M.: Crosstalk identification in xdsl systems. IEEE Journal on Selected Areas in Communications 19(8), 1488–1496 (2001)

Author Index